HAWAII

FAMILY ADVENTURE GUIDE™

by

JULIE APPLEBAUM

A VOYAGER BOOK

The Globe Pequot Press

OLD SAYBROOK, CONNECTICUT

Family Adventure Guide is a trademark of The Globe Pequot Press, Inc.

Library of Congress Cataloging-in-Publication Data
Applebaum, Julie
    Hawaii: family adventure guide / by Julie Applebaum. — 1st ed.
        p. cm. — (Family adventure guide series)
    "A voyager book."
    Includes index.
    ISBN 1-56440-968-6
    1. Hawaii—Guidebooks. I. Title. II. Series.
DU622.A68 1996
919.6904'42—dc21   96-47200
                                              CIP

Manufactured in the United States of America
First Edition/First Printing

ACKNOWLEDGMENTS

A big "mahalo nui loa" (thanks a whole bunch) to the following individuals who helped by being wonderful sources of information and photographs: Lori Kennedy, Aubrey Hawk, Heidi Nelson, Leslie Dance, Bernie Caalim-Polanzi, Donovan Dela Cruz, Babs Harrison, Christine Stanton, Diana Moody, June Tada, Yvonne Landavazo, Ruth Limtiaco, Molly Lawson, Nancie Brown, Valerie King, Donna Jung, Connie Wright, and Marie Saplan.

Thanks to all my friends, family, and coworkers, too numerous to list, who understood that I needed the space and time to create and willingly gave it to me. A special thanks to my dad, who proofread every word and whose support, infinite wisdom, and sense of humor always keep life in perspective.

HAWAII

Kauai

Oahu

Molokai

Lanai

Maui

Hawaii:
The Big Island

CONTENTS

INTRODUCTION

H awaii is a playground for young and old with activities, attractions, and historical sites galore. Everybody can find something they enjoy, and many activities are free, relatively cheap, or once-in-a-lifetime thrills that are worth the money. The sea is the ideal playground. You can swim, snorkel, scuba, surf, fish, sail, canoe, kayak, sailboard, bodysurf, parasail, cruise, or stroll along the shore picking up shells and exploring tidepools.

The ocean beckons around every curve in the road, but use caution before letting kids swim just anywhere. Hawaii has basically two seasons—summer and winter. In the summer, the north-facing beaches are usually calm, almost lakelike, and are safe for swimming, while the south shores often feature heavier surf and dangerous currents. The situation switches, and the differences magnify, in winter when the islands' north shores get pummeled by some of the biggest waves in the world, and the undertow is sometimes strong enough to pluck unsuspecting spectators right from the beach. Pay attention to the posted flags and signs before entering the water. Also, it's a good idea to ask the lifeguard about the current conditions.

If you venture to a small or deserted beach where lifeguards are absent, study the water before entering. Note the frequency and size of the waves. You can often judge the strength of the currents by watching how fast the sand is sucked into the water.

While in some places, such as Hanauma Bay, Oahu, the fish are so tame they'll eat right from your hand, in other places some creatures of the deep add an element of danger. Parents should always arrive at the beach equipped with a bottle of meat tenderizer. Certain weather patterns bring ashore pests known as Portuguese man-of-war, whose sting is sharp and painful, although usually not life-threatening. Meat tenderizer rubbed into the wound helps ease the pain.

Also, realize Hawaii is close to the equator and the ultraviolet rays beat down with full force here. Constant application of strong sunscreen is a necessity—otherwise a bad sunburn could ruin your vacation on the first day. Even on cloudy days the potential of sunburn remains serious, because ultraviolet rays burn through the cloud cover.

On every island there are several shops that rent water-sports equipment including surfboards, boogieboards, sailboards, and snorkeling and scuba gear. Additionally, many hotels, resorts, and condominiums offer rentals and lessons from the central activities desk.

Snorkeling is a very easy activity available to anyone who knows how to swim. In less than an hour, you can become acquainted with the basics and be able to master the equipment. If your hotel doesn't offer free snorkeling equipment, shop around before you rent. Often, dive or water-sport shops offer less-expensive alternatives than the larger hotels. A mask, snorkel, and fins usually cost $7.00 a day. By all means, consider using a disposable underwater camera, about $15, which helps capture the aqua-images permanently.

If you or your children want to try surfing, be aware that it takes many years to become an expert. Lessons are readily available, however, and with a little coordination you'll be good enough to stand up and ride the gentle waves.

Windsurfing, also called sailboarding, is a little easier than surfing because you are dependent on the wind instead of the waves. Windsurfing boards are much larger, more stable, and easier to stand upon than ordinary surfboards. The sail that propels you across the water is mounted on the board. Rental sailboards are usually more expensive than surfboards. Lessons are available on all major islands.

Boogieboarding is definitely a sport that water-safe kids will be able to master within a few minutes. The boards are made of heavy-duty foam and are about 3 feet long. Many boogieboarders also wear fins to help propel them toward a wave, but for beginners it's not necessary. Boards are for sale everywhere, from drugstores and supermarkets to surf shops. You can also rent them at the same places you rent snorkeling equipment.

Just as there are many water-sports rental shops scattered throughout the islands, there are also many companies that offer guided tours to the best spots in Hawaii's ocean playground. Generally, these tours are worthwhile, often led by guides knowledgeable about the local marine life and Hawaiian history. There are many to choose from, and each chapter of this book reveals a small sampling.

Every island also offers land-based fun, such as tennis, golf, horseback riding, bicycling, hiking, hunting, and freshwater fishing. There are also several land-based tours available, ranging from air-conditioned buses to passenger vans. These are a good way to get a general overview of the island but often lack the opportunity for in-depth exploring. The premise of this book is that you're more likely to discover the real nuances of each island on your own . . . equipped with this guidebook, a good map, and a sense of adventure.

For that reason, you also will notice the book does not include every restaurant or hotel/resort property. The restaurants that are mentioned are by no means inclusive of all the greats but are ones that have been personally taste-tested. Accommodations range from simple bed-and-breakfast inns to five-star luxury resorts, with an infinite variety of options and prices in between. To mention and review them all is enough material for another book, but a few of the more famous are included. Most of the larger properties offer children's programs that let the parents have a day off. The *keiki* (child) activities usually include a variety of outdoor activities, lunch, arts and crafts, and a souvenir T-shirt. Additionally, most of the larger properties offer baby-sitting services in which the caretaker will come to your hotel room.

The islands are full of kid-magnet attractions such as video arcades, movie theaters, and miniature gold courses; however, as these are similar to ones in your hometown, they were omitted from this book.

The book does focus on Hawaii-specific recipes for fun. Many of the ingredients of these recipes include visits to museums, where Hawaii's natural and cultural histories are explained and displayed. Many kids would prefer to be building sandcastles or "hanging ten" (local surfer's lingo) on a wave, but Mother Nature may call for another activity. It rains often in Hawaii (although the weather remains warm), and it's a good idea to have a choice of indoor activities.

Hawaii's history is fascinating. You can learn about the highly structured Polynesian culture that thrived in these islands before Captain James Cook arrived and exposed Hawaii to the rest of the world. The ancient Hawaiians lived a religious life, with separate gods for everything from fishing to fertility. Not only are examples of this culture evident in museums, remains ranging from *heiau* (religious temples) to petroglyphs (images or inscriptions carved on rocks), still exist on all islands.

Each island used to be led by one high chief, *ali'i*, until Kamehameha the Great united them all under one rule in approximately 1795. Kamehameha was the first of eight monarchs who ruled these islands until 1893, when the traditional Hawaiian government was overthrown.

As you drive throughout the islands, you'll notice that most places of historical importance are so noted by the presence of a Hawaiian warrior atop a pole. These "warrior-signs" were placed by the Hawaii Visitors Bureau to identify everything from scenic overlooks to old heiaus.

Hawaiian gods and goddesses live on, with a strong movement to revive culture among modern Hawaiians, through the ancient language of *hula* (dance) and through local legends and customs. In the Maui chapter, for example, you'll learn about the demigod Maui, who performed great feats of athleticism to slow down the sun, so his mother could dry her *kapa* cloth. In the Big Island chapter you'll meet Pele, the goddess of volcanoes, who has been angrily belching up lava since 1983.

Whether you're traipsing through the ruins of an ancient temple, or hiking on a mountain trail, remember that Hawaii's environment is extremely fragile. In fact, 98 percent of all plants and animals included on the federal endangered species list are endemic to Hawaii. Please remain on well-worn paths; a single misstep could damage a root or flower that is a food source for an endangered bird. Hawaii's beauty is in a precarious state, and environmentally conscious visitors can help preserve it for the next generation.

Throughout the book, a large variety of churches are mentioned as attractions and places to visit. This is not done with any religious significance or disrespect, but rather to emphasize the historical importance of the missionary era. Congregational missionaries, preachers, doctors, and teachers sailed here from New England in 1820. Determined to rid the native Polynesians of their "heathen" lifestyles, they built church after church, trying to save the local souls. They brought "white man's civilization" to these remote islands and forever changed the native culture. Many of the churches they built still stand, a testament to the hardiness and persistence of their founders, who traveled thousands of treacherous miles at sea to complete their mission.

People who have never been to Hawaii often mistakenly associate Oahu with the entire state. That's like eating only the fudge frosting on top of a cupcake. Sure, it's tasty and can be wonderfully satisfying all by itself. But when combined with the whole cupcake, the frosting is so much more enhanced. Yes, Oahu, known as the "gathering place," is wonderful. Yes, families can enjoy an action-packed vacation solely on Oahu. But a visit to all the islands truly offers the "whole cupcake" experience. Every island offers its own sense of identity and mystique, complete with an abundance of adventures for families of all ages.

On Oahu this guidebook will take you through Waikiki and a scenic Circle Island Tour that includes Pearl Harbor and the big-wave Country of the North Shore. On Maui, the Valley Isle, you'll travel everywhere from great whale-watching and snorkeling sites to the top of Mount Haleakala, to the edge of the island at Hana. On the Big Island your family shouldn't miss a trip to the country's only active volcano, acres of tropical rain forests, and lush coffee plantations. On Kauai the beauty of the majestic Na Pali Coast will linger in your memory long after you've returned home. On Lanai you can visit two of the state's most luxurious resorts, ride horses through virtually untouched country, and explore the mysterious Garden of the Gods. And, it will seem as if time has passed by the people of Molokai, the friendly isle, where small-town charms await visitors and miles of unspoiled coastline beg for exploration.

A few travel particulars: Hawaii law requires that children up to two years old be hooked into a car seat. You can reserve one when you make a reservation with a car rental agency. Expect a minimal added charge, computed daily. Also, when making reservations with any hotel, car agency, or airline, by sure to ask about family specials. Many hotels offer a "kids stay free" program in which *keiki* share their parents' rooms, sleeping on portable beds. Similarly, many restaurants offer free or discounted meals for kiddies—it pays to shop around. Don't forget to ask about accruing bonus miles on any frequent-flier accounts you maintain. Most car agencies and the larger, national resort properties can apply your total bill to a variety of airlines.

The restaurants throughout this book are listed according to the following price code, which reflects the average cost of dinner entrees: $— under $8.00, $$—$8.00 to $15.00, $$$—$15.00 to $21.00, and $$$$— over $21.00.

The area code for the whole state is 808. Calls originating in and destined for the same island are considered local, and calls from one island to another are long-distance, requiring you to first dial the numeral 1.

The prices and rates listed in this guidebook were confirmed at press time. We recommend, however, that you call establishments to obtain current information before traveling.

Maps provided at the beginning of each chapter are for reference only and should be used in conjunction with a road map. Distances suggested are approximate.

Oahu

Oahu is by far the most populated island. More than 836,000 of the state's 1.1 million residents live here. Honolulu is home to the state capitol, the financial district, medical centers, and universities. It's also home to Diamond Head Crater, Punchbowl Cemetery, Pearl Harbor, and the world-famous charms of acclaimed Waikiki Beach.

First-time visitors expecting Waikiki and Honolulu to be an idyllic, tranquil island paradise had better be prepared for a city that also has a frenetic pace and an accelerated pulse. Honolulu has evolved into a multicultural, cosmopolitan city, with a little bit of the laid-back "local-style" feel remaining—especially in our treatment of others. Enriching museums, cultural events, historical sites, a top-notch symphony, opera, and theaters compete for attention with sporting events, backcountry hikes and camps, botanical gardens, and a recently renovated zoo and aquarium. But, around it all exists an undeniable spirit of joie de vivre, the "aloha spirit," that embraces neighbors and newcomers alike.

As many people unfamiliar with the islands mistakenly associate Oahu with all of Hawaii, just as many mistake Honolulu and Waikiki for all of Oahu. The entire island encompasses 608 square miles and 112 miles of coastline, and Waikiki is just a crowded, concrete-laden 2-mile stretch of hotels fronting a sandy beach. The remaining land is filled with homes, offices, farms, a few remaining acres of pineapple and sugar cane, lush mountain ranges, and dry flatlands.

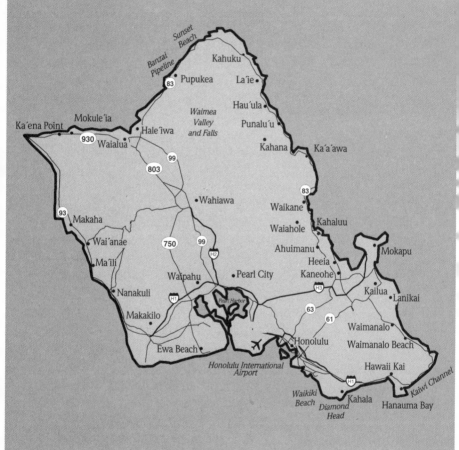

Ka´ena Point
Mokule´ia
Sunset Beach
Banzai Pipeline
Kahuku
La´ie
Pupukea
83
Hau´ula
Waimea Valley and Falls
Punalu´u
Hale´iwa
930
Waialua
Kahana
Ka´a´awa
99
803
83
Wahiawa
Waikane
Waiahole
Kahaluu
93
Makaha
Ahuimanu
Mokapu
Wai´anae
750
99
Heeia
Ma´ili
H2
Kaneohe
Waipahu
Pearl City
H3
Kailua
Lanikai
Nanakuli
H1
Pearl Harbor
63
61
Waimanalo
Makakilo
Honolulu
Waimanalo Beach
Ewa Beach
Honolulu International Airport
Hawaii Kai
Waikiki Beach
Kahala
Hanauma Bay
Diamond Head
Kaiwi Channel

Oahu

After landing at Honolulu International Airport, most visitors head directly for Waikiki, where the majority of hotel properties are situated. But there is a smattering of great resorts and bed-and-breakfast inns throughout the island.

For purposes of easy orientation, this chapter begins in Waikiki and will then expand to circle the entire island for a complete guide to Oahu's family adventures. After Waikiki, you'll be exposed to adventures in the surrounding communities of Downtown, Chinatown, Aiea, Nuuanu, Punchbowl, Makiki, and Manoa. Then you'll head to Leeward Oahu, the dry side of the island, and travel through Aiea, Pearl Harbor, Waipahu, Ewa Beach, Waianae, Makaha, and Kaena Point.

Back in Waikiki, you'll drive around the island in what's appropriately referred to by locals as a Circle Island Tour. This goes from the southeastern area (Kahala, Hawaii Kai, Waimanalo) to the Windward Side (Kailua, Kaneohe, Kualoa, Kaaawa, Kahuku) to the North Shore (Waimea, Sunset, Haleiwa) and back to Waikiki via the central plains of Wahiawa.

To begin with, Oahu is magnificently accessible via a public transportation system known as TheBus (296–1818, ext. 8287), on which a full Circle Island Tour costs just $1.00 for adults, 50 cents for students through high school age. Although you're not permitted to bring suitcases on board, you can ride TheBus to every adventure listed in this chapter. Pick up a schedule at the main office, 811 Middle Street, or at any satellite city hall. Oahu's public transportation is considered better than that of any of the other main Hawaiian Islands. If you're considering *not* renting a car, Oahu would be the only island where you wouldn't really miss it. Additionally, many hotels offer free shuttles to and from the airport.

Rental cars are readily available from a variety of companies, and a little research can garner some great deals. With kids, it's good to have your own set of wheels for easy access to pit stops and places to run off restless energy. If you require a car seat, check the rates to rent one from the car rental agency. Other kiddie equipment, such as strollers and cribs, is available for rent from some of the hotels and from a local company called Dyan's Rentals (527 Cummins St., 591–8207).

WAIKIKI

Waikiki Beach may be the most famous stretch of sand in the world. It's been the backdrop for many a Hollywood movie, and hundreds of famous celebrities, politicians, and foreign dignitaries have been photographed while enjoying its splendors. And for good reason. The weather is usually warm and sunny, the ocean calm and inviting. Developers must have known what they were doing as, one after another, huge hotel towers were built to house the millions of visitors that come every year for a taste of Waikiki's magic.

Don't let the multitude of hotels overwhelm you. As crowded as it is, Waikiki's status as the ultimate playground remains well deserved. Kids flock to the ocean here for hours at a time, teenagers rock-and-roll at the surplus of nightclubs, and couples stroll the golden sands by moonlight, marveling at the steely blue Pacific. Waikiki has something for everyone.

The ocean here offers an ideal outlet for almost any type of recreation you can imagine, whether it's simply bobbing around on a raft to soak up the sun, diving below the surface in a submarine, or barreling down a wave in a six-person outrigger canoe.

Most hotels feature an activities desk or a concierge that can help organize any activity to suit your fancy. Additionally, there are several beachside stands that offer everything from surfing lessons to luau tickets.

Many of the hotels, such as the **Hyatt Regency Waikiki,** offer children's programs. At the Hyatt, guests are given a free brochure, "Children's Guide to Fun Under the Sun," that doubles as a coloring book and lists kid-friendly things to see and do within walking distance of the hotel. Another booklet, entitled "101 Wonderful Things to Do on Oahu," is free for all guests. Camp Hyatt, the hotel's family program, offers special amenities, services, and activities, including scavenger hunts, hotel tours, and video games for children ages three to twelve.

Just a few blocks away from the Hyatt, the **Hawaiian Regent** hotel offers a Kid's Quest package, in which a second room is available at half price when guests book a certain category room at the regular rate. Or, if you want your kids in the same room as you, rollaways and cribs are provided for free. Guests eight years old and younger receive a complimentary fanny pack, sunglasses, and an inflatable beach toy. Kids ages nine to seventeen receive a unique bingo game featuring ancient Hawaiian petro-glyphs. Each Kid's Quest fun pack includes a coupon book with discounts at family-oriented attractions.

The Rainbow Express Young Explorer's Club is available for guests ages five to twelve years old at the **Hilton Hawaiian Village.** Activities include one-on-one encounters with sea creatures in the Touch-n-Feel pool at the Waikiki Aquarium. Kids love tickling a sea cucumber and holding a hermit crab. The children's program is offered year-round, seven days a week. Full- and half-day programs are available.

The programs at the Hilton, Hawaiian Regent, and the Hyatt Waikiki are just a few examples of the many benefits awarded to families traveling with children. For more information, it's best to consult a travel agent.

For kids who've seen surfboards only in the movies, it's a good idea to invest in some lessons—Waikiki offers ideal gentle waters for first-timers. The beachboys in Waikiki are experienced watermen and can have almost anyone standing up after a few basic hints. Expect to pay about $25 an

Children learn how to string leis at the Hilton Hawaiian Village's Young Explorer's Club. (Courtesy Hilton Hawaiian Village)

hour for a lesson and a board; if you want to rent just the board alone, it's about half-price.

Boogieboarding is a little tamer, and a lot easier to learn. And, again, Waikiki's gentle waters make it an ideal location for the inexperienced. While surfboards are about 6 feet long and weigh about twelve pounds, boogieboards are about 3 feet long and weigh about one pound. They also can be rented from beachside stands. There's no need to take a lesson to ride the waves, and even if your kids don't manage to "rip through the tubes," they'll still have a good time floating in the shorebreak.

The beach stands also offer outrigger canoe rides, in which six people and one beachboy armed with paddles take to the sea for a ride out into the water. The leader turns the boat around, and presto—the waves ride the canoe into shore. The sport of canoeing has been immensely popular since the days of old when Hawaiians first settled on these lands. It's great fun and easy to learn.

For more information about beachside services and rates, check at the big rack of standing-up surfboards at Kuhio Beach—the eastern tip of Waikiki. Additionally, if your hotel does *not* have an activities desk, contact the **Outrigger Hotel,** 2335 Kalakaua Avenue, 923–0711. You needn't be a guest to book activities here. Also, several beach stands are situated directly on the beach.

For a glimpse into the life below the ocean surface without even getting wet, there are different vehicles to consider. Underwater cruises aboard submarines are offered daily and transport you to a colorful world of pristine reefs, alive with yellow angelfish, spiny puffers, striped parrotfish, stingrays, turtles, and sometimes even sharks.

Beware, however, as bad weather can affect the schedule. Rough surface conditions don't necessarily affect a submarine but can make for an unpleasant shuttle ride out to the vessel. So call ahead if the wind is whipping up whitecaps or if breakers look unusually big.

On **Atlantis Submarines,** children must be 3 feet tall to ride. In Waikiki the most expensive and extensive trip, the Sea Quest Adventure, takes passengers 120 feet below the surface. Live narration is provided, as well as video monitors and personal audio headsets. For adults the fare is

$105; children up to twelve years old cost $39. Shorter and less expensive trips are also available. For more information, call 973–9800.

Voyager Submarines leave from Kewalo Basin, between Waikiki and downtown Honolulu. There are numerous dives daily, from 8:00 A.M. through 3:00 P.M. Each modern, air-conditioned submersible has comfortable seats opposite 30-inch viewports. Round-trip transportation is available from Waikiki hotels to Kewalo Basin, where passengers depart aboard a 90-foot yellow catamaran. The ride to the dive site takes about 10 minutes. For more information, call 592–7850; fares are $89 for adults, $49 children twelve and under. Again, children must be at least 3 feet tall.

Nautilus boats are semi-submersibles. Although they resemble submarines, these 58-foot boats do not submerge, and they are substantially less expensive than the submarine tours. Everyone has access to a large window below in the underwater cabin. Passengers cruise in cool comfort several feet below the surface and can stare across the sea floor at the constant swirl of marine life. It is also possible to ride topside for a different, off-shore view.

For adults the ride costs $45, for children, ages four to eleven, $25. Kids three and under are free. Trips are made daily at 9:00, 10:00, and 11:00 A.M., noon, and 1:00 and 2:00 P.M. The boat departs from Kewalo Basin, 1085 Ala Moana Boulevard. Check-in and tickets are available near Fisherman's Wharf Restaurant, also on Ala Moana Boulevard. For more information, call 591–9199.

The open-air **Waikiki Trolley** is a great way to get a complete overview of the town. The trolley runs from 8:30 A.M. to 4:00 P.M. and travels to many nooks and crannies of the city, including all of its historic sites. Passengers can get on and off an unlimited number of times. You can make a day of it—exploring, stopping for lunch, and hitting the road again. All-day passes for children under twelve are only $5.00; they cost $17.00 for adults. For more information, call 596–2199 for recorded information or 591–2561 to speak to a live operator. Tickets are available at the Royal Hawaiian Shopping Center in Waikiki, or you can simply board at any one of the stops, and the conductor will sell you a ticket.

On Seaside Avenue, in the heart of central Waikiki, the **IMAX theater** offers thrilling shows on oversized, 70-foot wide, 5-story screens.

Regular films include *Ring of Fire,* featuring life-size lava flows; *Hidden Hawaii,* with stunning views of remote locations; and *Search for the Great Sharks,* offering magnificent underwater footage. For more information, call 923–4629. The theater is at 325 Seaside Ave.; admission is $7.50 for adults, $5.00 for children eleven and under.

The **Damien Museum** is at the far end of Waikiki. Father Damien came from Europe to care for the people who were afflicted with Hansen's disease (leprosy) and exiled to the isolated Kalaupapa Peninsula on Molokai. He helped build homes, churches, and hospitals for hundreds of ill people and eventually died of the disease himself.

The museum is at 130 Ohua Avenue in Waikiki on the grounds of St. Augustus Church, between Kalakaua and Kuhio, about 3 blocks from the zoo. It's open 9:00 A.M. to 3:00 P.M., Monday through Friday. For more information, call 923–2690.

At the far end of Waikiki, just east of the Hilton Hawaiian Village Hotel, at the corner of Kalia and Saratoga roads, is the **Battery Randolph Army Museum.** Free guided tours are available and will give you a glimpse of the military's importance in the islands. Kids are allowed to play on a real tank and examine the structure of a cannon.

Military history is recorded here as far back as Kamehameha I (1753–1819). Exhibits include rifles, swords, and illuminating old photographs of popular sites, such as Waikiki and Diamond Head. The museum features a tribute to soldiers from Hawaii who fought in World War II, Korea, and Vietnam. The facility is open every day except Monday, from 10:00 A.M. to 4:00 P.M., for information, call 955–9552. Admission is by donation, but a self-guided audio tour costs $3.00. The museum validates parking for two hours.

Ala Moana Beach County Park is a popular hangout for locals and offers visitors recreational fun just outside of Waikiki. You'll see lots of people here surfing, swimming, picnicking, jogging, and rollerblading. In the middle of the park is **Magic Island,** a man-made structure that juts out from the coastline, providing a calm inside bay for young children.

The view from here looks back toward Waikiki and is nothing short of stupendous—especially during sunset. If you happen by on a Friday evening, you'll be treated not only to a spectacular sunset, but to a colorful panorama of sails as boats race back to the harbor—a long-standing local

Lindsay Amaral is delighted to sit on the shoulders of her strong uncle, Solo Taau. (Courtesy Lorrain Burgess)

tradition. The park isn't a good place to be, however, for too long after the sun sets.

The park is at the western end of Waikiki, across the street from the Ala Moana Shopping Center. Amenities include snack bars, a picnic area, restrooms, telephones, and lifeguards.

Imagine a supermarket of restaurants all in one place, and that's what one finds at **Makai Market at Ala Moana Shopping Center**—twenty-one different food shops, offering everything from chocolate chip cookies to exotic Asian delights, surrounding a huge central seating area. There are Filipino, Korean, Chinese, Japanese, French, Hawaiian, and American seafood, salads, and sandwiches. Whatever you like, you'll find it here in nearly endless variety. This is a great place to take a break or meet family or friends for a meal between visits to the Ala Moana Shopping Center stores. Complete meals are less than $10.

Another good place for lunch or dinner while shopping in the Ala Moana Center is **Fishmonger's Wife.** Fine fish dishes, interesting salads, reasonably priced sandwiches, and all-around good food are offered here. Located on the upper level, mountain-side of the mall; 941–3377. $$$.

At the far eastern end of Waikiki, across from Kuhio Beach and the Honolulu Zoo, **Kapiolani Park** is a great place to go for some old-fashioned, Frisbee-flinging fun. The park encompasses 140 acres and was built in the 1800s. It's named after Queen Kapiolani, King David Kalakaua's wife.

Locals flock here daily for soccer, rugby, Frisbee, picnics, kite flying, softball games, and volleyball. If you're visiting during spring, be sure to check out the Annual International Sport Kite Festival, during which the sky will be filled with colorful two- and four-handle sport kites that fly so fast, the whir of their fabric sounds like a jet engine.

In addition to a spacious grassy area, features of the park include jogging trails, bicycle paths, gymnastic equipment, and tennis courts. The Royal Hawaiian Band performs for free every Sunday from 2:00 to 4:00 P.M. at the bandstand. The bandstand also hosts other free outdoor concerts, publicized in the local newspapers. At the far end of the park, Waikiki Shell hosts several outdoor events, with an amphitheater designed for optimum acoustics.

The **Kodak Hula Show** is a free performance given on the lawn adjacent to the Waikiki Shell, on the Waikiki-side boundary of Kapiolani Park. It offers a nice alternative to the pricey luaus—although there's no food served here. The Kodak Hula Show is an institution in Waikiki—it's been around since 1937. Some of the performers—if not old-time originals—are sons and daughters of the original cast. The show features Hawaiian musicians and dancers and is scheduled every Tuesday, Thursday, and Friday at 10:00 A.M. Any willing participant from the audience is invited down for an impromptu hula lesson after the performance, so be sure to bring along a camera!

Families can get in touch with their "wild side" at the **Honolulu Zoo,** which more than 1,000 mammals, birds, amphibians, and reptiles call home. Special features for children include a petting zoo full of barnyard animals and a ladder that lets them climb to the eye level of a giraffe.

The Reptile House is also popular with children, as is the Elephant Encounter, but by far the most impressive feature is the African Savanna. This exhibit lacks the barriers or fences found in most zoos to keep the animals restricted to a certain place. Instead, creatures such as hippos, zebras, rhinos, lions, chimpanzees, baboons, and antelopes wander freely throughout land that's configured to resemble their natural African habitat. You'll feel as if you're walking through a wild jungle!

The zoo is located at 151 Kapahulu Avenue, at the entrance to Kapiolani Park; 971–7171. It's open daily from 9:00 A.M. to 4:30 P.M. Admission for adults is $6, and children ages six to twelve cost $1.00. (Kids five and under are let in free when accompanied by an adult.)

Just outside the zoo is a huge old banyan tree that's home to thousands of white pigeons. These pigeons are not indigenous to Hawaii but have flourished here and grown to an immense population. Nearby convenience stores (such as the ever-present ABC—Hawaii's version of a Circle K or 7-Eleven) sell birdseed that you can feed to the pigeons. The birds have been feeding off the visitors' generosity for so long that they have become tame enough to eat right from an outstretched hand.

For a chance to visit Hawaii's famous underwater world up close, don't miss the newly renovated **Waikiki Aquarium.** Founded in 1904, the aquarium is the third-oldest public aquarium in the United States. Here, you can look nose-to-nose at a reef shark and catch a glimpse of

Hawaii's colorful state fish, the humuhumunukunukuapua'a. The kids will love watching the comical expressions exhibited by the Hawaiian monk seals, whose faces are so cute they're almost human.

Besides the monk seals, displays include an underwater Coastal Garden, an Edge of the Reef tank, a Hunters of the Reef tank, a jellyfish exhibit, and a reef machine that simulates the effects of waves and underwater currents.

The aquarium is within walking distance of the zoo to the east, across the street from Kapiolani Park at 2777 Kalakaua Avenue. It's open from 9:00 A.M. to 5:00 P.M. daily, although visitors are no longer admitted after 4:30 P.M. Admission is $6.00 for adults, $4.00 for seniors and military, $2.50 for kids thirteen to seventeen, and free for children twelve and younger. For information, call 923–9741.

Up Kapahulu Avenue, past the zoo, try **Irifune** for a true sense of local-style Japanese cuisine in an out-of-the-way spot just northwest of Honolulu Zoo. Try the Mixed Kushiyaki, chicken and vegetables barbecued on a skewer. Simple, tasteful, inexpensive—Irifune doesn't waste anything on atmosphere or fancy tableware. Located at 563 Kapahulu; 737–1141. $– $$. Other dining choices on Kapahulu include **Zippy's,** a statewide chain offering great burgers and chili; **Harpos Pizzeria; Keo's Thai Cuisine,** and a variety of fast-food places.

Continuing on Kalakaua Avenue, shortly after the aquarium, you'll notice a beautiful art deco structure that's fenced off to prevent people from entering. This is the **Natatorium,** a saltwater swimming pool that was built in 1927 as a World War I memorial. Hawaii's most famous waterman, Duke Kahanamoku, broke the world record for the 100-yard freestyle here in 1911. Unfortunately the structure has been allowed to decay and is therefore no longer safe for swimmers. It's been closed since 1980, but there is a movement underway to restore and reopen the structure.

Sans Souci Beach, also known as **Kaimana Beach,** is a lovely strip of sand that fronts the New Otani Kaimana Beach Hotel at the very eastern tip of Waikiki. Locals frequent this area to take advantage of Waikiki's balmy weather and tranquil waters without the crowds. This is a great place to take children, because it's quiet and uncrowded compared to the more popular Waikiki beaches.

There's a slew of free entertainment throughout Waikiki as well as dinner shows offering everything from hula dancers and Hawaiian food to Elvis impersonators and magic shows. Freebies can be found at the following locations.

❋ A nightly torchlighting ceremony, Molehu I Waikiki, is held Saturday and Sunday at Kuhio Beach Park, the far eastern end of Waikiki, 6:15 to 7:00 P.M.

❋ The Royal Hawaiian Shopping Center features free weekday entertainment. On Tuesday and Thursday, at 9:30 A.M., Auntie Deborah Kakalia hosts quilting demonstrations and sells quilting kits. On Monday, Wednesday, and Friday, from 10:00 to 11:00 A.M., there are hula lessons with Puakeala. On Monday and Wednesday, from 11:00 A.M. to noon, there are lei-making lessons with Auntie Bella.

❋ The Sheraton Waikiki Hotel presents Na Mea Hula every Friday, 5:30 to 7:00 P.M., consisting of hula, lei-making, conch-shell blowing, and a torchlighting ceremony. Call 922–4422.

❋ The Outrigger East Hotel showcases local musicians playing Hawaiian music at the Aloha Bar every Saturday, Sunday, and Monday, 5:00 to 7:00 P.M. Call 926–6441.

There are a variety of different luau shows performed in Waikiki and throughout the islands that offer semi-authentic Hawaiian food and entertainment. Although locals may scoff at the glitzy, tourist-oriented performances, the luaus are good fun, geared for the whole family, and are definitely an experience worth attending.

In Waikiki the longest-running, and currently the only, luau is held at the Royal Hawaiian Hotel on Monday nights, 6:00 to 9:00 P.M. The cost is $74 for adults, $48 for children under twelve.

Two companies offer worthwhile luau experiences far removed from the hustle and bustle of Waikiki. Visitors are transported in air-conditioned buses to the leeward side of the island for a complete Polynesian extravaganza. **Germaine's "Too Good To Miss" Luau,** 946–3111, costs $44.50 for adults and $22.50 for kids ages six to twelve. **Paradise Cove Luau,** 945–3571, is $47.50 and $27.50, respectively.

There are dozens of good restaurants in Waikiki and the surrounding areas. The following few are just a small sampling of what's available. The concierge in your hotel or the local newspapers and telephone directories have more complete information.

❋ **Bali By The Sea.** Classic Continental cuisine with beautiful ocean views. The menu features traditional and regional cuisine with a Hawaiian accent and an extensive wine list. Try the chocolate soufflé for dessert. At 2005 Kalia Rd.; 941–2254. $$$.

❋ **The Golden Dragon.** Exquisite gourmet Chinese dishes that range from traditional to nouvelle cuisine. Chef Dai Hoy Chang's most famous recipes, including cold ginger chicken and lobster with curry sauce, are worth the visit. At Hilton Hawaiian Village; 946–5336. $$.

❋ **Cascada.** You'll almost feel as if you're in an Italian bistro instead of the ground floor of the new Royal Garden Hotel. The decor is upscale European, complete with alfresco ceiling paintings. The menu offers a good mix of light pastas and filling entrees. The food is tasty and fresh and the atmosphere elegant. At 440 Olohana St.; 945–0270. $$$.

❋ **Hanohano Room.** Spectacular views high above Waikiki Beach, along with fine dining, make this a popular restaurant. French entrees include beef, poultry, veal, and seafood dishes. Fresh fish served with local fruits and vegetables are also a notable attraction. At Sheraton Waikiki Hotel, 2255 Kalakaua Ave.; 922–4422. $$$$.

❋ **Hau Tree Lanai.** The atmosphere in this Diamond Head restaurant is like the Hawaii of old. The Hau Tree blends crisp service and out-standing food with its beachside location to guarantee a pleasing experience. At New Otani Kaimana Beach Hotel, 2863 Kalakaua Ave.; 923–1555. $$$.

❋ **Halekulani Hotel.** For a truly elegant meal in traditional resort style, one can always rely on the Halekulani Hotel's **Orchids** or **La Mer.** But, for an atmosphere just a bit less formal, you can't beat the **Halekulani's House Without A Key.** $$. La Mer is the premier dining room for the prestigious Halekulani resort. Because the food is incredible, the view is magnificent, and the service swift and sure, the award-winning La Mer ranks at the top of the finest restaurants in the islands. $$$$. While La Mer upstairs is a five-star dinner house,

Orchids at Halekulani has earned four stars and is open for breakfast and lunch as well as dinner. Breakfast or lunch on the veranda is pure delight, while dinner is a gustatory revelation. $$$. At 2199 Kalia Rd.; 923–2311.

☀ **Hy's Steak House.** At this restaurant you can dine in either a cozy, librarylike dining room or a modern, art deco eatery. Steak is the specialty, but the menu includes a wide choice of poultry and fresh fish, as well as a special children's menu. At 2440 Kuhio Ave., Honolulu; 922–5555. $$$.

☀ **Matteo's.** Classic Italian specialties prepared in gourmet style, served in an intimate atmosphere. One of the island's best restaurants. At 364 Seaside, Honolulu; 922–5551. $$$$.

☀ **Monarch Room.** For sheer class and old-fashioned style, it's hard to beat the Royal Hawaiian Hotel. With a wide range of fine entrees, from lobster to veal, the food is excellent, the service beyond comparison, and the decor the reason why many still believe the Pink Palace is the best hotel in Hawaii. The Monarch Room caters to families with a special children's menu. At 2259 Kalakaua Ave.; 923–7311. $$$$.

☀ **Oceanarium Restaurant.** Here's a place where the entertainment is as good as the food. The "entertainment" is inside a 280,000-gallon aquarium, while the dining is just outside the heavy acrylic windows. The best views, however, are from the tables closest to the tank on the lower level, especially at feeding times (for the fish) at 9:00 and 11:30 A.M. and 12:30, 6:30, and 7:30 P.M. daily. Seafood is the house specialty, of course, but there are beef and chicken dishes, too, and a children's menu. At 2490 Kalakaua Ave.; 922–1233. $$$.

☀ **Parc Cafe.** One of the best-kept secrets in Hawaii is the Parc Cafe, home of the "gourmet buffet," in the Waikiki Parc Hotel. Featuring a brightly lit decor, attentive service, a kids' menu, and some of the best food in the islands. Carved-to-order beef and lamb, fresh fish dishes, rotisserie duck and chicken, a creative salad bar, fresh soups, a dessert bar, homemade potato chips, and a do-it-yourself yogurt bar. The Wednesday noon Hawaiian Buffet is a local-style treat; don't pass up the taro root au gratin. At 2233 Helumoa Rd.; 921–7272. $$$.

❋ **Prince Court.** Situated on the third floor of Waikiki's lush new Hawaii Prince Hotel, and overlooking the Ala Wai Harbor, this quietly elegant new dining establishment features crisp service, excellent buffets, and wonderful interpretations of Hawaii Regional Cuisine. The breakfast buffet is $13.50 and spectacular. **Hakone,** on same floor, offers traditional Japanese dishes. At 100 Holomoana St.; 956–1111. $$$.

❋ **Sarento's.** At the top of the Ilikai Hotel, the view is almost as good as the food. Both are spectacular. Private tables ideal for viewing the sunset are available with a reservation, and you can't go wrong with any of the menu choices. At 1777 Ala Moana Blvd.; 955–5559. $$.

❋ **Suntory Restaurant.** In the Royal Hawaiian Shopping Center, Suntory offers upscale Japanese cuisine—everything from *teppen-yaki* and *yakitori* to *shabu-shabu.* Try the fresh lobster teppen-yaki. This place is a favorite of visitors and locals, so reservations are recommended. At 2233 Kalakaua Ave.; 922–5511. $$.

❋ **Tahitian Lanai.** There are only a few restaurants still around that are reminiscent of "Old Waikiki." In the old days, the Tahitian Lanai was the hottest piano bar in town, and many famous people have made impromptu performances. Today, breakfast is the most popular meal. Locals come from far away for the special popovers, banana muffins, and waffles. Nestled on its own little lagoon, the restaurant has outdoor seating for an incredible view. The atmosphere is pure Hawaiian —with individual thatch-roofed huts, a menu that offers fantastic fried taro as well as children's dishes, and an aloha spirit that radiates from every staff member. At 1811 Ala Moana Blvd.; 946–6541. $.
In between Waikiki and downtown Honolulu are what locals refer to as the McCully, Makiki, and Kapiolani Districts—mostly places where people live and work, with little interest for visitors. There are, however, some great restaurants around here.

❋ **Alan Wong's.** Formerly the executive chef at Mauna Lani's Canoehouse and Le Soleil, Alan Wong has brought his talents to King Street at McCully Court. The menu changes daily, and the pupus, entrees, and desserts feature the latest and greatest in Hawaii Regional Cuisine. His most famous pupus include hoisin BBQ baby back ribs and shredded Kalua pig wrapped in taro pancake on poi vinaigrette with Lomi Tomato Relish. Open for dinner only, reservations needed. At 1857 S. King St., 5th Floor; 949–2526. $$$.

✳ **Auntie Pasto's.** If you love good Italian food at the kind of prices you pay in Italy, not New York, you'll love this Beretania Street storefront bistro. Serving a wide array of pasta dishes, from a top-of-the-line lasagna to a creamy pesto, Auntie Pasto's feels like eating at a friend's house. Reservations are not accepted, so get here early if you don't want to wait in line. At 1099 S. Beretania St., at the corner of Pensacola; 523–8855. $.

✳ **Ichiryu Noodle House.** When you get the yen for saimin or rahmen (the difference is in the soup stock), this is a place to assuage that hunger. Ichiryu Noodle House is on the corner of South King and Pensacola Streets, not far from downtown Honolulu, and offers fifty-two varieties of rahmens, noodles (hot and cold), saimin, and soba udon. Take-outs are available. At 1103 S. King St.; 591–8033. $.

✳ **Cafe Sistina.** An upscale Italian eatery, Cafe Sistina offers a great variety of pastas, fish, and poultry. Free jazz performances are given every Sunday by local musicians. At 1314 S. King; 596–0061. $$.

✳ **Phillip Paolo's.** In a remodeled old home and patio not far from downtown or Waikiki Beach, Phillip Paolo's "Home of Fresh Pasta, Seafood & Salads" features Italian-style seafood at its best. At 2312 S. Beretania Ave.; 946–1163. $$$.

✳ **Caffe Aczione.** A charming little hideaway in the McCully District, this cafe is frequented by university students and coffee lovers. The menu features a huge variety of specialty coffees and fountain drinks, as well as a yummy assortment of baked goods. Lunches offer salads and sandwiches, with plenty of vegetarian choices, and the dinner menu features pastas and pizza pies. The menu is limited, but the food is fresh and wholesome, the portions large, and the tab small. At 1684 Kalakaua Ave.; 941–9552. $.

✳ **Chiang-Mai.** Specializing in Northern Thai cuisine, Chiang-Mai's menu offers a variety of curries, salads, soups, and noodles. There's also a large vegetarian section to choose from. The food is fresh and tasty, and the special Thai sticky rice is done to perfection. Be sure to regulate the "hotness level": if you don't care for ultra-spicy food, mild versions of all dishes are available. At 2239 S. King St.; 941–1151. $$.

✻ **I Love Country Cafe.** There's always a crowd at this small plate-lunch place, and after one meal there, you'll understand why. The menu is quite diverse, ranging from low-fat, low-cal boneless, skinless grilled chicken breast with papaya salsa to cholesterol-laden Philly cheesesteak. There are plenty of vegetarian selections and tasty fruit smoothies. This is a favorite local lunch spot, so either arrive early or expect a wait. At 451 Piikoi St.; 596–8108. $.

✻ **A Taste of Saigon.** For a really interesting lunch or dinner, order the combination roll-ups. The waiter brings a dish of very thin, flat rice cakes, a tray full of assorted greens, vegetables, and broiled meats, and two sauces, one peanut and the other sweet-and-sour. Soak the rice cakes in water to make them flexible, then load on any combination of ingredients. Roll up, dip in sauce, and prepare to be enchanted by the taste. Wash it all down with some of the special iced coffee, and you'll be a Viet-food fan forever. At 2334 S. King St., Honolulu; 947–8885. $.

✻ **Yanagi Sushi.** This little restaurant may have the best sushi in all Oahu. If you are an inexperienced sushi-er, this is a great place to start. The quality is superb and you may order a wide variety. At 762 Kapiolani Blvd.; 537–1525. $.

✻ **Grace's Inns.** A mini-chain of "local-style" fast-food shops. Plate lunches are standard fare with such delicacies as chicken katsu, sweet-and-sour pork, and chili with rice, as well as hamburgers, hot dogs, etc. Not gourmet but filling and inexpensive. Grace's Inns are at 98–280 Moanalua Rd., Aiea; 94–866 Moloalo St., Waipahu; 1296 S. Beretania; and 1111 Dillingham Blvd. $.

✻ **Mekong Thai.** In two locations, this family-run restaurant features outstanding Thai food in a low-key, friendly atmosphere. Try the spring rolls appetizer and the satay for a main dish. Be sure to have a spice tolerance—Thai food is not for the weak. (You can request mild seasonings.) At 1295 S. Beretania and 1726 S. King; 591–8842. $.

Just beyond Waikiki are two shopping centers, Ward Centre and Ward Warehouse, both of which offer a great variety of eateries.

* **The Chowder House.** Simmering bowls of either red, Manhattan-style chowder or creamy, Boston-style chowder are served. Chowder House has a nice variety of other seafood dishes, with luncheon specials and a children's menu. In Ward Warehouse, 1050 Ala Moana Blvd.; 596–7944. $$.

* **Kincaid's Fish, Chop & Steak House.** Yet another reason to visit the Ward Warehouse shopping center is this excellent eatery, where there are always interesting daily seafood specials. Open for lunch and dinner, Kincaid's has a wide variety of standard dishes on the menu, including entrees just for kids. It's a great place to have a business lunch or meet a friend for sunset cocktails. In Ward Warehouse, 1050 Ala Moana Blvd.; 591–2005. $$$.

* **Compadres.** From the interesting, reasonably priced Mexican menu, try the smoke-oven specialties: baby back ribs or *pollo borracho* (drunken chicken)—a whole bird smoked, marinated in white wine, and then grilled. At Ward Centre, 1200 Ala Moana Blvd.; 591–8307. $$.

* **Keo's at Ward Centre.** Excellent Thai-style cookery in the elegant setting of Ward Centre's posh shops; 596–0020. Dishes are listed with mild, medium, and hot seasoning strengths. If you haven't had experience with Thai dishes, stick with mild. Also at Kapahulu, 737–8240. $$.

* **Mocha Java Espresso & Fountain.** This delightful coffee bar in the Ward Centre pavilion features a wide selection of gourmet coffees and pastries. Stop in for an espresso milkshake after a busy afternoon window shopping the boutiques; 597–8121. $.

* **Ryan's Parkplace Bar & Grill.** Related to the famous Cutter's restaurants on the Mainland, this Ward Centre eatery features an elegant brass-and-hardwood bar with almost every beer and ale made. The food, which is quite good and reasonably priced, includes lots of pasta dishes and special dishes for kids; 591–9132. $$.

* **Yum Yum Tree.** Similar to Mainland-based Marie Callendar's chain,

the Yum Yum Tree features pies and baked goods but also offers a diverse menu that includes kids' entrees and has everything from pastas to hamburgers. Try the Portuguese Bean Soup—it's a specialty and it's wonderful! Five locations, at Ward Centre, 523–9333; Kahala Mall, 737–7938; 970 N. Kalaheo Ave., 254–5861; Westridge Shopping Center, 487–2487; and Mililani Town Center, 625–5555. $.

✺ **A Pacific Cafe.** This is the newest arrival at Ward Centre, and it's definitely worth a visit. The menu features the best of Hawaii Regional Cuisine, and the flavors will explode in your mouth and leave your taste buds wanting more. Reservations recommended; 593–0035. $$$.

DOWNTOWN

Downtown Honolulu is the financial and commercial heartbeat of the city, but it's also home to several historic structures representative of Hawaii's multicultural roots. Within its boundaries are the only royal palace in the United States, a 155-year-old church built from coral blocks, and a living museum dedicated to preserving life as it was during the missionary era.

Juxtaposed among these old relics are sparkling new high-rises, the state capitol, Chinatown, and the Aloha Tower Marketplace. Downtown is a wonderful place to stroll and people-watch. While lawyers, bankers, and politicians hustle to their next appointment, merchants in Oriental herb shops sell such unusual products as snake tails and bat eyes. With its art galleries, flower shops, and coffee kiosks, combined with its Oriental flavor, its business sense, and its history, downtown is a potpourri of the old and the new—and it's compact, relatively clean, and possible to see in a day.

Honolulu TimeWalks offers interpretive walking tours of the city that are educational, a great bargain, and a guaranteed good time. The tour subjects change regularly and include such topics as "The Revolution of 1893" and "The Scandalous Days of Old Honolulu." During the tour, the guides, often in period costume, will take you to the exact location of historical events pivotal to Hawaii's past. They paint the picture so well, you'll almost feel as if you're watching history unfold. The most popular tour is "Ghosts of Honolulu," led by storyteller extraordinaire Glen Grant. His tours fill up quickly, so it's best to call a few days in advance to make a reservation; 943–0371.

Iolani Palace was built in 1882 during the reign of King David Kalakaua and is among the most significant historical structures in all Hawaii. It's the only royal palace in the United States and is designated a National Historical Site, representative of an era when kings and queens rode regal horse-drawn carriages. There were royal celebrations that lasted for days during Kalakaua's reign.

It was important to King Kalakaua that Hawaii be on a par with Europe in its manifestations of majesty, and he designed the building to resemble Queen Victoria's royal residence in England. It was the first place west of the Mississippi to have running water, electricity, and phone service.

Sadly, the palace is also the site of the Revolution of 1893, when a select group of local businessmen, officially known in history books as the Committee of Safety, overthrew Hawaii's monarchy and deposed its ruler, Queen Liliuokalani, sister of the then-deceased Kalakaua.

Guided tours by well-trained docents are given Wednesday through Saturday, from 9:00 A.M. to 2:15 P.M. The tours last for forty-five minutes, and reservations are recommended because each one fills up quickly. Admission for adults is $8.00, children five to twelve get in for $2.00. Children under five are not admitted—there are too many priceless antiquities around to risk exposing to youthful, energetic toddlers. For recorded information call 538–1471; to make reservations, call 522–0832.

It's a good idea to plan your tour for a Friday morning. After the tour, you can enjoy a picnic on the lawn and listen to the free concert given every Friday from 12:15 to 1:15 P.M. by the Royal Hawaiian Band.

Situated kitty-corner from Iolani Palace is **Kawaiahao Church.** The church was constructed from 1836 to 1842 under the supervision of its missionary minister, Hiram Bingham. More than 14,000 coral blocks were taken from offshore reefs to build the structure, and its 154-year-old weather-beaten facade remains as a hearty testimony to the craftsmanship. This is Honolulu's oldest church. During the heyday of the monarchy, it functioned as the royal chapel, where kings, queens, princes, and princesses came to pray. It was also the site of weddings, funerals, and royal inaugurations. Today, services are held every Sunday at 10:30 A.M. The church is located at the corner of South King and Punchbowl Streets; 522–1333.

Directly across King Street from Iolani Palace is **Aliiolani Hale,** the state judiciary building. Kamehameha V, a predecessor of King Kalakaua, originally directed its construction in 1872 as a royal palace. Kamehameha V died before the structure was completed, and it was later redesigned as a court building because Kalakaua had alternative palace plans.

After the monarchy was overthrown in 1893, all eyes in Honolulu were focused on the steps of Aliiolani Hale. It was here that the first proclamation was read by the members of the Committee of Safety. The proclamation stated that the sovereign nation of Hawaii no longer existed and the land would be controlled by a provisional government. Thus Hawaii began its journey to statehood, which ended with its designation as the fiftieth state in August 1959.

The **bronze statue** in front of Aliiolani Hale is a tribute to King Kamehameha the Great, who was the first Hawaiian monarch to consolidate all of the islands under one rule. This was no small feat because each island was under the domain of a different chief or king. Kamehameha and his warriors endured a series of bloody battles and finally triumphed. The result was an organized society with a defined caste system of chiefs and commoners that flourished until the monarchy was overthrown.

As an everlasting tribute, June 11 is King Kamehameha Day, a state holiday in Hawaii, and on this day the statue is draped with hundreds of floral leis bursting with a rainbow of color—quite a fragrant spectacle.

Mission Houses Museum is a living museum designed to show visitors the importance of the missionary era in Hawaii. The missionaries arrived in 1820 from the eastern coast of the United States with a goal to convert the "heathen" natives to the ways of their Christian god. Their success and the resulting impact on Hawaiian society were tremendous. European-style clothing became commonplace, Christian marriages performed, and the hula, a rhythmic form of communication, was pretty much discontinued. Missionaries believed the ancient dance to be vulgar and distasteful, and it remained mostly absent from the culture until King Kalakaua assumed control in 1874 and reinstated the hula.

At the Mission Houses Museum, guides and hosts are dressed in period clothing. These actors make believe they are the missionaries who made that long pilgrimage overseas years ago. They welcome questions about their journey, their lifestyle, their religious motives, and, most interestingly, their interactions with the native Hawaiians.

The museum grounds encompass two main houses, a printing-house annex, a library, and a gift shop. Each building is restored and furnished to its former architectural and decorative design.

The museum is open Tuesday through Saturday from 9:00 A.M. to 4:00 P.M., on Sunday from noon to 4:00 P.M. Admission is $5.00 for adults, $4.00 for children under eighteen. It's located at 533 South King Street; 531–0481.

While the entire family may not be interested in visiting an art academy, there truly is something for everyone at the **Honolulu Academy of Arts.** This institution boasts an international collection of works by respected artists set among a maze of indoor/outdoor hallways. The kids will be able to occupy themselves in the many picturesque courtyards. There is a restaurant and gift shop on the grounds.

The Academy is at 900 S. Beretania Street, across the street from Thomas Square. It's open Tuesday through Saturday from 10:00 A.M. to 4:30 P.M., Sunday from 1:00 to 5:00 P.M., closed Mondays. Guided tours are conducted Tuesday through Saturday at 11:00 A.M. and Sunday at 1:00 P.M. There's a general admission of $5.00, but the first Wednesday of every month is free. For more information, call 532–8701.

Kakaako Waterfront Park is a new park situated smack in the middle of an industrial area and offers a nice respite for recreation between Waikiki and downtown. It's at the oceanside end of Coral Street, off Ala Moana Boulevard. The park features wide paved walkways often filled with rollerbladers and bicyclists. It's a great place for a midday picnic, although the facilities are minimal; you'll have to bring your own supplies.

Soon this park will be home to the **Children's Discovery Center,** scheduled to open in summer 1997. The center will have state-of-the-art interactive exhibits that offer hands-on experiences. It's sure to be great for kids of all ages. Don't miss the chance to visit this fantastic facility, where you can feel what it's like to walk on the ocean floor, visit with children in other countries, and learn about the physical properties of bubbles. For more information, call 592–5437.

Another oceanbound tour is on **Royal Hawaiian Cruises'** *Navatek* ship. The luncheon cruise lasts from noon to 2:00 P.M. and travels along the "gold coast" of Kahala, where all the million-dollar mansions are situated. On Friday, the cruise features music by one of Hawaii's most renowned entertainers, Auntie Irmgard Aluli and her accompanying group, Puamana. The luncheon buffet on Friday, Saturday, and Sunday features Hawaiian food, with international cuisine offered Tuesday through Thursday. There is no lunch cruise on Mondays. The cruise costs $47 for adults, $28.50 for children ages two to eleven; kids under two are free. In season (January through April), the *Navatek* sails on a morning whale-watching cruise that lasts from 8:30 to 11:00 A.M. and costs $39 for adults, $24 for children ages two to eleven. There is also a year-round sunset dinner cruise that sails nightly, from 8:15 to 10:15 P.M., and costs $75 for adults, $55 for children ages two to eleven.

The *Navatek* is constructed with a double-hull swath design that virtually eliminates the rocking and rolling from the ocean currents. It's ideal for passengers who are prone to motion sickness.

Imagine that when the **Aloha Tower** was built in 1926, it was the tallest structure on the island. As you travel in an elevator to the top of the tower, it's amazing to note how the high-rises of Honolulu and Waikiki far surpass this tiny structure. Be sure to take a ride to the top—it's free, and the panoramic views of the harbor and surrounding cities are spectacular. It's open from 8:00 A.M. to 9:00 P.M.

The tower was recently restored, and the surrounding marketplace full of restaurants, recreation venues, and boutique-type shops opened in November 1994. Today residents and visitors arrive to dine in the specialty eateries and stroll through the open-air mall. But in the old days, before jet travel carted hundreds of tourists at a time to these fair shores, visitors arrived via steamer ship and all passengers disembarked at Aloha Tower.

Whenever a ship was due in, it was known as "Boat Day" in town. Locals would greet the incoming visitors in outrigger canoes and on surfboards in the water. It was always a celebration, complete with food, music, and dancing.

Although jet travel has rendered the tower's usefulness as an embarkation site relatively unimportant, it is the departure and arrival point for American Hawaii Cruises' *Independence,* which casts off on

Tuesday evenings.

Kids will love visiting Aloha Tower, especially the state-of-the-art virtual-reality complex, where the latest and greatest in electronic arcade games exist. Most noteworthy is the laser-tag arena, in which participants don specially equipped vests and enjoy an old-fashioned game of team tag, modernized with laser lights.

The tower is a fun place to be on Friday evenings during the *pau hana* (after work) hour. Free Hawaiian entertainment by well-known local musicians is featured at the open-air Pier Bar, weather permitting, usually from 5:00 to 7:00 P.M.

Gordon Biersch Brewery Restaurant, Hawaii's first full-fledged brewery, offers a tasty selection of beers and just as tasty menu. The cheeseburger has that good barbecued taste that reminds you of outdoor picnics, but the best menu item has to be the garlic french fries! At Aloha Tower Complex, 101 Ala Moana Boulevard; 599–4877. $$.

There are several other restaurants in Aloha Tower Marketplace, ranging from casual cafeteria-style to Tex-Mex to steak and seafood.

With its isolated location in the middle of the Pacific, Hawaii understandably enjoys a rich maritime historical heritage. The **Maritime Center,** adjacent to the Aloha Tower Marketplace, displays that history in a wonderful interactive setting. The center actually is the site of a former boathouse used by King David Kalakaua in the late 1800s. The facility has been wonderfully restored to house an incredible 2,000 years of Hawaii's oceangoing history.

Exhibits are both indoor and outdoor and include videos; three-dimensional figures; interactive, hands-on displays; and a do-it-yourself audio tour with portable cassette players. The tape uses realistic sound effects and voices to present the displays in a fun, educational manner.

You'll see how the first Polynesians arrived and be able to appreciate the danger and duration of their journey—dependent on wind, weather, celestial navigation skills, and the seaworthiness of their hand-carved canoes.

Kids will gravitate to the surfing exhibit, the highlight of which is a film portraying the brave local experts who think nothing of sliding full-force down the face of 30-foot waves on Oahu's north shore.

Another popular display focuses on whales. Especially noteworthy is the complete skeleton of a humpback, one of only two on display worldwide. The carcass was discovered on Kahoolawe, an uninhabited Hawaiian island. You'll really get a feel for the whale's immense proportions when standing next to the 750-pound skull.

The center is open 8:30 A.M. to 5:00 P.M. daily, except Christmas Day, and offers free parking. Admission is $7.50 for adults, $4.50 for children ages six to seventeen (under six free); 523–6151.

Right next to the Maritime Center, the **Falls of Clyde** is the only remaining fully rigged, four-masted ship afloat in the world. Now a National Historic Landmark, this ship was part of the Matson Navigation Company and was used as a cargo and passenger liner from 1898 to 1920. Since 1960 the ship has been used as a floating museum. The ship is open daily, 9:00 A.M. to 5:00 P.M.; admission is $7.00.

At the Maritime Center, not only will the *Falls of Clyde* catch your eye, but you'll also be drawn to the **Hokule'a,** an authentic replica of a Polynesian voyaging canoe built in 1976. It recently sailed 6,000 miles to Tahiti and back, manned by a crew that used traditional Polynesian navigational methods. Although some modern materials were used during its construction, the design was kept as traditional as possible, using lots of petroglyphs (ancient rock carvings) and old drawings as the basis.

Hawaii has maintained a rich Chinese heritage since the first laborers arrived in the mid-1800s to work in the sugar plantations. Their passage was a ticket to a form of indentured servitude that typically lasted five years and provided cheap labor for the sugar barons. When their time was up, however, most of them stayed, started businesses, and established the **Chinatown** that exists today.

In 1900 a major fire burned Chinatown to the ground. But the immigrants painstakingly rebuilt, and some of the old buildings that exist today are not only fine architectural examples of that era, but also a testimony to the determination of its people.

A stroll through Chinatown is likely to be filled with unusual and exotic sights, smells, and tastes—it's a virtual symphony of senses. (It's a good idea to keep a close watch on your children around this area. While it's basically safe and well policed, some parts are representative of Hon-olulu's "seedy" side.)

Be sure and check out the recently restored **Hawaii Theatre** at the corner of Bethel and Puahi Streets. Inside are murals representative of the art deco style popular during the 1920s and 1930s.

For a look at Hawaii's finest lei-makers, and a wonderfully fragrant treat, you won't want to miss the many lei stores situated on Maunakea and Beretania Streets. Prices are very reasonable here, and locals often come from all parts of the island to purchase leis for special occasions.

You'll walk by meat markets, where windows display hanging ducks, drying and readying for the next meal. There are acupuncture and herb shops advertising, believe it or not, powdered monkey brain—sure to cure whatever ails you! If that doesn't suit your fancy, there are always signs advertising coiled snake skin and mashed antelope antler.

If you still have an appetite, there's an immense variety of great food priced very inexpensively. You can pick from Chinese, Korean, Viet-namese, Hawaiian, Filipino, Thai, Japanese, and even Italian, as well as the American standard represented by those "golden arches."

Over the past few years, Chinatown has benefited from a rebuilding—many old structures have been refurbished and transformed into galleries and restaurants. **Indigo Restaurant,** an elegant new upscale hideaway in the heart of downtown Honolulu, offers "Eurasian" Cuisine: classic Euro-pean dishes with an Asian twist. The menu features meal-size pizzas with unusual toppings, and a variety of fresh fish dishes ranging from salads to pastas. Come prepared to sample new flavors; some of the dishes are served with different dipping sauces on the side. Open for lunch and dinner, reser-vations recommended. At 1121 Nuuanu Ave.; 521–2900. $$$.

Two organizations offer **walking tours** that present a good overview of the area for a reasonable price. The **Chinese Chamber of Commerce** sponsors a narrated tour every Tuesday from 9:30 A.M. to noon. The tour begins at the office at 42 North King Street and costs $5.00; kids under twelve are admitted free. For more information, call 533–3181.

The **Chinatown Historical Society** offers a walking tour that covers the heart of the district. The tour goes from 10:00 A.M. to noon daily, Monday through Friday. Guides will take you through colorful, exotic shops; historic buildings; and the famous open market. This tour costs $5.00 for adults; kids twelve and under pay $3.00. The tour meets inside Asia Mall at 1250 Maunakea Street. For more information, call 521–3045.

Heading west out of Downtown, you'll soon run into the **Dole Cannery Square,** constructed around the canning factory of Hawaii's most famous fruit. The cannery has been converted into a retail center and food court. It's fun to walk around the complex and view the antiquated machinery that's still in place. It's an unofficial museum of Hawaii's pineapple industry. The cannery is at 650 Iwilei Road; 531–2886.

For a fun family picnic amid stately trees, **Foster Botanical Gardens** is an ideal locale. The gardens encompass fifteen acres of manicured lawns and are situated on the outskirts of downtown Honolulu, at the corner of Vineyard Boulevard and Nuuanu Street. The gardens are open from 9:00 A.M. to 4:00 P.M., and admission is $5.00 for adults, $1.00 for children ages six to twelve. Guided tours are offered Monday through Friday at 1:00 P.M. For more information, call 522–7065.

The hills and valleys behind Downtown and Waikiki are dotted with small communities called Manoa, Makiki, Nuuanu, and Punchbowl, all of which possess unique characteristics and histories and feature outstanding hiking trails and important cultural sites.

Manoa Valley is the site of the University of Hawaii and Punahou School (K–12), the oldest private school west of the Mississippi. In the back of the valley, **Lyon Arboretum** will be a fun, but usually wet, adventure.

There are many ongoing scientific projects at Lyon, and you'll be impressed with the variety, quality, and abundance of plants at this place. The arboretum is open Monday through Saturday, 9:00 A.M. to 3:00 P.M.; 988–7378. To get there from Waikiki, follow McCully to Beretania Street, and turn left. Turn right on Punahou Street, which turns into Manoa Road. The arboretum is at 3860 Manoa Road. Donation suggested.

On the way to Lyon Arboretum, look for Manoa Marketplace off Manoa Road. Try **Paesano** for lunch or dinner and you'll be treated to one of Oahu's best Italian restaurants. The menu features a wide selection of pasta, meat, chicken, veal and seafood. Reservations recommended for dinner. At 2752 Woodlawn Dr.; 988–5923. $$.

Take a drive to **Tantalus** and **Round Top,** an area high in the hills above **Makiki** that offers breathtaking views of the city and a few good hiking trails. This is a great area for exploring, as the trails receive regular maintenance and are well-kept. There are eleven different trails to take here, but use good judgment; not all of them are suited for young children.

To get the **Makiki/Tantalus Trail** from Waikiki, head up McCully Avenue, turn left on Beretania, right on Keeaumoku, then right on Wilder. At the first light, turn left onto Makiki Street. You'll cross Nehoa Street, then go left on Makiki Heights Drive, which eventually winds into Tantalus Drive. You'll soon enter the Makiki Recreation Area and pass Hawaii Nature Center on your right. Eventually a chain in the road will force you to park and walk.

On foot, once you pass the chain, the road narrows and becomes **Kanealole Trail.** From here, a variety of trails cross over and run parallel to Kanealole. You can bring a picnic and spend the whole day up here enjoying the view, or you can do a quick twenty-minute escape to nature, where it's unbelievable that busy Waikiki is less than 10 miles away.

If your family includes really young children who are unable to enjoy the hiking trails, by all means you should still drive to the top of Tantalus for a king-size view of the island.

To get to the **Manoa Cliff Trailhead,** and a great family hike, follow Round Top Drive until you pass Forest Ridge Way. Look for a large turnout that offers parking on both sides of the road. The **Moleka Trail** is easily navigable and begins on the right. It's only a half-mile long and the views are outstanding. The trail leads to a bamboo forest and continues on to a wide area with a panoramic view.

The trail to the left leads to Round Top Drive, where it splits into three sections. The **Makiki Valley Trail** slices across the valley to the right; Ualakaa Trail veers left, goes for about a half-mile, and joins with the Makiki Valley Trail to **Puu Ualakaa State Park.** The **Makiki Branch Trail** goes straight for a half-mile and ends at the bottom of the valley at the Division of Forestry Baseyard.

These trails are very safe and are well-maintained by the Division of Forestry and Wildlife. One note of caution: This area is *always* muddy and mosquito-laden, so dress accordingly and bring some repellent along.

Even nonartistic kids will be captivated by the beautiful setting of the **Contemporary Museum.** An old estate was converted into a museum, and the exhibits are situated literally all over the place. The grounds are chock full of interesting modern sculptures, and visitors may stroll about at their leisure. With the exception of a colorful permanent display of David Hockney works, the exhibits are always changing and reflect different themes in modern art.

The museum is at 2411 Makiki Heights Drive and is open 10:00 A.M. to 4:00 P.M., Tuesday through Saturday, and noon to 4:00 P.M. on Sunday. Closed Monday. A great restaurant and wonderfully stocked gift shop are on the premises. Admission is $4.00. For more information, call 526–1322.

The **Nature Center,** a geared-for-kids facility, is also in Makiki. It provides a hands-on approach that turns learning about Hawaii's unique flora and fauna into a fun experience. Guides lead visitors on trails that feature native plants, flowers, and trees. The trails are geared toward younger children, but everyone is welcome. Participants get a chance to touch, see, feel, and smell nature in its most pristine environment—all under the supervision of resident naturalists.

On weekends the Nature Center hosts community programs for families that further explore Hawaii's natural environment through earth care projects, nature crafts, and interpretive hikes.

A nonprofit organization, the Nature Center is truly something not to be missed. It's at 2131 Makiki Heights Drive; 955–0100. It's open 8:00 A.M. to 4:30 P.M. Free admission.

A little farther back into the mountains sits the **National Memorial Cemetery of the Pacific** and the Honolulu Memorial. The area is known as Punchbowl because it's situated in the middle of an extinct volcano and actually resembles the shape of a punch bowl.

This may be a rather somber site to visit, but after Pearl Harbor, it's the second most attended place in all of Oahu and an important testimony to Hawaii's brave heroes. The cemetery is filled to capacity with 33,143 gravesites, including one for Ellison Onizuka, the Hawaii astronaut who died in the *Challenger* shuttle disaster and 776 casualties from the December 7, 1941, attack on Pearl Harbor.

The impressive Honolulu Memorial on the northwest wall of the crater was dedicated on May 1, 1966. It honors the sacrifices and achievements of American armed forces in the Pacific during World War II and the Korean Conflict, plus those missing from the Vietnam conflict. Park your vehicle behind the memorial and explore the map galleries to see where important battles took place.

From the back of the memorial, walk toward the ocean on the Outer Drive and follow the Memorial Walk up to the overlook area. You'll be rewarded with one of the best views of Honolulu—from Diamond Head in the east all the way west to Ewa Beach.

The National Memorial Cemetery of the Pacific and the Honolulu Memorial are open daily from 8:00 A.M. to 6:30 P.M.; 566–1430. To get to Punchbowl from Waikiki, take McCully to Beretania and turn left. Turn right on Pensacola, which eventually curves left and turns into Awaiolimu. From here, look for Puowaina Drive, which leads to the main gate.

Heading west of Waikiki on H–1, a detour on the Pali Highway (Route 61), leads to lush **Nuuanu Valley,** home to many religious temples and shrines, representative of the vast variety of ethnic groups that call Oahu home.

Volunteers guide visitors through the royal mansion known as the **Queen Emma Summer Palace.** Queen Emma was married to King Kamehameha IV, and the couple used this beautiful home as a summer retreat. The Daughters of Hawaii have facilitated its meticulous restoration, and many of the family's personal belongings are on display. The architecture and interior decor are reminiscent of Great Britain; Queen Victoria was good friends with King Kamehameha IV.

The palace is at 2913 Pali Highway and is open 9:00 A.M. to 4:00 P.M. daily. Admission for adults is $4.00; children under twelve get in for 50 cents. For more information, call 595–3167.

Hold on to your hats as you climb up the paved walkway to the **Pali Lookout.** You'll feel as if you're at the windiest spot in the planet! (Although there's no scientific information to prove this and it's probably a bit of an exaggeration, the winds do whip fiercely here.) It's so windy that water from the nearby waterfalls (if it's rained lately) is often carried upward by the winds. The setting offers an unobstructed view of the lush windward side of the island and is nothing short of spectacular. Be sure to bring a jacket or sweater—the winds create quite a chill in the air, making it at least 20 degrees cooler here than it was back in Waikiki.

Some historians claim this is the site of a major battle during King Kamehameha's quest to consolidate all the islands under one rule. Kamehameha won and drove some 16,000 warriors to their deaths over these very cliffs. One look down, and you can easily imagine the despair of the losing side.

You can take the **Judd Loop Trail** from the parking lot at the Pali Lookout. To find the trail, exit the H–1 West on the Pali Highway (Route 61). You'll pass Queen Emma Summer Palace on your right, then bear right on Nuuanu Pali Drive. The road will fork, but keep bearing right, staying on Nuuanu Pali Drive. Look for a stone bridge over a small stream, after Polihiwa Place. There will be another small bridge marked 1931 that covers a reservoir spillway. Park in the small dirt lot just before the second bridge.

The trail is a little more than 1 mile, and the whole loop will take less than one hour. It's a wonderful forest walk that includes one of Honolulu's most popular isolated swimming holes. It's a good idea to have kids wear tennis shoes, even when swimming, as there may be broken glass hidden in the mud. The trail is very easy to follow and passes through groves of banyan and mango trees.

From the parking lot go down to the Nuuanu Stream and cross the stream immediately (do not take the trail heading downstream). A wide trail leads away from the stream, through a bamboo grove. Ignore the side trails along the stream and bear right along the slope. Climb gradually through eucalyptus and Norfolk Island pines. Again, ignore the side trails heading uphill or down to the stream. Enter the Charles S. Judd Memorial Grove of Norfolk Island pines. As the trail descends, bear left into a shallow gully. The turn is marked by a short metal stake. Cross the gully and bear right, parallel to it. Almost immediately you reach the junction with the Nuuanu Trail, which leads off to the left. (The Judd loop continues straight downhill and back to the starting point.) You can continue on the **Nuuanu Trail,** which is a little more advanced and is not recommended for young children. The two trails combined cover about 3.5 miles. If your kids are young, stick to the Judd loop.

Maunawili Demonstration Trail is one of Oahu's easiest and most accessible trails. Soon after passing the Pali Lookout, you will go through a tunnel. Almost immediately, a sign points to a scenic overlook. Pull off into the parking area and walk back up the highway for about 100 yards, where you'll see a break in the guardrail and a sign for Na'ala Hele, the Hawaiian Trail and Access System.

This trail is great for children because it's relatively flat, with minimal gains and losses in elevation. It offers scenic views as it twists along the windward side of the Koolau Mountain Range. The noisy traffic diminishes and you find yourself in a beautiful tropical forest.

To hike all the way to the end will take more than three hours. You can find a nice, scenic, secluded spot for a picnic not too far in. Remember: As with all Hawaiian trails, recent rainfalls make for treacherous footing.

Route 61, the Pali Highway, continues all the way to Kailua and the windward side of the island, which is included in a later section of this chapter.

From Waikiki on H–1, if you don't detour on Route 61, you'll head right toward **Bishop Museum.** Exit at Likelike Highway and turn right. The second right leads straight to the museum.

Bishop Museum features fine exhibits of the natural and cultural history of Hawaii. On display are royal cloaks crafted from millions of colorful feathers. The difficulty involved in constructing them made them priceless, and only the highest *ali'i* (chiefs) were allowed to don them.

You'll get a firsthand glimpse into the past, in which precontact Hawaii thrived as a Stone Age culture. There are weapons, cooking utensils, and even a replica of a grass hut, or *hale,* that was used for shelter.

There is a series of fantastic nature exhibits that cover the evolutionary adaptations unique to the Pacific Basin. Before man arrived, the Hawaiian Islands were even more isolated than the Galapagos, which were the primary focus of Charles Darwin's theory on evolution. As a result, species developed here in a completely natural, symbiotic state. For example, rather than forming nests in trees to keep eggs safe, birds were ground nesters because they had no predators.

JULIE'S TOP FAMILY ADVENTURES ON OAHU

1. Hiking Diamond Head
2. Visiting Iolani Palace, the United States' only royal residence
3. Enjoying a sunset picnic at Ala Moana Beach Park
4. Hiking to Manoa Falls
5. Exploring the Pacific's unique flora and fauna at Hawaii Nature Center
6. Snorkeling or SNUBA-ing at Hanauma Bay
7. Wading through Pupukea Tide Pools
8. Watching the marine creatures at Sea Life Park
9. Climbing to the windswept Pali Lookout
10. Strolling through Bishop Museum

The cave exhibit is especially fascinating. You can peek into an assimilation of a newly formed lava tube and learn about the unusual life-forms that exist on the barren, hot lava.

There is a planetarium on-site that lets you gaze into the skies above Hawaii and contemplate the vastness of the universe.

The museum is located at 1525 Bernice Street; 847–3511. There is a restaurant and gift shop on the grounds. The facility is open daily from 9:00 A.M. to 5:00 P.M. Admission is $7.95 for adults, $6.95 for children ages six to seventeen, and free for children under six.

Aiea, the next town heading east, is pretty much a residential community. But above all the homes, restaurants, and businesses is an important site of Hawaiian history and a fun hike. At the top of Aiea Heights Drive sits **Keaiwa Heiau State Recreation Area.** At first glance, this ancient structure will probably look like a bunch of old stones piled together somewhat haphazardly, but don't let its simplicity belie its importance. Ancient Hawaiians used the heiau as a place of worship, a sort of pre-Western temple. Different heiau served different purposes; some were for healing, some for refuge from war or crime, and some were for quiet meditation. Keaiwa was a healing place where *kahuna* (priests) concocted magical potions that cured sickness and disease.

Remnants of the extensive herb garden that once flourished around the stone heiau still exist. Kahuna used every part of these plants—the roots, leaves, bark, and flowers—to mix the concoctions that, when combined with prayer, worked to heal.

As with any significant archaeological site, it's important to tread carefully here, with respect. You may see small rocks wrapped in *ti* leaves scattered about. These were left by locals as a sign of respect, and visitors are encouraged to convey the same attitude of reverence. This doesn't mean you should feel pressured to find a rock and a ti leaf, but you should encourage your family to properly appreciate this holy spot.

From here, you can follow the park road to the 4.5-mile **Aiea Loop Trail,** which begins here. It's a fun, easy hike that's suitable for families and takes about three hours. You'll pass through damp forests of eucalyptus trees and come out on one of the ridges of the Koolau Mountain Range, with scenic, majestic canyons on both sides of you. The views of the mountains and Pearl Harbor below are wonderful, and the feel and smells of the eucalyptus trees are a nice alternative to the sun-soaked, suntan lotion–laden waters of Waikiki, just a few miles away.

To get to the park, take H–1 west to Route 78 toward Aiea. Exit at Halawa Heights/Stadium, which puts you on Ulune Road. Follow Ulune for a few miles until it dead-ends, and turn right on Aiea Heights Drive. Follow Aiea Heights Drive all the way up the long hill and it will end at the park. The park is open from 7:00 A.M. to 6:30 P.M.

Continuing west, on the way to Pearl Harbor, near the Honolulu International Airport, **Kelly's Coffee and Pastry Shop** is a great place to stop if you've got a case of the hungries. The place where the locals go for "ono grinds" (good eats), Kelly's has all the standard stuff with plenty of coffee or iced tea to wash it down, and offers a nice selection of light snacks or pastries for dessert. It's under H–1 where Puuloa Road intersects Nimitz Hwy., at 2908 Kamehameha Hwy.; 836–3444. $.

The **Arizona Memorial at Pearl Harbor** is consistently the most visited, most recognized attraction on Oahu every year. Although Pearl Harbor captured worldwide attention on December 7, 1941, with the surprise attack by Japanese planes that catapulted the United States into World War II, the military controlled the area long before that. In 1887 King Kalakaua signed the Sugar Reciprocity Treaty that provided for profitable, duty-free exportation of sugar in exchange for the U.S. Navy's full control of the harbor.

A visit to Pearl Harbor consists of an onshore museum/display area, a short film, and a boat ride to the memorial. The visitor center at Pearl Harbor emphasizes the area's strategic location and the military's presence in Hawaii since 1887. Today, all five services are represented here. Oahu is the headquarters of CINCPAC (Commander in Chief Pacific), which oversees 70 percent of the earth's surface, from California to the east coast of Africa and to both poles.

The museum displays materials from World War II naval history. There are actual letters written by servicemen stationed here to loved ones on the Mainland. The letters paint a poignant picture of young men who lost their lives.

There is a great system of maps that show the route of the Japanese planes and models of the ships that were damaged. There's even some old wreckage displayed in glass cases.

The film depicts life in the islands before the attack, the military happenings in other parts of the world, and the far-reaching devastation caused by Japan's bombs. It's an emotional and impressive film, made even more meaningful by the elderly veterans who are always there. By the time movie is over and you're shuttled to the boat, there are more than a few damp handkerchiefs.

The boat takes you to the USS *Arizona* Memorial, where the remains of 1,100 men are entombed forever within the hulk of the once-mighty battleship. The memorial was built in the 1960s, and Elvis Presley staged a benefit concert that helped raise more than $60,000 for the building fund. The structure straddles the sunken ship, and looking out into the water, you can see the *Arizona* sitting on the ocean floor. It is still leaking oil and shows no signs of stopping. The walls of the memorial are decorated with all the names of soldiers who lost their lives on December 7, 1941.

The visitor center is open daily, 7:30 A.M. to 5:00 P.M., but closed Thanksgiving, Christmas, and New Year's Day. The shuttle boat runs from 8:00 A.M. to 3:00 P.M. daily (it starts at 7:30 A.M. in the summer). There is no admission. Call 422–2771 for recorded information or 422–0561 for more information.

The facility does become quite crowded; it's best to arrive before 10:00 A.M. for the shortest wait. On the average, expect a ninety-minute wait from when you arrive and are given a ticket until your number is called and you're ushered into the theater. During that ninety minutes, however, you can walk around the museum. There are a gift shop, snack bar, and restrooms.

Getting there: If you're driving from Waikiki, take H–1 west, exit at 15A, and follow the signs. The entrance is actually along Route 99, the Kamehameha Highway. The *Arizona* Memorial shuttle bus (839–0911) offers $6.00 round-trip transportation from several Waikiki hotels (kids under six ride for free).

Paradise Cruises (593–2493) offers a different type of cruise around the harbor from 8:30 A.M. to noon but does not stop at the USS *Arizona* Memorial or the visitor center. Admission is $26.50 for adults, $13.25 for children ages three to eleven.

USS *Bowfin* Submarine Museum and Park is situated so close to Pearl Harbor, it's unfortunately often dwarfed by its famous neighbor. Here you can venture below the deck of the USS *Bowfin,* a fully restored World War II submarine nicknamed "The Pearl Harbor Avenger." Visitors are treated to a glimpse of the tight quarters in which the crew ate, slept, worked, and probably prayed during the rigors of World War II and Korea. The *Bowfin* journeyed on nine successful patrols and was a Naval Reserve training vessel until being decommissioned in 1971.

Next door to the submarine is a museum that chronicles the advancements in submarine technology from 1776, when the first attempt at building a submersible vehicle was made, to today, when high-technology, nuclear-powered machines patrol the waters.

Admission is $8.00 for adults, $3.00 children ages four to twelve. Children under four are permitted in the museum, but cannot go aboard the ship. The facility is open 8:00 A.M. to 4:30 P.M. daily, closed Thanksgiving, Christmas, and New Year's Day. For more information, call 423–1341.

Continuing west on H–1 from Pearl Harbor, you'll soon arrive in the small residential community of **Waipahu.** Don't miss a visit to the **Hawaii Plantation Village,** a living museum dedicated to the many immigrants who arrived in Hawaii to labor in the sugar cane fields.

An illuminating guided tour takes visitors through a historically re-created plantation that displays lifestyles during the early nineteenth century. It's a wonderful multicultural experience comprising eight villages, each one representing a different ethnic group.

Admission is by a suggested donation of $5.00. The village is located at 94–695 Waipahu Street; 677–0110. If you visit in September, be sure to attend the annual Plantation Heritage Festival for a great slice of local, multiethnic life. There are cultural performances, arts and crafts, a variety of unusual foods, rides, and games. The village is open 9:00 A.M. to 4:30 P.M., and tours are given at the top of every hour, Monday through Saturday, with the last tour leaving at 3:00 P.M.

LEEWARD COAST

This is the dry, desertlike side of the island. In recent years, it has become the site of increased development. You'll notice Hawaii's first outlet mall in Waikele, where **Discovery Zone** (671–5437) offers a fun respite for kids with bargain-hunting, shopping-hungry parents.

Beyond Waikele, the new resort development is called **Ko Olina.** So far, all that's been completed is Ihilani, a beautiful five-star luxury resort, and an award-winning golf course. This area is sure to grow in years to come—the weather is outstandingly sunny and it offers a calmer, more scenic alternative to Waikiki. And, it's only about thirty minutes (during non-peak traffic hours) from many of the popular sites around the island.

At the new resort property called Ihilani, **Azul** is *the* place for dinner, with Chef Suki Sugiura's own special Mediterranean and Pacific Rim cuisine. Appetizers are incredible and entrees out of this world. **Naupaka Terrace,** open for all three meals, also offers Chef Suki's special cuisine. The restaurant's open-to-the-sea dining area is Hawaii at its best. **Kyu-An** specializes in traditional Japanese fare, but again with Chef Suki's magic touch. Ihilani Resort, 92–1001 Olani Street; 679–0079. $$$.

The beach at Ihilani is man-made, is accessible to non–hotel guests, and is one of the prettiest sites on the island. The tranquil setting and warm water are ideal for kids, and the sandy beach will appeal to any sun-worshipping teenager or parent.

In an effort to steer some of the development away from Honolulu and its traffic hassles, there is a new residential community here called Kapolei. It's one of Hawaii's first attempts at "affordable housing," though one look at the real estate section of the newspaper will lead Mainlanders to consider that term an oxymoron. Nevertheless, attractive prices have lured thousands to the leeward side of the island, and Kapolei will undoubtedly continue to grow and prosper in the future.

When you head out this way, be sure to take a detour on Route 760 to **Ewa Beach Park** or **One'ula Beach Park.** Both beaches are spacious, sunny, and quite scenic.

Don't miss a ride on the historic **Ewa Beach Railway.** Operated by Oahu's Historic Railway Association, the little train travels the same route

Face painting is a favorite activity for young keiki at Ihilani Resort. (Courtesy Sheila Donnelly & Associates)

used by locomotives during sugar's heyday. Tracks were laid here in 1889 to carry the sugar from the central plains of the island to ships docked at the harbor. When automobiles and trucks arrived, the trains were rendered obsolete and unfortunately were left to rust and decay. Today, they have been painstakingly restored, so you'll feel as if you are one of the plantation workers making the short trek.

The train station is at 91–1001 Renton Road. The narrated ride lasts about ninety minutes and costs $8.00 for adults, $5.00 for children ages two to twelve. Two trips are made every Sunday, and seating is on a first-come-first-served basis. For directions or reservations, call Oahu Railway Association at 681–5461.

Back on H–1 heading west, the interstate turns into Route 93, Farrington Highway, which runs north to the tip of the island at Kaena Point. This is the **Waianae Coast,** marked by a series of beach parks, mostly maintained by the city or state. Many of the beaches are not good for swimming or for children, because of either dangerous currents or rocky shorelines—those beaches, although picturesque, are intentionally not included in this family adventure guide.

The first swimmable site is **Nanakuli Beach County Park,** in tiny Nanakuli town. The park features basketball courts, a baseball field, restrooms, and a little playground for kids, in addition to a spacious beach. Lifeguards are here daily, and it's a good idea to consult them about the current safety level. The ocean on this side of the island can be rough and dangerous in winter.

Another little town, **Maili,** doesn't have much other than a 7-Eleven, a gas station, and a few residential developments. It's just south of Waianae, and the beach here is truly pretty. The park is well-maintained, clean, and a great place for family outings. The beach is ideal for snorkeling, swimming, boogieboarding, and surfing. Restrooms are on-site.

Continuing north on Farrington Highway, you'll soon arrive in the little towns of **Waianae** and **Makaha.** As the highway curves north, the sparkling blue sea beckons stronger here than almost anywhere else on the island. The different shades of blue, contrasting with the sparkling white sand, framed by lava rock promontories and the Waianae Mountains, are so pretty that you'll be compelled to pull over and contemplate the view.

Makaha Beach County Park is best known as the site of the Annual Buffalo Big Board Riding Championship. "Buffalo," refers to Richard "Buffalo" Keaulana, one of Hawaii's best-known and top-rated lifeguard/surfers. If you're here during the winter, pull over and witness some of the biggest waves in all Hawaii. (Don't even *think* of entering the water during the winter, however. Even some of the most experienced swimmers and surfers have had to be rescued from here.) On the other hand, summer visitors will enjoy the calm waters, which are ideal for families.

To find Makaha Beach, look for the landmark black rock called Lahi Lahi. There will probably be a smattering of local fisherman congregated around the rock. Behind you looms the Waianae Mountain Range and Mt. Ka'ala, Oahu's highest peak at 4,020 feet.

Visit **Kaneaki Heiau** for a great chance to see a replica of the seventeenth-century *heiau* (temple) that was built in praise of the Hawaiian god Lono, who represented agricultural harvests and fertility. The heiau has been restored by the Bishop Museum, and visitors here will see grass huts and a spirit tower where *Kahuna* prayed to the gods.

After you pass Makaha, the road gets a bit rugged. There are plenty of places to pull off and enjoy a picnic. Farrington Highway ends at **Kaena Point.** This is the only coastal section of the island without paved roads, so it's not possible to drive around the entire island.

It is possible, however, to hike around Kaena Point to Dillingham Field, Mokuleia, and the north shore of Oahu. Of course, if you hiked completely around, you'd have to turn around and hike back because your car would be stuck at the leeward side, so don't worry about making the complete trip. Parts of the journey require a little rock climbing and may be a bit difficult for youngsters, but by all means get out and explore the point.

Swimming is *not* safe here—strong winds whip the water full of whitecaps. On any given day, the largest waves in Hawaii will be at Kaena Point, and the giant tumblers are awe-inspiring to watch.

Hawaiian legend says that Kaena was a departure point for spirits making the journey from earth to heaven, and numerous heiau are situated here.

SOUTHEASTERN COAST

It is possible to drive around the island if you exclude the aforementioned Leeward Coast. From Waikiki, you can go either way—east or west—but for simple geographic preferences and to go against normal traffic-jam patterns, this guide heads east.

The Circle Island Tour starts at the southeastern side of the island, continues on the windward coast, travels around the bend at Kahuku, through the North Shore, and back to Waikiki via the central plains. It's a beautiful drive that offers an immense variety of sights and adventures. Plan at least a full day to be able to fit in a select choice of activities.

Your first stop should be Hawaii's most famous mountain—**Diamond Head.** Actually named Mt. Leahi, the crater earned its nickname from some gullible English sailors who mistook glimmering calcite crystals for that precious gem. It's so well known and well depicted in paintings, diaries, and visitor publications, it has become one of the more enduring symbols of Hawaii, along with pineapples, coconut palm trees, and plumeria leis. A visit to Oahu simply would not be complete without being able to tell your friends back home that you climbed to the top of Hawaii's state monument.

To get here from Waikiki, take Kalakaua Avenue south to Diamond Head Road. Keep driving around the mountain and look for the sign reading DIAMOND HEAD CRATER. It's right across the street from the Kapiolani Community College, recognizable for its series of brown buildings opposite Diamond Head.

After turning in, you'll pass through a tunnel and emerge at a large parking area surrounded by an even larger grassy field. The area used to be heavily manned with military equipment when it was a focal lookout point during World War II. There are still some vestiges of war here—gun emplacements and tunnels are built right into the mountain. Today it is home to a Hawaii National Guard depot and the Federal Aviation Administration.

The area is clean and safe, and signs point clearly to the trail. Try to ignore the pesky vendors who have set up stands at the trailhead, selling everything from bikinis to tuna sandwiches to T-shirts that verify the wearer actually climbed Diamond Head. Locals consider these businesses an eyesore at an otherwise beautiful natural setting, and the majority opinion dictates that such stands should be limited to Waikiki. Nonetheless, the constitution and a business license allow them to "sell" their products here. The issue is being debated in the courts, but the outcome is anyone's guess. On the plus side, you can stock up on cold water for the hot hike ahead.

The hike is ideal for grandparents, young children, and everyone in between. It's an easy, forty-five-minute trek that offers breathtaking panoramic views of Waikiki, downtown, and the Leeward Coast to the west, and Kahala, Kaimuki, and the eastern shores in the other direction.

The 0.7-mile trail leads from the crater floor to the bunker and lookout at the 760-foot summit. The structure up here was built in 1908 to serve as a U.S. Coast Artillery Observation Station. Although the trail is used frequently and very well maintained, you will definitely develop a hearty thirst. Bring plenty of water, a flashlight, and binoculars—and most importantly, a camera with enough film.

Most of the trail is defined by sturdy guardrails. The only tough part necessitates climbing about 100 steep cement steps—sure to leave even the most physically fit a little short of breath. The rest is uphill but easy. Flashlights are recommended because one section—about 75 yards—is *inside* the mountain and therefore quite dark.

While hiking, it's intriguing to think that this tuff cone is suspected to be more than 350,000 years old. Geologists say it was formed when lava was forced out of a fissure and connected with the ocean in one gigantic explosion of steam and ash. The last eruption here is thought to have been more than 200,000 years ago.

The Clean Air Team, as part of a litter-control project, sponsors free guided hikes from Honolulu Zoo to Diamond Head every Saturday. The group meets at 9:00 A.M. near the main entrance to the zoo, at the corner of Kalakaua and Kapahulu Avenues.

After hiking, treat the family to the best milkshake in all Hawaii. Just a few minutes' drive from Diamond Head, **KC Drive Inn** serves an "Ono Ono" shake that is guaranteed to be a memory your taste buds will savor for a long time. (*Ono* means delicious.) KC Drive Inn is at 1029 Kapahulu Avenue; 737–5581. $.

In the funky little town of Kaimuki, don't miss a chance to taste Vietnamese food at **Hale Vietnam.** This is a great place to sample the popular appetizers: Vietnamese-style summer rolls (same concept as Thai spring rolls, but with a different twist) and stuffed chicken wings. There are also a variety of curries and *pho* (soup). Open for lunch and dinner, at 1140 12th Ave.; 735–7581. $$.

Heading east on H–1 from Waikiki, eventually the highway ends and turns into Route 72, Kalanianaole Highway. You'll first pass through the tony town of **Kahala.** It's a nice detour to veer off Kalanianaole and head down Kahala Avenue. The multimillion-dollar mansions on both sides of the road are where Hawaii's richest and most famous live. Remember that all beaches in Hawaii are public, so everyone has access to the silky sands that front even the most luxurious homes. Look for the "right of way" signs and enjoy a wonderful, calm stretch of sand ideal for children.

Kahala Mall is a good stopping point for a variety of restaurants.

* **Bernard's New York Deli.** This is the place for fresh, New York–style deli food. Even the service and atmosphere will remind you of the Big Apple; 732–3354. $.

* **The Patisserie.** The best store in this mini-chain is at Kahala Mall, though there are others around Honolulu that offer good value on baked goods and quickie meals; 735–4402. $.

* **Yum Yum Tree.** Similar to Marie Callendar's chain, the Yum Yum Tree features pies and baked goods but also offers a diverse menu with everything from pastas to hamburgers. Five locations, at Kahala Mall, 737–7938; 970 N. Kalaheo Ave., 254–5861; Westridge Shopping Center, 487–2487; Ward Centre, 523–9333; and Mililani Town Center, 625–5555. $.

* **California Pizza Kitchen.** Currently at three locations—Kahala Mall, Pearlridge Center, and Waikiki—this fast-growing chain makes pizza like you've never tasted before. Santa Fe Chicken Pizza, for instance, has grilled chicken breast, sautéed onions, and cilantro, topped with fresh tomato salsa, sour cream, and guacamole. Also, there are salads, pastas, and desserts. Take-outs are available. At Kahala, 737–9446; Pearlridge, 487–7741; Waikiki, 1910 Ala Moana, 955–5161. $$.

Kahala Avenue ends at the newly renovated **Kahala Mandarin Oriental Hotel.** Formerly the site of the Kahala Hilton, this five-star resort is frequented by movie stars such as Sylvester Stallone and Gary Shandling. The beach here is well protected and very shallow—ideal for children. You can walk about 50 yards out, and the water level won't change.

It's worthwhile to park and walk around the grounds—filled with a man-made lagoon, waterfalls, and flower gardens. A pair of dolphins live in the lagoon, and feeding time is a sight to watch. Kids will delight as the dolphins perform amazing antics in expectation of a lunch reward. Feeding times are 11:00 A.M. and 2:00 and 4:00 P.M., and the show is free, although parking costs $6.00. You can get free parking if you eat at one of the resort's restaurants. **Plumeria Beach Cafe** offers oceanfront dining, fabulous lunch and dinner buffets, and a kiddie menu. $$. **Hoku's** is the signature restaurant and presents the fine cuisine in an air-conditioned room overlooking the scenic resort. $$. For more information, call the Kahala Mandarin Oriental Hotel, 5000 Kahala Avenue; 739–8888.

Continuing east on Kalanianaole Highway, you'll pass through the residential communities of Aina Haina, Niu Valley, and Kuliouou before arriving in **Hawaii Kai.** Previously swampland, this now-exclusive area was developed in the late 1960s by Henry Kaiser, a wealthy businessman with a million-dollar dream. Kaiser succeeded and Hawaii Kai has grown tremendously; it's now home to award-winning restaurants, two shopping centers, a Costco, and a movie theater.

❈ **Cha Cha Cha Salsaria.** Located in the Costco Shopping Center in Hawaii Kai, Cha Cha Cha offers a casual combination of Mexican and Jamaican tastes. Tortillas are made fresh daily. The salsa is spicy and the beer is cold. At 333 Keahole St.; 395–7797. $.

❈ **Roy's.** If seafood is your favorite, a visit to Roy's is absolutely required; Roy's does seafood right! It's truly a fine showcase for Hawaii Regional Cuisine. Go early to get a window seat so you can watch the sunset over Maunalua Bay. At 6600 Kalanianaole Highway; 396–7697. $$$.

People come from all over the island to use the boat harbor along the coast here at **Maunalua Bay.** On any given day, you'll see a dozen craft out in the water, some fishing, some waterskiing, some just cruising.

Commercial vendors have long used the calm waters here to take willing participants on parasailing trips and jet-ski and wave-runner rides. Parasailing involves being strapped onto a large parachute and lifted into the air by the boat's forward momentum. You travel about 30 feet above the water and enjoy wonderful views, the wind in your hair, and a daring adventure.

Jet Skis and **wave runners** provide less passive adventures. Jet Skis are like a motorized floating motorcycle on which the participant stands or kneels, turning a mechanism on the handlebars to make it go forward. Wave runners allow the rider to sit and are therefore a bit easier to manage. Rates vary, as do age requirements, so it's best to call for more information. The outlets based in Hawaii Kai are Aloha Ocean Sports, 396–4889 or 396–2810; Fun Island Watersports, 395–4386; and Marine Sports, 396–6982.

For **waterskiing** enthusiasts, the Suyderhoud Water Ski Center in Koko Marina Shopping Center will take all levels of expertise and specializes in beginners. The fee is $49 and includes about a half-hour on the water combined with on-land instruction and a descriptive video. There is no real age requirement; as long as your kids are watersafe, they can learn to ski. For more information, call 395–3773.

Continuing on Kalanianaole past Maunalua Bay, the road ascends Koko Crater. **Hanauma Bay State Underwater Park** will be on the right. A visit to Hanauma Bay definitely will be one of your family's Oahu highlights. The natural inlet surrounded by coral reefs creates a warm-water safe haven for Hawaii's most colorful exotic fish and has a well-deserved reputation as a world-class snorkeling site.

Snorkeling equipment is available for rent at the visitor center (about $10 a day), so you needn't lug your own down the tiresome hill leading to the beach. Supplies are limited, so be sure and get there early. Once you've donned the requisite mask, snorkel, and fins, a whole new underwater world unfolds. Coral and more than 1,500 different types of shells sit in a rainbow spectrum of colors, forming a reef that feeds and shelters thousands of multicolored fish.

The water is so clear that even children who don't know how to swim can simply walk along the shoreline and still see multitudes of fish.

The aquatic life here is protected by state law, meaning you can look but can't touch, and you most definitely cannot try to bring anything home as a souvenir. As a result, the fish here are so tame and so used to visitors that they will eat right from your hand. Fish pellets are sold on the premises. It's a good idea to bring an underwater camera so Mainland friends and family will really believe you had fish eating from your outstretched palm.

Recently, constant overuse by Oahu's six-million-plus annual visitors has begun to affect Hanauma Bay. After so many years of being hand-fed, the fish were beginning to quit nibbling on the reef, upsetting the natural symbiotic relationship. Even worse was the reef's condition—severely compacted and broken from thousands of tromping feet. As a result, the crowds at the beach are now kept to a minimum—when it gets too full, a friendly policeman is situated at the entrance and will not let any more cars into the park. Also, the bay is closed to the public every Wednesday morning—allowing park staff and Mother Nature time to repair and replenish. The suggested donation is $5.00 per car.

It's best to arrive early in the morning—before 9:00 A.M.—to guarantee admittance. Additionally, early morning hours offer the clearest water as the sand has yet to be kicked around by hundreds of fins, creating a kind of gray murkiness.

For a fun adventure, and if weather's permitting, take a walk over the rocks, around the eastern edge of the bay, for a real surprise. Once you've rounded the corner, notice the large natural hole in the ground. This is called the **Toilet Bowl** by locals because as the water recedes before a wave, the level in the hole drops, similar to how a toilet flushes. When a wave comes in, the water level rises.

It's fun to stand inside the toilet bowl and let yourself rise and fall with the tide. It's quite safe but not recommended for young children, because it's sometimes hard to get out. Also, pay close attention to the weather. Storms arrive quickly in Hawaii, often without warning. During a storm, big waves will pound violently on these rocks, making the short walk and the toilet bowl very dangerous—even for experienced locals.

Continuing on the highway, what follows next is one of the more spectacular scenic routes in all Hawaii. The road was built right on the edge of the mountain and the dark blue ocean contrasts with the black lava cliffs and creates a truly awe-inspiring sight. There are a few scenic turnoffs for picture-taking purposes.

Be sure to stop at the **Halona Blowhole,** a lava tube through which the ocean shoots forcefully every time a wave comes in. The spray can reach several feet high and can even douse the onlookers watching from the cement overhang above. During humpback whale season, from November through April, this is a great spot to scan the horizon for that telltale plume or fluke. (A fluke is the end section of a whale's tail. During mating season the male whales slam their flukes against the ocean surface with a resounding slap that can be heard from several yards away, or as much as a hundred yards on a quiet day.)

Just west of the blowhole, toward Hanauma Bay is a delightful little cove, known by locals as **"Cockroach Bay"** but recognized by the rest of the world as the site where Burt Lancaster passionately kissed Deborah Kerr in *From Here to Eternity.*

A short scramble down the rocks leads to a picturesque sandy beach, as calm as it is beautiful. If it's windy or stormy, however, don't swim. You'll probably be the only people there—not many people know about this secluded sight. The channel is strong here and can suck even strong swimmers out to sea.

About two minutes past the blowhole, you'll see **Sandy Beach** on your right. Sandy's is popular with local boogieboarders and surfers, but it's not recommended as safe swimming for visitors. More broken necks, backs, and drownings occur here than at any other beach in the entire state! Lifeguards here have been known to ask visitors to remain on shore. It is beautiful, however, and it's quite entertaining to watch the local athletes expertly maneuver the big waves.

A few miles after Sandy Beach, the road wends through a golf course and veers left around a big bend. Directly below is **Makapu'u Beach,** the *best* bodysurfing spot in all Hawaii. Again, however, unless you're an expert, it's best to experience Makapu'u from the sand. As Sandy Beach ranks first in the number of annual injuries, this ranks a close second.

This beach is also beautiful and great for picnics and parties. During the summer, when the waves and currents are weak, it's quite safe to swim.

Offshore are two tiny islands that are sanctuaries for seabirds. Man-ana, the larger one, is known as Rabbit Island because a rancher tried breeding rabbits there in the late 1880s. It worked and descendants of those original rabbits still live there. Kaohikaipu, the smaller island, is called Turtle Island by locals because it looks like a turtle lying in the water.

Just across the highway from Makapu'u, **Sea Life Park** is a fun-filled and educational marine park that's home to dolphins, sea lions, penguins, and the world's only wholphin (a cross between a whale and dolphin—imagine that!). Although not entirely endemically correct (penguins are not indigenous to the tropics), the park is wholly entertaining and will be one of your children's favorite Hawaii activities.

One of the more popular exhibits is the 300,000-gallon Hawaiian Reef Tank, filled with colorful creatures from Hawaii's waters, including reef fish, sharks, eels, and turtles. You can walk 3 fathoms down a ramp and go nose-to-nose with more than 2,000 different specimens.

At the open-air Hawaii Ocean Theatre, penguins, sea lions, and dolphins entertain audiences under the patient tutelage of their trainers. The

Children greet the penguins up close and personal at Sea Life Park. (Courtesy Monte Costa/Sea Life Park)

penguins usually steal the show with their comical tricks.

At Whaler's Cove, dolphins help tell tales of Old Hawaii in a beautiful lagoon, in which sits a ⅝-size scaled-down replica of the *Essex,* a nineteenth-century whaling ship.

Some of the other attractions include the Penguin Habitat, the Shark Galley, Turtle Lagoon, and the *Kolohe* (crazy) Kai Sea Lion Show, featuring the park's residents in a variety of comedy routines.

Sea Life Park is open daily, 9:30 A.M. to 5:00 P.M. On Friday, it remains open until 10:00 P.M. and a free Hawaiian concert is performed at 8:30 P.M. There are a restaurant and gift shop on-site.

Also here is the Pacific Whaling Museum, which boasts the largest collection of whaling artifacts and memorabilia in the Pacific. Entrance to the museum is free, but admission to the rest of the park is $19.95 for adults, $9.95 for juniors ages four to twelve. A free shuttle bus transports tourists without wheels to and from Waikiki. For more information, call 259–7933.

Route 72 soon leads to the agricultural town of **Waimanalo.** As soon as you hit the 7-Eleven, you've arrived. The landscape is dotted with small farms and old homes. Residents are primarily Hawaiian. At one time this was the center of a thriving sugar plantation. When the plantation closed in the 1940s, so did financial security for residents. But the land is rich and fertile, and things have picked up in recent times. Today, most of the bananas, papayas, and anthuriums that fill Honolulu's homes and hotels come from Waimanalo.

Waimanalo Beach Park is a great place for learning how to body-surf or boogieboard. The waves are small enough so you won't get hurt, but forceful enough to let you maneuver about. There are a picnic area, restrooms, a pay phone, and a lifeguard on duty. This is Oahu's longest stretch of sandy, swimmable coastline—3.5 miles long. It's a veritable paradise for beachcombers!

Just beyond Waimanalo Beach Park, look for the turnoff immediately after the McDonald's. The sign for **Sherwood Forest** is small and difficult to see, but the beach is definitely worth a stop. The beach is calm, inviting, and a great place for the whole family. The waves aren't big enough to surf, and the water is safe year-round for young children.

The only potential hazard here is the frequent appearance of Portuguese man-of-wars. Look around the shoreline for any that have washed up. They look like quarter-size opaque bubbles, with a long, bluish tail. A sting is really no big deal and feels much like a bee sting, providing you have no serious allergic complications.

If there are no man-of-wars on the sand, then it's a green light to jump in the water. If you do get stung, the quickest remedy is—believe it or not—meat tenderizer. In fact, most local beachgoing moms and dads always bring a bottle of meat tenderizer with them to the beach . . . just in case.

Right next door to Sherwood's, just a few minutes' drive down the highway, is **Bellows Beach.** At one time this was an Air Force base. Today it's an R&R retreat for active duty personnel, complete with cabins, a grocery store, and campgrounds. The beach park is open to the public every weekend, from noon on Friday to 6:00 A.M. on Monday, and on every federal and state holiday, from 6:00 A.M. to 6:00 A.M. the following day. As with Sherwood's, water is safe year-round for kids of all ages, the only danger being an occasional appearance of Portuguese man-of-wars.

Camping is allowed with a permit from the City and County of Honolulu Parks and Recreation Department, Box 621, 1151 Punchbowl St., Honolulu, HI 96809; 587–0300.

WINDWARD SIDE

After Bellows, Kalanianaole Highway rolls through more agricultural/residential areas until arriving at Kailua and the lush, green windward side of the island. **Kailua** and **Kaneohe** are residential communities that seem to beat at a slower pace than those neighborhoods closer to Honolulu. There's a Marine Corps Air Station in Kaneohe, and many military personnel call this area home.

There are no major resorts here and just a few bed-and-breakfast inns. The result is untouristy, uncrowded beaches. Windsurfers crave the constant winds on this side of the island, and on any given sunny day, you'll see at least a few colorful sails jumping over the waves.

To get to Kailua proper, turn right on Kailua Road from Kalanianaole Highway. Kailua winds through central downtown—past old-fashioned storefronts, eateries, and sailboard stores. The street dead-ends at Kalaheo

Avenue and the beach.

It is possible to get to Kailua directly from Waikiki instead of traveling though Kahala, Hawaii Kai, and Waimanalo. Take H–1 west and exit at Route 61, the Pali Highway. Continue on 61 through Nuuanu, the Pali Lookout (already discussed in an earlier section), and through the tunnel. Eventually, you'll see a sign pointing to Kailua Road and the entrance to town.

Kailua Bay and Kailua Beach County Park outranks all other beaches on the island as the top choice for windsurfers. Not only do the experienced love to come here, but a variety of commercial outlets take first-timers here to learn.

In addition to windsurfers, the water often is chock-full of boats, Jet Skiers and kayakers—all competing for the right of way. All this activity creates congestion that can be hazardous to a casual swimmer. You get the feeling that you've got to be moving on something fast, or get out of the way! If you're there strictly for swimming, it's best to stay in the shallow waters of the lagoon. The park does offer great picnic facilities, showers, restrooms, lifeguards, and a snack bar.

For experienced windsurfers looking to rent a board and sail, or for the inexperienced itching to learn, contact one of the following vendors.

Naish Hawaii, 155A Hamakua Drive, 262–6068. Robbie Naish is a champion windsurfer and his company is well known for its custom boards, sails, hardware, accessories, and repairs. The windsurfing school offers half-day lessons for $55 ($75 for two people). Lessons include one and one-half hours of teaching and two and one-half hours on the water.

Kailua Sailboard Company, 130 Kailua Road, 262–2555. Here you can rent a board and try it on your own first. Windsurfers rent for $25 for a half-day and $30 for a full day. Group lessons are offered for beginners and cost $39 for three hours. During the week, the company brings its equipment right to the beach; on weekends the staff will help you with a pushcart or roof rack at no extra charge. Boogieboards and two-person kayaks are also available to rent at $10 and $39, respectively.

Lanikai Beach is the jewel of the crown for windward residents who count their blessings daily that tourists have yet to begin flocking here. It's breathtakingly beautiful: a mile-long expanse of soft white sand and shimmering aquamarine ocean. The surf is generally mild, and the beach is completely swimmable year-round. Lanikai is just south of Kailua. To get there, follow Kalaheo Avenue south to Mokolua Drive, where you'll see posted signs.

Just beyond Mokapu Peninsula and the military base sits **Kaneohe Bay.** A host of oceangoing recreational businesses operate from here and offer a different experience from the similar venues at Waikiki.

All Hawaii Cruises, 942–5077, offers hotel pickup if you didn't drive out here yourself. For $69, your outing will include a four-hour sail complete with a barbecue lunch, offering a dry way to witness the underwater world. Admission is $59 for juniors ages thirteen to seventeen, $49 for ages four to twelve, free for children under four.

Continuing on the Circle Island Tour, look for Route 83, the Kahekili Highway, which will take you all the way up the windward coast to the North Shore, where it turns into the Kamehameha Highway. The drive is beautiful, with the majestic wind-carved Koolau Mountains looming on your left and undeveloped expanses of pristine coastline on the right.

Up in the hills to the left are the **Haiku Gardens,** so beautiful they have become a favorite place for locals to have outdoor weddings and host special occasions. The gardens are free and anyone is welcome to walk around. In the early 1800s, Hawaiian chiefs gave the land to an engineer from England named Baskerville. He took great care to develop this area in a way that would enhance, not detract from, its natural beauty. There are a series of spring-fed lily ponds, a few homes, and acres of flowers, fruits, and ornamental trees. Later a restaurant was built, today the site of the Chart House, specializing in steak and seafood.

The next valley over from Haiku is known as **Valley of the Temples,** situated in the green hillsides high above the ocean. You can't miss the white Christian cross that's permanently planted up there. Valley of the Temples is a universal-faith cemetery that's so beautiful, it's become a popular visitor attraction.

If it's rained lately, be sure to scan the cliffs surrounding the valley for picturesque, rainbow-hued waterfalls. They're quite common here.

The Valley of the Temples Memorial Park is at 47–200 Kahekili Highway, 239–8811, and it's open 8:00 A.M. to 4:30 P.M. Admission is $2.00 per adult, $1.00 for children up to age twelve.

Byodo-In Temple is the main attraction of the Valley of the Temples. It's a replica of Japan's 900-year-old Byodo-In. This temple was built in 1968 on the centennial of the first wave of Japanese immigrants to arrive in the Islands. Kids will love having the chance to strike a three-ton brass bell; anyone is allowed to strike it after making an offering.

The grounds exude a sense of peace and contentment; gentle streams trickle slowly over well-placed boulders, koi frolic gracefully in a special pond, and birds chirp from distant trees. There is a small gift shop and snack bar.

The county's newest and largest botanical garden is **Hoomaluhia Regional Park,** a 400-acre park in the hills above Kaneohe. The park is planted with groups of trees and shrubs from tropical regions around the world. It's a peaceful, lush green setting, with a stunning pali backdrop. Hoomaluhia is not a landscaped flower garden, but more of a natural preserve. A network of trails wind through the park and up to a thirty-two-acre lake (no swimming allowed).

The little visitor center (233–7323) has displays on flora and fauna, Hawaiian ethnobotany, and the history of the park, which was originally built by the U.S. Army Corps of Engineers as flood protection for the valley below.

The park is at the end of Luluku Road, which starts a little more than 2 miles down Kamehameha Highway from the Pali Highway. It's 1.5 miles up Luluku from the highway to the visitor center.

The park is open 9:00 A.M. to 4:00 P.M. daily (except on Christmas and New Year's Day), and admission is free. Guided two-hour nature hikes are held at 10:00 A.M. on Saturdays and 1:00 P.M. on Sundays.

Senator Fong's Plantation and Gardens is the creation of Senator Hiram Fong, Hawaii's state senator from 1959 to 1976. Upon retirement, he set out to create his dream garden. After a lot of hard labor and dedication, his dream was realized in this idyllic spot.

Guided tram tours take visitors through the 725 acres and run from 10:30 A.M. to 3:00 P.M. Admission is $8.50 for adults, $5.00 for children ages five to twelve. The gardens are located at 47–285 Pulama Road at the outskirts of Kaneohe, near Kahaluu. For more information, call 239–6775.

The next two towns on the Kahekili Highway, **Waiahole** and

Waikane, are rural agricultural areas, where much of Oahu's taro is grown. Taro is a tuber root that Hawaiians grow to make poi, a sticky starch that accompanies every meal. (Be sure to sample some if you attend a luau.) The route is well maintained and a pleasure to drive. Inspirational beauty greets you at every turn.

Kualoa Ranch County Regional Park is situated against a backdrop of the spectacular Koolau Mountains. A variety of recreational fun is to be had here—everything from horseback riding to helicopter tours to Jet Ski rentals. Reservations are required; call 237–8515 for more information.

The beach park is spacious, pristine, and inviting. It's considered by many to be the best on this side of the island. Although the shoreline is rocky, swimming is safe year-round. If you're here at low tide, you can walk on the reef all the way to Chinaman's Hat, the little island sitting offshore. It's so named because it closely resembles the wide-brimmed hats the Chinese laborers wore to protect themselves from the glaring sun.

If you do trek to the island, be sure to wear some old, but well-soled, tennis shoes. Also, keep a constant watch on your kids. If a big wave were to suddenly hit, it would be very easy to slip off the reef.

This area possesses great historical significance and is included on the National Register of Historic Places. In Old Hawaii, all of the chiefs sent their royal children to be educated at this sacred site.

The park across from the ranch contains complete facilities, including restrooms, picnic tables, and lifeguards. It's open daily 7:00 A.M. to 7:00 P.M., and overnight camping is allowed with a permit.

In the lush, green town of **Kaaawa,** don't miss the **Crouching Lion Inn.** Just look for the many cars and tour buses parked at a hillside restaurant. The inn has been serving guests for more than fifty years and is an institution on this side of the island. Diners enjoy scenic views during lunch and dinner.

Look for the lion-shaped rock in the hills above the inn. Hawaiian legends say that the formation is really a god who was frozen in that position as a form of punishment.

The Crouching Lion Inn serves lunch daily from 11:00 A.M. to 3:00 P.M. and dinner from 5:00 to 9:00 P.M. It's at 51–666 Kamehameha Highway; 237–8511. $$.

Swimming is a good year-round activity at **Kahana Bay Beach County Park,** though it's never crowded. There are picnic facilities, restrooms, a small boat launch, and lifeguards here. It's quite picturesque and representative of all the quaint pockets of beach on this side of the island. It's worth getting out of the car and exploring.

Across the highway is **Kahana Valley State Park,** an idyllic spot for a picnic. It offers restrooms, picnic tables, and a freshwater stream that runs deep into the valley. Locals often kayak up the stream to the isolated area at the base of the cliffs.

In between the next two small towns, Punaluu and Hauula, look for the small marker identifying **Sacred Falls Park.** The 5-mile trail within the park is among the most popular on Oahu.

Although the hike is long, it's fairly easy for most families. Mountain apple trees flourish here and, when ripe (during the late summer months), offer a tasty treat. The hike begins at the ocean and ends deep in the crevices of the mountain, where a waterfall tumbles 90 feet down into a large pool. Although cold, the pool is swimmable. Be sure to bring warm clothes and lots of mosquito repellent.

The trail is well maintained and easy to follow. The only hazards come during the stream crossing—it's quite slippery. There are two additional notes of caution regarding this hike. If it has rained recently, or if rain is in the forecast, *do not attempt this hike.* This area is prone to severe flash floods, and the water level can rise to dangerous levels before you have a chance to get to high ground. Secondly, don't start hiking in late afternoon. When the sun falls, it's pitch black here, and you won't be able to navigate among the potential anklebusters of roots and rocks.

In Punaluu, don't miss **Paniolo Cafe.** This old-time country pub is run on the premise that a stuffed-full customer is a happy customer. The R'snake Burger is a half-pound of lean beef and is big enough for two normal hungry people (though Paniolo charges for an additional setup). Chi Chi and Mai Tai drinks are served in sixteen-ounce mason jars, and the Old-Time Burger is a huge half-pounder with crisp french fries. At 53–146 Kamehameha Hwy.; 237–8020. $.

Next is **Laie,** where the main attraction is the **Polynesian Cultural**

Center, which, along with Pearl Harbor and Punchbowl, is among the most-visited sites on the Island. The center provides a glimpse into the lifestyles and cultures of the South Pacific Islands.

Here you'll be greeted by islanders representing the seven different Polynesian groups—Fiji, Hawaii, New Zealand, Tahiti, Samoa, the Marquesas, and Tonga. Visitors are led through the villages either along waterways in a canoe or on a walking tour. Everyone is given the chance to explore the villages, learn the songs and dances, taste the foods, and watch demonstrations of ethnic arts and crafts. A Polynesian extravaganza, complete with hula dancers, fire dancers, and Hawaiian food, is held every night.

A big allure is the IMAX theater, a five-story wraparound movie screen that will make viewers feel as if they're actually paddling a canoe around the sands of Samoa or tromping over trails in the hills of New Zealand.

The center is open from 12:30 to 9:30 P.M. daily except Sunday. Admission is $27 for adults, $16 for children ages five to eleven, and children under five get in free. A variety of packages are available, including an

Children dress in traditional Polynesian costumes for May Day celebrations. (Courtesy Anthony Anjo/Hawaii Visitors Bureau)

all-day pass with dinner buffet and evening show for around $40 for adults, $27 for children. Transportation is also available to and from Waikiki hotels. For more information, call 923–1861.

Brigham Young University, or BYU-Hawaii Campus, is also in Laie. Several signs point visitors in the direction of the beautiful Mormon temple.

After passing through Laie, you'll arrive in **Kahuku,** the last town on this side of the island. Once a thriving sugar town, Kahuku is now best known for its shrimp farms and fields of aquaculture. You'll see signs advertising fresh (and they do mean fresh) Hawaiian prawns, and there's even a roadside stand with some picnic tables for people who can't wait until they get home.

The Kahuku Mill Shopping Center is on the north end of town. Although it features a few normal mall characteristics, this is no normal place of commerce. It's actually the old sugar mill, de-rusted and painted in bright colors so it looks like a modern sculpture. If you look carefully, however, you'll be able to see the huge gears and other machinery once used to refine sugar.

After the shrimp farms, a large, well-manicured golf course will appear on the right. This is the Turtle Bay Hilton Resort. The resort is a full-destination property, meaning it offers tennis, golf, horseback trips, and even ATV (three-wheeled all-terrain vehicle) rides on the sand.

The guided horseback ride takes visitors on a sandy stroll through the complex and into a bit of the natural terrain. Non-guests can participate for a fee, and reservations are required. The forty-five-minute rides are offered daily, except Monday. Admission for adults is $30, kids ages nine to twelve are $20. Riders must be at least 4 feet, 6 inches tall. For more information, call 293–8811.

NORTH SHORE

After passing Kahuku and driving around the northern tip of the island, you'll arrive at the fabulous North Shore, a haven for surfers and surf photographers from all over the world. When locals say they're going to spend the day in the "country," they're referring to the North Shore, a series of beaches and small towns that radiate relaxed charm and beauty. The water can be very rough here and the currents strong, sometimes even in summer. Kids should be cautioned to stay close to shore.

Note that the Kahekili Highway (Route 83) turns into the Kamehameha Highway (Route 99) after the road bends left, or west.

Sunset Beach is famous worldwide for its huge winter swells, but in the summer it can be as calm as a bathtub. It's appropriately named for its spectacular sunsets, but it's more popular as the site of the World Cup of Surfing. There are no picnic tables or restrooms here, but there is a lifeguard on duty.

Directly after Sunset, **Ehukai Beach** is across the road from the Sunset Beach Elementary School. Ehukai is the site of the famous "Banzai Pipeline," a major attraction for surfers. The pipeline is where the waves break in a round, cylindrical shape, creating a hollow tube. The best surfers are able to disappear inside the tube and emerge a few seconds later on the other side.

Like Sunset Beach, Ehukai is calm and safe during the summer. But in the winter months, do not enter the water under any circumstances.

A large group of **tide pools** at **Pupukea** offer an ideal place to see marine life in its natural state. To get there, park across the street at the Shell gas station. Look for the long wall that forms a sheltered pool at low tide.

Here safety is an issue only during rough winter swells; when the ocean looks mean and menacing, it's best to stay on dry land. Make sure you wear foot gear and beware of stepping on spiny sea urchins. (They look like porcupines and can poke right through tennis shoes.) It's also a good idea to wear a mask; you'll be able to see much more.

Look for Pupukea Road at the intersection of Kamehameha Highway and Foodland Market. Follow the road up the mountain to beautiful **Pu'u O Mahuka Heiau State Monument.** At the beginning of the access road, you'll see a sign warning against any further travel. However the road is well maintained and safe, and the sign is often ignored.

The heiau occupies about five acres and is marked by a series of stone steps leading to a lower level. It was a *luakini* temple, different from the healing temple described in Aiea. Human sacrifice was practiced here to honor the war god, Ku. The many stones wrapped in fresh ti leaves are evidence that people still come here to pray.

Continuing on Kamehameha Highway, **Waimea Bay** is the picturesque beach around the corner from Pupukea. Waimea boasts the biggest rideable surf in the world; wintertime waves can reach 40 feet! During the summer, however, the bay is calm, inviting, and a great place for a family picnic.

Waimea Falls Park is an 1,800-acre historic nature park situated in Waimea Valley. The well-marked entrance is directly across from the entrance to Waimea Bay. A visit to the North Shore should definitely include a side trip here—the sites are spectacular and offer exposure to a valley rich with tropical splendor and the history of Old Hawaii.

The Waimea Valley experience is divided into four stages, beginning with an exploration of ancient Hawaiian living sites. Here, visitors interact with native Hawaiians as they re-create the daily activities that took place here during the 1700s. Stage Two showcases the evolution of the hula through a performance by the Waimea Valley Dancers. The Hawaiian dancers also offer guests the opportunity to participate in a variety of cultural games. Stage Three features an acrobatic cliff-diving show performed at the park's 45-foot waterfall. Stage Four includes narrated exhibits of endangered plants, animals, and birds.

Visitors are given the option to explore the park at their own pace, or participate in a variety of tour packages. Waimea Valley by Night is a relatively new activity offered Friday through Sunday. A narrated tram tour presents the rich history of the valley. On the way to a fiery cliff-diving show at the falls, the tram pauses at twenty staged vignettes where actors dressed in authentic costumes of Old Hawaii reenact the activities of valley residents in the early 1900s.

Admission is $19.95 for adults, $9.95 for juniors ages six to twelve, and free for children five and under. The park is open daily 10:00 A.M. to 5:30 P.M.; 638–8511. There is a restaurant/snack bar on-site.

Waimea Adventure Tours offers ATV (all-terrain vehicle) rides and mountain-bike tours that explore the park's pristine north valley. There are also kayak rides along the Waimea River. For more information, call 638–8511.

Haleiwa Beach Park is at the entrance to Haleiwa town, a few miles beyond Waimea. The park features a sandy beach, playing field, basketball courts, picnic tables, and restrooms. Jet Ski and windsurfing lessons are available nearby.

The rustic seaside town of Haleiwa sits at the junction of Farrington Highway (Route 930), which continues west along the coast, and Kamehameha Highway (Route 83). The main street is a mixture of funky restaurants, fast-food joints, boutiques featuring hand-crafted clothes and jewelry, a few small-scale shopping centers, art galleries, and ramshackle wooden buildings housing surf stores.

You'll see a big crowd in front of **Matsumoto's Shave Ice Store**— and for good reason. Many locals swear that the Matsumoto family makes the best shave ice on the island. (Shave ice is comparable to a snow cone.) The most popular flavor is Rainbow, which includes a little bit of everything. For those with a sweet tooth, this is a definite must-visit.

Another "for good reason" crowd will be a little farther down the road at **Kua Aina Snack Shop**—reputed for the best burgers this side of Honolulu. $.

Jameson's By The Sea has become *the* place to eat, drink, and visit in Haleiwa. It draws crowds and waiting lines even when other nearby restaurants are wide open. The patio atmosphere, with Waialua Bay across the way, adds to the experience. And, don't forget to visit the Fudge Factory, which shares space with the restaurant; you won't be able to resist a sample and a take-home supply. At 62–540 Kamehameha Hwy.; 637–4336. $$.

If you pass Haleiwa and continue heading west, Kamehameha Highway changes to Farrington Highway, which ends at Kaena Point. **Wailua** is adjacent to Haleiwa and is an old, but scenic, sugar town.

Farther down, **Mokuleia** is the last nice stretch of beach on this side of the island. It's quite a picturesque site, with picnic facilities, restrooms, lifeguards, and a playground area. The few structures here are part of a camp frequented by local children and church groups during the summer.

Across the highway from Mokuleia, **Dillingham Airfield** offers a wide variety of **airborne tours.** Be sure to bring binoculars and a good camera if you choose to flight-see Oahu. The Honolulu Soaring Club offers glider rides that will provide a panoramic view of the North Shore. Flights last about twenty minutes and cost $90 for two people or $60 per person. Flights are offered daily on a continuing basis, from 10:30 A.M. to 5:00 P.M.

There's always a pilot with you to make sure your glider is a return trip.

You can also travel up in the air and back in time aboard a fully restored 1940-vintage open-cockpit biplane. These flights last twenty to thirty minutes. Cost depends on the route: the North Shore Scenic trip costs $125, the Pearl Harbor trip costs $175. Flights are available seven days a week, starting at about 10:00 A.M. on a first-come, first-served basis. For more information, call 677–3404.

If you don't detour to Mokuleia and the west side, you'll pass through Haleiwa and the central plains of Oahu on the way back to Waikiki.

CENTRAL OAHU

You can't miss the **Dole Pineapple Plantation,** clearly visible from Route 99. You can taste Dole's field-fresh pineapple slices and juice, and the cool Frosty Dole Whip. You'll also get to browse through a collection of unique Hawaiian souvenirs and edibles, including Morrow's nut products and Hawaiian Plantations brand preserves and condiments. You can buy some fresh-from-the-ground pineapple and walk through the Dole gardens to see the different varieties. Dole Plantation is open daily. Call 621–8408.

Right next door to the Dole Plantation is the **Helemano Plantation,** a facility that trains mentally challenged adults. Open to the public daily, the plantation has a bake shop, two gift shops, a garden, and a restaurant that offers a lunch buffet, salad bar, and sandwich bar. At 64–150 Kamehameha Highway; 622–3929.

Look at the intersection of Routes 803 and 80 for **Del Monte Pineapple Variety Garden,** a small but well-marked and informative roadside garden. Most varieties of pineapple grown worldwide are present and are identified with descriptive signs. There is also a little information about the history of pineapple production in Hawaii. The garden is free and well worth the stop.

The first thing you'll notice at **Wahiawa Botanical Gardens,** especially if it's been raining, is all that red, stain-provoking dirt. Be sure to wear shoes and clothes that you don't care about. The gardens encompass twenty-six acres, with an international collection of exotic trees, ferns, and flowers. The gardens are at 1396 California Avenue and are open daily 9:00 A.M. to 4:00 P.M., except holidays.

The Circle Island Tour concludes back at Waikiki, and if you've made the trip, you'll certainly have been exposed to the most beautiful sites on Oahu, from scenic Makapu'u Beach to the Windward Side to the North Shore. Oahu has more than twice as many attractions, parks, and fun things to do as all the other islands, so don't feel pressured to visit every site—maybe you'll want to save some fun for your next trip.

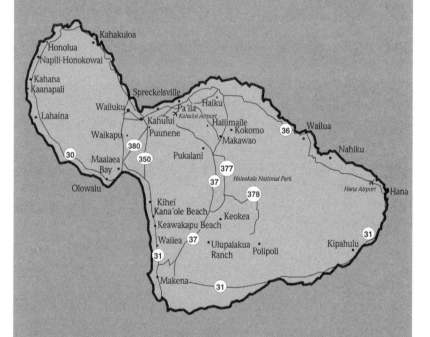

Maui

Maui

M aui, the Valley Isle, is the third most populated and second most visited Island. Every year about two million visitors grace its shores. With 150 miles of coastline, Maui offers more miles of swimmable beaches than any other island. Many of these beaches are pristine, shallow, and ideal for children.

The island is named after Maui, a mischievous mythological figure of ancient Hawaii whose antics are recorded in historic chants. One legend says that Maui dragged the Hawaiian Islands out of the ocean with a giant fishhook. Another tale tells of how Maui's mother, Hina, was having a hard time drying out her *kapa* cloth because the sun moved too quickly across the island. So, from the majestic crater of Haleakala, Maui lassoed the sun and forced it to crawl across the sky at a slower pace. Haleakala, known today for its long hours of sunlight, means "House of the Sun."

Geographically, the island is dominated by Haleakala, the world's largest dormant volcano, and the West Maui Mountains, always picturesque with their ever-present umbrella of lovely green mist.

The resorts and condominiums are concentrated in Kaanapali, Kihei, and Lahaina; the rest of the island is comprised of delightful small towns and nature preserves just begging to be explored.

Beautiful Maui is a sure bet for any vacationer. The lush eastern coast of Hana is replete with isolated waterfalls, fragrant gardens with giant ferns and wild orchids, and old-fashioned Hawaiian charm, while the southern and western coasts of Kaanapali, Lahaina, Kihei, and Wailea offer sunny skies, great snorkeling, and dazzling resorts. In between, there are dozens of gardens, state parks, and pristine rain forests that create a brilliantly colored sparkle over the land.

There's no Circle Island Tour on Maui as there is on Oahu, because the roads do not circumvent the entire island. This chapter begins in Lahaina, the most famous city on the island. From there, it will cover a circular route as much as possible as it shifts west to Kaanapali and Kapalua and continues over the northwest tip to Kahakuloa and drifts to Kahului. From Kahului, we'll head east to Hana and the end of the road at Kipahulu. Then, we'll travel the other direction from Lahaina, south along the coast to Kihei and Wailea, to the end of the road at Makena. Inland from Lahaina sits massive Haleakala to the east and Iao Needle Nature Preserve to the west.

Most people fly into Maui's biggest airport, in Kahului; there is a smaller airport in West Maui. Some airlines, including United, Delta, and Hawaiian, fly direct to Kahului from West Coast cities on the Mainland such as Los Angeles, San Francisco, and Seattle. Otherwise, you'll have to first land at Honolulu International Airport and catch an interisland flight on Aloha (484–1111), Hawaiian (838–1555), or Mahalo Airlines (833–5555). Sometimes the connecting flights can be booked as a package deal with your main airfare. If not, expect to spend about $100–$150 per person. Aloha and Hawaiian Airlines offer frequent-flier mileage that will be accepted by a major Mainland carrier.

Even though many of the island's resorts offer free airport pickup, and most of the excursion companies, such as snorkeling and sightseeing tours, offer transportation to and from your hotel as part of the package, it's a good idea to rent a car on Maui. It's easy to navigate around the island, and having your own set of wheels will reward you with miles and miles of beauty to explore.

Whether you're strolling through Lahaina or your own hotel lobby, it's likely you'll feel overwhelmed with all the tours to choose from—sightseeing, snorkeling, hiking, helicopter, bicycling, and so on. Tour desks are everywhere and offer an extensive menu of choices and venues, ranging from bicycles to catamarans to helicopters. These tours are great because most are led by guides knowledgeable in Maui's flora, fauna, and history, but don't think that packaged tours are a necessity to discover Maui's charms. Armed with this book and a good driving map, you'll be able to devise a do-it-yourself tour that's guaranteed to please.

One thing you're sure to notice immediately upon arrival is Maui's fascination with the mighty humpback whale. Not only are there an immense variety of whale-watching tours, but whaling museums and historical paraphernalia also abound. The humpbacks frequent Hawaii's waters from November through April, on their migratory way from Alaska. While in Hawaii's warm winter waters, they fatten up to prepare themselves for the long journey back. They also mate and give birth here; it's not uncommon to see males courting females and mothers swimming side by side with their young calves.

Of all the islands and all the channels in between, the southwest coast of Maui offers the best glimpse of these mighty creatures. The whales seem to favor the warm, protected waters within the boundaries of Kahoolawe, Lanai, Molokai, and Maui. The area of ocean that surrounds Maui has been designated as the Hawaiian Islands Humpback Whale National Marine Sanctuary.

From Kaanapali in the west to Makena in the south, several dozen commercial boat operators offer tours that will guarantee a whale sighting (in season). It pays to shop around, as some will offer discounts to children and free transportation to and from your hotel. Others offer breakfast and/or lunch and include a snorkeling trip along with the whale watching.

If you opt for a tour that includes a snorkeling excursion, and it's during the whale-watching season, be sure to stick your head underwater and listen carefully. One thing that differentiates humpbacks from other whales is their ability to sing. While no one has yet been able to decipher what their songs mean, it is clear that they communicate. Researchers from the Pacific Whale Foundation in Kihei say the singers are "escort males" that protect the females and their offspring. Intriguingly, all humpback whales sing the same song, over and over again.

But even if you can't hear the song, the whale-watching trip will be an unforgettable experience. You have to keep your eyes on the horizon and look for spouts. As soon as you see a spout, keep looking in that same area for a whale to breach. A breaching whale rises out of the water, arches its humongous body, and splashes back into the Pacific. It's an amazing feeling to witness such an impressive force of nature. When you see a mammal weighing several tons throw its body out of the water and land with a resounding "thump," it's quite awe-inspiring. Full-grown humpback whales can be more than 45 feet long and weigh more than forty tons!

The waters surrounding the Hawaiian Islands are designated a safe haven for these return visitors. Commercial whale-watching tour operators are prohibited from chasing a whale and from moving too close. Nothing, however, prohibits the sometimes curious whales from investigating *you*! Most boat captains, upon sighting a whale, will simply turn off the engine, or take down the sails and drift. Oftentimes, a whale will swim right up to the boat, then turn on its side so it can check out the passengers with its large eye. Once you've stared right into the eye of a whale, you'll never forget the experience.

WEST MAUI

Visitors flock to the historic city of **Lahaina,** considered by many to be a smaller version of Oahu's Waikiki. There are enough shops, historical sites, restaurants, museums, art galleries, and fun activities to please a variety of discriminating tastes.

Not only is modern-day Lahaina a playground for locals and visitors, its colorful history shows it's been a center for fun, frolic, and politics since the early 1800s. By the time King Kamehameha the Great died in 1819, the islands were consolidated under one rule and the king's successor, Kamehameha II, designated Lahaina as the first capital city. Kamehameha the Great had already commissioned the **Brick Palace,** Hawaii's first building, in 1801, and ruins from that original structure still remain in Lahaina. Although Kamehameha II later moved the central seat of government to Honolulu, where it remains today, Lahaina continued to be a hotspot of activity.

During the boom of the whaling industry, Lahaina was the world's greatest port, accommodating more than 500 ships at once in its bustling harbor. Whalers were known for their good-time revelry, and a jail was built in 1859 to hold contestants from various barroom brawls and vagrants who couldn't handle their liquor.

Then the missionaries came and tried to bring Christianity and order to a society proud of its drunken disorder. Churches and schools were built as followers of God's Word tried to squelch the alleged debauchery and rid the saloons of liquor.

Today, Lahaina retains some of that mischievous lifestyle by holding onto its reputation as a "good-time" town. But it's a lot more wholesome and low-key than Waikiki, and residents try hard to keep it that way for 364 days a year. The one day when the rebellious ghosts come alive is Halloween. The whole town celebrates Hallow's Eve with a daylong party and parade. Everyone in costume is invited to participate, including children, and storekeepers and restaurateurs open their doors to hordes of celebrators. Locals come from throughout the state to join in the fun. It's by far the biggest Halloween party in all Hawaii. If you're on Maui at the end of October, don't miss it.

The rest of the year, Lahaina is frequented by an equal blend of tourists and locals looking for some fun. Friday evenings are known as "Art Night." Galleries offer free snacks and drinks, and artists are present to answer questions about their work. It's a fun time, but unless your kids have a strong artistic bent, they may not find it interesting.

The best way to visit all the historic sites in Lahaina is with a self-guided half-day **historical walking tour.** The sites are clearly marked on **Front Street,** the town's main artery. You can pick up a free map that highlights the best places at the headquarters for the **Lahaina Restoration Foundation,** in the Master's Reading Room, on Front and Dickenson Streets; 661–3262.

The **Baldwin House Museum** is one of the first stops. It was home to the Doctor/Reverend Dwight Baldwin, his wife, Charlotte, and their eight children. Baldwin was the first Western dentist and doctor in the islands, and his home, built in 1834 and the oldest building in Lahaina, quickly became a local fixture.

The museum is open daily, 10:00 A.M. to 4:30 P.M. Admission is $3.00 for adults, $5.00 per family, and kids get in free when accompanied by a parent. For more information, call 661–3262.

Don't miss a visit to the **Holua Stone,** a historic rock just right of the Brick Palace. You'll notice it right away, because it looks like a huge chair. Precontact Hawaiians believed this stone had healing powers and if you sat in it and let the waves wash over you, you would be cured. ("Precontact" is used to refer to the Hawaiian civilization before the arrival of Western explorers, such as Captain James Cook.)

The **Wo Hing Temple** is another highlight of the tour. It's at the far north end of town, across the street from the Lahaina Whaling Museum. The temple has been converted to a museum and is home to a Buddhist shrine and many exhibitions depicting Chinese heritage in Hawaii, especially Lahaina. Also, don't miss a visit to the cookhouse next door, where film clips are played that show Lahaina in 1899 and 1906. The museum is open daily, 10:00 A.M. to 4:00 P.M. Admission is by donation. For more information, call 661–5553.

Even if you cringe at the thought of shopping for yet another souvenir T-shirt, don't miss a visit to the Crazy Shirts store at 865 Front Street in northern Lahaina. Within the store is a wonderful **Whaling Museum** full of harpoons, navigational instruments, gaffs, and pieces of engraved scrimshaw. Free admission; 661–4775.

At the southern end of town, it's impossible to miss the huge 50-foot-high **banyan tree.** It was planted in 1873 to commemorate the fiftieth anniversary of the first missionary arrival in Lahaina and covers more than two-thirds of an acre with its shade. It's the largest banyan tree in America. Nearby are the Brick Palace and the remnants of a fort built in the 1830s to prevent cannons fired by angry whalers from destroying a missionary compound. Although today the fort looks like nothing more than a rock pile, it was once 20 feet high. It was built from coral rocks hauled onto shore from the reef.

Behind the banyan sits the **courthouse,** built in 1859. The jail in the basement has been converted into the home of the **Lahaina Art Society,** where artworks sit behind bars until purchased. The four cannons at the courthouse were salvaged from a sunken Russian barge.

One of Lahaina's most famous landmarks, the **Pioneer Inn,** is on the other side of the banyan. The inn (661–3636) was built in 1901 for interisland passengers. Although it's been remodeled, it maintains its old-fashioned charm. Many people think it was built to house the rowdy sea-men when whaling was king, but by 1901 the whaling industry was no longer prominent. The inn is decorated as a tribute to Lahaina's former industry, with swinging doors and signs warning against improper behavior.

In the harbor, the ***Carthaginian*** is the only brig in the world authentically restored to its original splendor. The 93-foot brig was built in 1920 and today sits in Lahaina Harbor as a floating whale museum. Onboard, you can hear recordings of the whales' song (explained in the introduction to this chapter). Admission is $3.00 adults, $2.00 seniors, $5.00 for the whole family, and free to children who are accompanied by an adult. It's open daily 10:00 A.M. to 4:00 P.M.; 661–8527.

For a movie with spectacular scenes, visit the **Omni Center,** similar to the IMAX theaters on Oahu, at Waikiki and the Polynesian Cultural Center. The five-story screen will make you feel as if you're really flying over the Na Pali Coast or swimming with sharks. The Hawaii Experience

Family adventure is never far away at any one of Hawaii's Beaches. (Courtesy Aston Hotels & Resorts)

Omni Theater is at 824 Front Street and offers showings at the top of every hour, from 10:00 A.M. to 10:00 P.M. Admission is $5.95 for adults and $3.95 for children younger than thirteen. Call 661–7111 for information.

For nighttime entertainment, the **Old Lahaina Luau** has a great reputation so you'll need to make a reservation a few days ahead of time. Although it's smaller than many of the resort-sponsored shows, it is known for being family oriented and homey. It's held on the beach from 5:30 to 8:30 P.M. daily. Admission is $57 for adults, half-price for children under thirteen, and free for kids under three. For more information, call 667–1998.

Various hotels in the Kaanapali/Wailea area also offer Polynesian extravaganzas and, except for a few different dance numbers, are basically equal in terms of value, entertainment, and good food.

Beaches in Lahaina aren't too popular because Kaanapali is so close and its beaches are top-notch. A good family spot here, however, is at the west end of town, at **Lahaina Beach** near Mala Wharf. To get there, simply follow Front Street to Puunoa Place, which leads to the beach. It's perfect for young kids because it's shallow and safe.

While touring Lahaina, look for the "L" painted on the hills above town. When the missionaries arrived, one of their first projects was to build a school for their own children and the children of natives whom they were able to convert. **Lahainaluna,** completed in 1831, was not only the first school in all Hawaii, it also was the first school and had the first printing press west of the Rockies. It was a boarding school for children throughout Hawaii and even California. It's still an educational institution, as one of Maui's public high schools, and it still functions as a boarding school. Every year in April, the students celebrate the memory of the school's most famous alumnus, David Malo, who wrote *Hawaiian Antiquities* (published in 1898 by the Bishop Museum Press).

Hawaii's first newspaper was produced from here, in the **Hale Pa'i** (printing house), which put Lahaina on the map as a printing capital of the islands.

Lahaina Harbor is a busy site, with dozens of boat companies headquartered there. Most of the boats have a ticket booth right on the pier.

There are a huge variety of options for ocean tours: snorkeling, whale-watching, dinner cruises, sunset cruises, snorkel/whale-watching combos, barbecue lunch cruises, Continental breakfast cruises, and so on. All tours will offer snorkeling instruction if needed, and most of the crew are locals who have a fine appreciation for Maui's waters and are willing to share their marine biology knowledge. It's best to walk around the harbor and shop for the excursion most suited to your budget and family.

The following boat operators offer different combinations of touring activities, with snorkeling almost always included in the experience. This list is not inclusive but merely offers suggestions of companies that have been around a long time and have a good reputation.

* *Trilogy* **Excursions,** 661–4743, cruises to Lanai and serves a breakfast and gourmet lunch on the way. Once on Lanai, you're given a quick tour of Lanai City, then taken to Hulopoe Bay for snorkeling. *Trilogy* also goes to Molokini.

* **Club Lanai,** 871–1144, also goes to Lanai, where a mini-resort is set up for snorkeling, kayaking, Jet Skiing, cycling, playing volleyball and horseshoes, and even guided wagon tours of the Pineapple Island.

* **Lahaina Divers,** 143 Dickenson Street, 667–7496, offers guided scuba and snorkel dives and rents equipment. Multiple locations on the island.

* **Dive Maui,** in the Lahaina Shopping Center, 667–2080, rents equipment and offers guided snorkel and scuba tours.

* **Hawaiian Reef Divers,** 667–7647, rents snorkel and scuba gear as well as boogieboards and offers a daily boat tour to Molokini.

* **Captain Nemo's Emporium,** 150 Dickenson Street, 661–5555, offers guided tours and a variety of rental equipment, including boogieboards.

For a truly wonderful sensation of flight, try **parasailing.** You sit in a swinglike harness that's attached on one end to a huge parachute and on the other end to a winch on the boat. As the boat speeds up, the wind catches the parachute and lifts you high in the sky. Not only are the views spectacular, the fun "weightless" experience is truly one you'll remember long after your vacation ends. For more information, call **Lahaina Parasail** at 661–4887. Kids must weigh more than forty-five pounds to participate.

There are dozens of wonderful places to eat in Lahaina, and many of the restaurants offer kiddie menus. What follows is a small sampling and is by no means comprehensive.

* **Cheeseburger in Paradise.** Burgers and breezes are the highlight here, though there are salads and fish, too. The trademark cheese-burger is as juicy and tasty as you'll find in the islands, while the views of Lahaina Harbor from the upstairs level are spectacular. Lunch and dinner only; special kids' menu. Great place for cooling off and relaxing after a hard morning in the T-shirt shops. At 811 Front St.; 661–4855. $.

* **David Paul's Lahaina Grill.** One of the hottest, most popular spots for dinner in Lahaina, and with good reason. Try Chef David Paul's sig-nature dish, Tequila Shrimp and Firecracker Rice. The different fla-vors are blended perfectly to create a unique and superb taste. A fine wine list accompanies the menu; the restaurant has its own 1,200-bottle climate-controlled cellar. Be sure to make a reservation since this place is always packed. At 127 Lahainaluna Rd.; 667–5117. $$$.

* **Gerard's.** This gourmet, yet casual, restaurant, founded by a master French chef, offers fresh food and hearty entrees from lamb, pork, veal, poultry, sweetbreads, and salt roast duck. A delicate blend of French ideas with Maui-grown ingredients produces such enchant-ments as ahi with béarnaise sauce. Dinner only. At Plantation Inn, 174 Lahainaluna Rd.; 661–8939. $$$$.

* **Kimo's.** Located in the heart of Lahaina, this restaurant gets busy—for good reason. The food is wonderful, with the atmosphere provided by a torch-lit balcony overlooking the ocean; they also have a special children's menu. Kimo's is worth a wait. At 845 Front St.; 661–4811. $$$.

* **Kobe Steak House.** A Japanese country-inn-style eatery where six to eight guests sit around a large table with a grill in the middle. The chef does his thing right there in front of you, slicing and dicing

("faster than a Vegematic," he claims) in the *teppan-yaki* style of cooking. It's all stir-fried, and the vegetables and meats are done to perfection. Served with rice and chopsticks (knife and fork optional). The show is as good as the food. Dinner only; special menu for kids. At 136 Dickenson St.; 667–5555. $$$.

❋ **Longhi's.** One of Lahaina's longtime standards, Longhi's Front Street location is a favorite gathering place for visitors as well as locals. Food is Italian-oriented, though there are plenty of the basics. The menu is provided verbally, by the waiter, who may start out by asking what you like—salads, sandwiches, pasta, and so on—then expanding on the choices. At 888 Front St.; 667–2288. $.

❋ **Song's Oriental Kitchen.** Take-out shop with a few outdoor tables. Huge bowls of *saimin,* chicken *adobo* plate lunches, and other local delicacies abound on the menu. Good food, friendly service, low prices. In the rear of The Wharf shopping plaza; 667–1990. $.

Heading west from Lahaina, on Route 30, the first beach worth stopping at is **Puamana Beach County Park.** The views from here are beautiful, and it's a great spot to enjoy a picnic in the shade.

Continuing on Route 30, look oceanside for **Wahikuli State Wayside Park,** another ideal picnic spot. Across the street, facilities include restrooms and tennis courts. Shortly beyond Wahikuli, Route 30 (the Honoapi'ilani Highway) leads west to **Kaanapali,** an outstanding 4-mile stretch of coastline. Developers sure knew what they were doing when they chose this area for a full-scale resort. The weather is almost always strikingly sunny, and the beaches are among the best on the island. Although the coastline is heavily developed with condos and hotels, you needn't be staying here to enjoy the beach—access is easy and widespread. On the far east end is the Hyatt Regency Maui; from there starts the string of properties ending with the Royal Lahaina Resort. In addition to accommodations, the area includes Whaler's Village (description follows), a shopping center, restaurants, and world-class golf courses.

The beaches are beautiful here and safe year-round. The waters are warm and shallow—ideal for young children. Snorkeling is paramount at the **Black Rock,** bordering the Sheraton Maui at the far end of the resort.

Black Rock, also known as Pu'u Keka'a, is a large chunk of lava that's part of the recently restored Sheraton property. While you'll no doubt see lots of local kids jumping off the rock for a quick thrill, the better action is underwater. Here, snorkelers are treated to schools of brightly colored fish frolicking in clear water. (Don't worry—those cliff jumpers can spot snorkelers and are careful about where they land.)

For fabulous scenic vistas, you can climb to the top of the rock. There are guardrails and a paved path, so it's very safe and easy. Ancient Hawaiians believed that this was one of several sites from which the spirits of the dead departed earth and entered the spiritual world.

Kaanapali Beach is a great spot to learn how to windsurf. Lessons can be arranged through any of the hotels' activities desks, or from **Kaanapali Windsurfing,** 667–1964.

In Kaanapali (and at Kapalua and Wailea as well), most of the hotel/ resort properties offer children's programs that will occupy your kids for the better part of a day with a variety of recreational and cultural activities. Camp Kaanapali, for example, offered by the **Aston Kaanapali Shores** (667–2211) will take kids ages three to eight, Monday to Friday, 8:00 A.M. to 2:00 P.M. The program costs $10.00 per child, plus an extra $6.00 for lunch. At the **Hyatt Regency,** Camp Hyatt is a comprehensive program with special amenities, services, and activities, including scavenger hunts, a ride on the Sugar Cane Train, sand-castle building, arts and crafts, beach picnics, hotel tours, and video games for children ages three to twelve. Night camp is also offered every evening from 6:00 to 10:00 P.M.

Also at the Hyatt, kids will love the **Tour of the Stars.** An in-house astronomy expert leads guests on a tour of the night sky through a deep-space telescope known as "Big Blue." The telescope is equipped with a computer that is programmed to identify and locate 1,000 objects including planets, star clusters, nebulae, and galaxies. This is all done from the hotel rooftop nine stories up. There are three one-hour shows nightly, at 8:00, 9:00 and 10:00 P.M. Admission is $12.00 for adults, $6.00 for children twelve and under.

You can ride throughout the area on the free Kaanapali Trolley and to Lahaina on the Lahaina Cannery Shuttle. A one-way ride on the shuttle costs $1.00 for adults, 50 cents for children three and older. It goes from

Kaanapali to the Cannery Mall, to Hilo Hattie's, to the Wharf, and back to Kaanapali.

Whaler's Village Mall and Museum is filled with shops and restaurants and is definitely worth a visit. The free display area on the upper level offers an in-depth look at Maui's whaling industry, whaling life, and the brave men who hunted these fearsome mammals. Kids will be fascinated by the real whale skeleton. There is also a reconstructed section of an old whaling ship, accompanied by authentic photographs, drawings, and artifacts from actual ships.

Miles and miles of sugar cane still grow in fields across the highway from Kaanapali Resort. Although the sugar industry is no longer the powerful moneymaker it was in the late 1800s, a few scenic sweet acres remain. The Lahaina, Kaanapali and Pacific Railroad, today known as the **Sugar Cane Train,** used to haul the crops from the inland valleys to the coast, where ships waited in the bay, ready to transport the cane to refineries.

The train is a fun excursion and offers a glimpse into a historic way of life that changed Hawaii for generations. The narrow-gauge trains are modeled after steam locomotives that were used in the 1890s and take visitors on the same tracks on which crops were hauled. The trains run from 8:30 A.M. to 4:30 P.M. daily. An hour-long round-trip costs $9.00 for adults, $4.50 for children. For more information, call 661–0089 for recorded information, or 661–0080 to speak to a live operator.

All of the resort properties in Kaanapali offer great choices for dining. Here are a few of the many.

※ **Cook's at the Beach.** An all-purpose, do-everything basic eatery, it's located near the Westin Maui's swimming pool and has permanent umbrellas for shade control over its open-air tables. Cook's has breakfast, lunch, and dinner service; a children's menu; an island breakfast buffet; a Sunday champagne brunch; a nightly all-you-can-eat prime rib buffet; and an evening Hawaiian music and hula show. The buffet is another of those good bargains, but soups, salads, and entrees are better than average, too. At 2365 Kaanapali Pkwy.; 667–2525. $$.

※ **The Sound of the Falls.** This the Westin Maui's premier dining room, replete with its own lagoon and waterfall; the usual sparkling glassware, shining cutlery, and snow-white napery; and superb service, plus some of the best food in the state! At 2365 Kaanapali Pkwy.; 667 2525. $$$.

❀ **The Villa Restaurant.** Surrounded by rockscaped lagoons and waterfalls at the south end of the Westin Maui Hotel, the Villa is a real surprise—it now has what may be the best seafood menu in West Maui. Serving dinner seven days a week, it has an open-air atmosphere of casual elegance. A solo guitarist serenades diners from a small stage near the top of the waterfall, and if more entertainment is needed, the nearby Villa Lounge features a variety of after-dinner musical acts. The nearby Villa Terrace is an open-air buffet featuring all-you-can-eat seafood, pasta, salads, and desserts, or items from the Villa menu. At 2365 Kaanapali Pkwy.; 667–2525. $$.

❀ **Leilani's on the Beach.** Sit as close to the ocean as you can and enjoy the passing parade as you sip tall, cool refreshments or nibble the edibles. Food is reasonably priced standard fare of fish, steaks, chicken, and lamb specialties, with a special kids' menu. Open for lunch and dinner or just beverages from 11:30 A.M. to 1:00 A.M. On Kaanapali Beachfront walkway at Whaler's Village; 661–4495. $$.

❀ **Rusty Harpoon.** The view is great, the ambience pleasant, and the food good. Harpoon is located at the west end of the Whaler's Village shopping mall and projects out toward Kaanapali Beach. Though only a short patch of beach is visible, it's enough to provide a continuous floor show during lunch or dinner. The restaurant is in a huge lanai open to all the breezes, which makes dining doubly pleasant. Children's menu. At Whaler's Village; 661–3123. $$.

❀ **Pavillion.** The all-purpose dining center for the Hyatt Regency Maui Hotel in Kaanapali, this poolside restaurant is open 6:00 A.M. to 6:00 P.M. daily. It offers breakfast and lunch only, but a light-fare menu is available all day, and there's a menu for kids. Recently remodeled, it now features a Pacific Rim cuisine that blends exotic dishes with the standards. Menus may include Okinawan velvet corn soup, won ton salad, Korean barbecue beef with kim chee, and Singapore chili shrimp. Pavillion includes both indoor and terrace tables.

❀ **Swan Court.** Superlatives abound for this five-star dining experience in the Hyatt Regency Maui Resort. Go for breakfast first so you can experience the lagoon-side ambience in bright early daylight (Swan Court is not open for lunch). Then, starve yourself for a day and make a dinner visit to what may be Maui's most elegant restaurant. If you can't do both, then at least make an early evening reservation, so you can get a table nearest the lagoon, where you can enjoy the swans floating serenely around the cooling waterfall, the sunset colors and the incredible service. At 200 Noheakai Drive; 661–1234. $$$$.

Continuing on Honoapi'ilani Highway beyond Kaanapali, you'll pass through the towns of **Honokowai** and **Kahana,** easily noticed by the plethora of apartments and condominiums. This is a great area to stay if you're traveling on a budget. Although you won't get the variety of amenities offered by such destinations as Kaanapali Resort, or Kapalua, farther west, you can find great values, and the beaches remain sunny, beautiful, and—compared to the other resorts—relatively uncrowded.

To get to **Honokowai Beach County Park,** take the Lower Honoapi'ilani Highway, which runs parallel along the coast to the Upper Honoapi'ilani Highway. The beach park is easy to find, directly across the street from the Food Pantry. As long as it's not too windy here, the shallow waters are a great place for children to play on an uncrowded beach. There's also an oversized lawn, framed by lots of palm trees and dotted with picnic tables.

The **Ironwood Ranch** in Kapalua offers tours of this area on horseback. Gentle horses can take beginners for a one-and-a-half-hour ride that costs $75 and includes refreshments. Riders can opt for visiting pineapple fields, mountains, or tropical rain forests, or going on a sunset trip. Rates vary according to the length of the ride. For more information, call 669–4991. The ranch offers hotel pick-up from the Kaanapali and Kapalua resort areas. To participate in rides, children must be at least eight years old and 4 feet tall, and must be accompanied by an adult.

If you simply want to rent a bike and cycle at your own speed, expect to pay about $19 a day, less for multiple-day rentals. **West Maui Cycles** has two outlets: at 4310 Lower Honoapi'ilani Highway in Kahana, 669–

1169; and at 193 Lahainaluna Road in Lahaina, 661–9005. The cycle shop is open weekdays 9:00 A.M. to 6:00 P.M., weekends 10:00 A.M. to 3:00 P.M.

The **Kapalua Bay Resort** is a few minutes west of Kaanapali and encompasses the Ritz-Carlton Kapalua, the Kapalua Bay Hotel, and the Kapalua Bay Villas, which are individual condominium units featuring complete kitchens. This full-fledged resort features top-rated golf, tennis, restaurants, and accommodations. If the wind is mild or absent, beaches here can be ranked among the best on the island. However, the pesky, all-too-frequent wind can be annoying and often forces beachgoers to head back east to Kaanapali, Kihei, or Wailea. Despite the wind, the waters are always calm, sheltered by a series of lava promontories that stick out of the coastline and form tranquil bays.

You can get here via either Lower or Upper Honoapi'ilani Highway, although the lower route is easier and more scenic. Check out **A & B Rentals,** at 3481 Lower Honoapi'ilani Highway, 669–0027, open daily 9:00 A.M. to 5:00 P.M. Here you can rent snorkel gear for $2.50 per day and $10.00 per week, plus a selection of other water toys such as boogieboards, surfboards, and even fishing poles.

The Ritz-Carlton Kapalua, located at One Ritz-Carlton Drive, 669–6200, provides a choice of four restaurants:

- ❊ **Banyan Tree Pool Restaurant.** Ritz-Carlton Kapalua has strategically located this plantation-style dining room right next to its three-tiered swimming pool so that hungry bathers can drop in for a refill. Try the white bean soup, a local favorite. Open for lunch and dinner; piano and guitar players entertain in the evening. Kids' menu. $$$.

- ❊ **Beach House.** It's a long walk from the beach back up to the main dining rooms, so the Ritz-Carlton thoughtfully provided a convenient oceanfront bistro adjacent to Fleming Beach. This open-air dining area features high-quality sandwiches, crispy salads, and the ever-present hamburger. Kids' menu. $.

- ❊ **Terrace Restaurant.** Pacific Rim delicacies are featured at this Ritz-Carlton restaurant. Roasted, air-dried duck with ginger plum sauce and wok-seared ahi are two of the house specialties. The Terrace has both indoor and outdoor tables with marvelous views of the ocean and islands. Entertainment in the evenings. $$$.

☀ **The Grill.** Paniolo rack of lamb, Molokai sweet potato lasagna, and seared Kahuku prawns are but a few of the Hawaiian Cuisine delights presented nightly at The Grill at the Ritz-Carlton. The Grill offers superb food in elegant, clublike surroundings. The adjacent Sunset Lounge features sophisticated entertainment nightly and shares the pleasant sounds with The Grill patrons. $$$$.

Following are some of the other dining options in the area.

☀ **The Garden.** Open and delightfully airy, The Garden serves dinner, offering buffets and menu service with equal aplomb. Meals here are of the high quality one would expect from this resort; there also is a menu for kids. The Pool Terrace extends the service to pool and beach levels. At One Bay Dr.; 669–5656. $$$.

☀ **The Plantation House.** The expansive Plantation Golf Course's clubhouse has half its top floor devoted to this restaurant and it's not a waste of space. The food is exceptionally good for golf-course dining, and the ocean views are an unexpected bonus. At Plantation Club Drive; 669–6299. $$$.

☀ **Roy's Kahana Bar & Grill.** Maui branch of the Hawaii Kai restaurant opened in Oahu by Chef Roy Yamaguchi, the Kahana features an ever-changing array of incredible specials and an equally intriguing fixed menu. The Asian spring rolls are a great starter and mesquite-smoked Peking-style duck an equally impressive entree. Desserts are simply sumptuous. At 4405 Honoapi'ilani Hwy., Kahana Gateway; 669–6999. $$.

The first beach you'll arrive at is **Napili Bay.** This is a good site for swimmers and just-learning surfers, and the beach is beautiful. To get to the beach, follow the beach access signs near the condominiums.

There are restrooms, showers, and concession stands at popular **Kapalua Beach.** It's a good spot for snorkeling, although better fish sightings will be had farther down the road at Fleming's. The crescent-shaped beach is truly beautiful and, in the absence of heavy winds or storms, is a safe spot for kids of all ages. To get there, look for the public parking lot near the Napili Kai Beach Club. You'll have to walk through the short tunnels to get to the beach.

If you keep traveling up Lower Honoapi'ilani Highway, you can't miss **Fleming's Beach Park,** where the scenic beauty is not even the best part. The beach is ideal for snorkeling along the edges of the coast, surfing the outside break, and, for toddlers, wading in the gentle shorebreak. Use caution when trying any of these activities in winter, when storms create dangerous currents and pounding surf. There's plenty of parking, showers, and barbecue grills—a great place for a picnic.

Farther down the road, **Mokuleia and Honolua Bays** are Marine Life Conservation Districts, which means that fishing is prohibited and therefore they are colorful, lively spots for snorkeling. However, as calm and tranquil this area is in the summer, it gets equally choppy and dangerous in the winter.

To find the bays, look for a trail about 250 yards from mile marker 32 on the highway. The trail for the beach is on the left; it's a bit of a hike down, so it's not recommended for small children unless you can carry them. But even if you choose not to walk down to the water, it's still a picturesque spot to stretch your legs and watch the surfers gliding through the sparkling blue Pacific.

Continuing on the highway, the road winds around the whole northwest tip of Maui, eventually turning into Route 33, the Kahekili Highway, and ending up in Wailuku. The road is rugged and the bane of car rental companies, but it is doable and the sights along the way are extraordinarily beautiful. You'll pass isolated old homes and churches, and new waterfalls will greet you around many of the corners. If it's misty, you'll feel as if you're driving through the clouds, to an idyllic spot that time has ignored. You'll pass through a few charming, picturesque towns, the biggest of which is **Kahakuloa**.

Please be cautious along this road; at many spots there's room for only one car and you have to pull over or back up to let another car pass. If the weather is rainy, it's not a good idea to travel here; mudslides are prevalent. As you come over the tip of Maui, you'll leave the quiet hills and valleys for the next city, **Wailuku,** mostly a residential community.

CENTRAL MAUI

Wailuku is also accessible from Lahaina, from which there are two routes that cross Central Maui. Route 30, a continuation of the Honoapi'ilani Highway, travels to Iao Valley and Wailuku. Route 35, the Mokulele Highway, leads to Kahului, where it branches off to Upcountry and Haleakala, or changes to Route 36, the Hana Highway.

Coming from Lahaina, the Honoapi'ilani Highway continues through the central plains of Maui to Wailuku, passing the small village of **Waikapu.** In Waikapu, the **Maui Tropical Plantation** is a model of a working plantation and is a great place to visit for a glimpse into the lives of agricultural workers. Kids will love the forty-five-minute tram ride that takes you through the taro patches surrounding the village. There are fields of pineapple and sugar cane, and groves of banana, mango, macadamia nut, and papaya trees. An abundance of tropical flowers gives the place a rich fragrance.

On-site facilities include a restaurant, gift shop, and nursery that will ship merchandise home for you. Admission is free, but the tram ride costs $8.50 for adults, $3.50 for children ages five to twelve. The plantation is open daily 9:00 A.M. to 5:00 P.M.; 244–7643.

Route 30 eventually turns into High Street. **Kaahumanu Church** is Maui's oldest stone church that's still standing. It was built in 1837. It's easy to find, located right off High Street, but it's usually closed on weekdays. Sunday services are held here at 9:00 A.M., and many of the hymns are sung in Hawaiian.

From Route 32, be sure to take a side trip up Route 320 leading to Iao Valley and Iao Needle. On the way, a nice stop is the **Tropical Gardens of Maui.** This is a delightful little garden filled with tropical fruits and flowers. The gift shop has a variety of homegrown plants, fruits, and flowers, along with information about how to ship these beauties home and grow them successfully. The gardens are open Monday to Saturday, 9:00 A.M. to 4:30 P.M.; the gift shop and nursery are open until 5:00 P.M. Admission is $3.00 per person. Children under eight years old are admitted free. For more information, call 244–3085.

On the way to Iao Valley, stop at **Kepaniwai Park,** a historic spot that's been turned into a great picnic site with plenty of tables and pavilions. Kamehameha won an important battle against Maui's warriors here, during his mission to gain control of all the islands. Today, you can walk

JULIE'S TOP FAMILY ADVENTURES ON MAUI

1. Going on a whale-watching trip (in season)
2. Watching the sun rise atop Haleakala
3. Snorkeling at Molokini
4. Driving on the road to Hana and continuing beyond to the Seven Pools
5. Horseback riding on the slopes of Haleakala
6. Visiting the rare animals at Keiki Zoo Maui
7. Riding the sugar-cane train in in Kaanapali
8. Driving across the northwest tip of the island to Kahakuloa
9. Taking a windsurfing lesson at Kaanapali Beach
10. Exploring lush, green Iao Valley

among a Hawaiian grass shack, a Portuguese villa, a Chinese pagoda, a New England–style house, a bamboo house, and a Japanese teahouse.

Iao Needle is a 2,250-foot cinder cone, around which are several popular hiking trails that are great for families. You can't miss the large stone monolith rising up from the lush green valley. This was also the site of a great fight between Kamehameha and the Maui warriors. Historical accounts say the battle was so intense, the soldiers' blood turned the stream red.

From the parking lot, an easy walk is the **Tableland Trail.** It climbs for about 2 miles, and the beautiful expansive views encompass all of the valley. If swimming in the pools is on your agenda, simply walk down to the valley floor and follow the stream. (Note: If it has rained lately, this area may be muddy and hard to navigate. Bring clothes that you don't mind getting dirty, and plenty of mosquito repellent.) If altitude changes are too difficult for your group, try the **Waihee Trail**—it stays level and journeys over two suspended bridges to the stream.

Just behind Kaahumanu Church sits **Bailey House Museum.** It's situated in the old Bailey House, named after the former manager of the Wailuku Sugar Company, Edward Bailey. It was built in the mid-1800s and contains the biggest collection of Hawaiian artifacts in all of Maui. You'll find displays of Hawaiian *tapa* (a cloth made from the bark of mulberry trees) and quilts, lots of memorabilia from the sugar days, and an extensive exhibit on missionary lifestyles. The museum is at 2375–A Main Street, and it's open Monday through Saturday, 10:00 A.M. to 4:00 P.M. Admission is $4.00 for adults, $1.00 for children ages six to twelve. For more information, call 244–3326.

From Wailuku, Route 32, Kaahumanu Avenue leads toward the town of **Kahului.** Most visitors drive right through this area after landing at the airport, on their way to the popular resort sites of Kaanapali, Kapalua, Kihei, or Wailea. But there are a lot of great sites packed into this little town.

At the **Hawaiian Alii Coral Factory,** you can watch as coral that's been harvested from local waters is transformed into colorful jewelry. The factory is located at 804 Keolani Place in Kahului. It's open daily, 8:00 A.M. to 5:00 P.M.; 877–7620.

The **Kanaha Fish Pond** is not only a stopover for migrating Canadian geese and ducks, it's home to two species of endangered Hawaiian birds, the stilt and the coot. You'll probably need binoculars to see them clearly. The coot looks almost like a duck; it's dark gray or black and can be seen in its floating nests on the pond. The stilt is a long, skinny bird, with sticklike pink legs, a white stomach, and black back. The pond is at the junction of Routes 36 and 37, less than 2 miles from the airport. There is an observation shelter at Route 37.

At the **Alexander and Baldwin Sugar Museum** in Puunene, the exhibits detail not only the sugar industry, but the lifestyles of the immigrants who arrived on Maui to harvest the cane. Particularly interesting are the explanations of how the rainfall was funneled into irrigation systems to insure healthy crops.

The museum is at the intersection of Hanson Road and Route 350 (Puunene Avenue). It's open Monday through Saturday, 9:30 A.M. to 4:30 P.M.; 871–8058. Admission for adults is $4.00, children ages six to seventeen are admitted for $2.00.

From Kahului, Route 36 heads northeast to Hana. **Kanaha Beach County Park** is a wonderfully scenic place for a picnic and is an ideal spot for beginning windsurfers. The wind and waves are gentle here, creating a safe environment in which to learn the basics of this fun activity. To get here, follow Hobron Avenue toward the water and turn right into Amala Street. Signs will lead you right to the park.

Maui's biggest airport in Kahului is not only the site of most visitors' interisland arrivals and departures, it's also the headquarters for many **helicopter and aerial tour companies.** A variety of flight-seeing opportunities are available, from daylong sojourns over all of Maui, to shorter, hour-long flights that highlight a certain geographical/natural wonder. Shorter trips fly to Haleakala Crater and remote spots of West Maui Mountains, where inaccessible valleys open up before your eyes. Other tours offer such niceties as a champagne brunch in Hana, or an excursion to the spectacular sea cliffs and remote beaches of Lanai or Molokai. Prices vary depending on the trip.

Both **Paragon Airlines,** 244–3356, and **Scenic Air Tours,** 871–2555, offer daylong, narrated trips over the whole island in ten-seater planes. **Biplane Barnstormers,** 878–2860, features open-cockpit biplane rides for as little as $59 per person.

Helicopters can get passengers into even more remote spots than airplanes. Passengers are usually given headphones to drown out the noisy whir of the blades and to enjoy piped-in music and a narration explaining the sights below. Some companies even offer a video of your flight that you can take home as a souvenir. Well-known Maui companies that fly out of Kahului include **Hawaii Helicopters,** 877–3900; **Sunshine Helicopters,** 871–0722; **Blue Hawaiian Helicopters,** 871–8844; **Alex Air,** 871–0792. Prices range from $99 for a thirty-minute ride to $179 for an hour-long ride. Children ages two and up must pay full fare because the F.A.A. requires that they occupy their own seat.

Just a few miles uphill of Kahului, don't miss a meal at **Haliimaile General Store.** Neither a store nor general in nature, this off-the-beaten-track spot has become one of Maui's best-known gourmet restaurants. Owned and operated by Chef Beverly Gannon and her husband, Joe, it features such international entrees as Szechuan barbecued salmon, rack of lamb Hunan style, paniolo ribs, and blackened chicken with corn and roasted pepper sauce. Dessert delicacies include super-smooth piña colada cheesecake and chocolate macadamia fudge pie. The restaurant is at 900 Haliimaile Road, in the old Haliimaile General Store building; 572–2666. $$.

Beyond the airport, a few minutes' drive east, **Sprecklesville** is a little secluded spot that's great for children. Part of the beach is sheltered by lava rock piles on one side and a long reef in the water, making the setting tranquil and scenic. It's easy to find; just look for directional signs on the side of the road.

Continuing on Route 36, **H. P. Baldwin Beach County Park** is about 7 miles past Kahului, and well-marked signs make it easy to find. The park contains full picnic facilities, restrooms, and showers. The protected swimming area is great for kids of all ages, and the sands framing the beach are fun for shell collecting.

Paia Town and Hookipa Beach are the next two must-stops on the road east of the airport. They are easy to find—just follow the well-marked signs off the Hana Highway. Paia is full of local color—old-fashioned storefronts house a variety of boutiques, coffee shops, and restaurants. Check out Just You and Me Kid (579–9433), where parents and kids can get matching aloha wear. If you're heading all the way to Hana, Paia is a good place to stock up on gas and supplies—some restaurants in town will even offer to pack your lunch in a disposable cooler.

Paia is most noted for Hookipa Beach, about 10 miles from town, where top-rated windsurfers come from all over the world to enjoy the hefty tradewinds. Bring binoculars, because you're sure to see at least a dozen colorful sails bobbing about in the water. It's a great place to sit and watch the windsurfers' athletic maneuvers. Several contests are held here throughout the year, the best of which is the O'Neill International Windsurfing Championship every spring. The world's top windsurfers compete in the O'Neill for $10,000 in prize money.

Windsurfing is now a multimillion-dollar industry, with many of the biggest, most reputable companies headquartered here in Paia or in Kahului. Many of the companies offer hotel pick-up, lunches, and lessons from world-class athletes. If watching the windsurfers slice through the water is not your style and you'd rather join the crowds in the ocean, you can rent equipment and take lessons from **Sailboards Maui,** 397 Dairy Road, 871–7954; **Maui Wind Safari,** in the High-Tech Surf Sports Store at 425 Koloa Street, 871–7766; or **Maui Windsurf Company** 520 Keolani (Airport Road), 877–4816.

Mama's Fish House, a seafood gourmet's heaven, easily found on the side of the road before Hookipa Beach, has a spectacular beachfront location. The *papio* in their Hana ginger teriyaki sauce is merely sensational, as is the papaya seed dressing on the chilled salad. At 799 Poho Pl.; 579–8488. $$$.

THE ROAD TO HANA

Just as a sunrise on Haleakala is a must-do for any Maui vacation, so too is the **Road to Hana.** A stay on Maui simply would not be complete without taking your family over the 54 miles and fifty-plus one-lane bridges that lead to one of the most beautiful spots on earth.

The road begins just after Paia, as Route 36 leads into Route 360—the daunting yet beckoning Hana Highway. Actually, the road is more impressive, interesting, and scenic than the town itself. There reportedly are more than 600 hairpin turns in this curvaceous coastline, but the views are so captivating it's hard to keep count. The going is definitely slow, but the scenery is spectacular and you wouldn't dream of speeding by. From Kahului, it takes about four hours to get to the town of Hana and four hours to get back. So either start early or plan to spend the night.

The Road to Hana has earned an undeserved bad reputation. Throughout Maui, you'll see tank tops, T-shirts, sweatshirts, golf hats, and water bottles all imprinted with the famous slogan: I SURVIVED THE ROAD TO HANA. What began as a joke has become a misleading deceit. There's really nothing to "survive" about the road. It's a safe, well-maintained route that is never scary—just long and winding. It does rain often, however (the lush rain forests got that way for a reason), so the road can get a bit slippery. And make sure you bring plenty of mosquito repellent—the little buggers are quite fierce in this damp area.

This is the tropical Hawaii that everyone imagines. The road leads through rain forests where waterfalls plummet down craggy cliffs into isolated pools framed by fragrant tropical flowers. At periodic turnoffs you can dip your toe in these little pools, or jump completely in and let the waterfalls tumble over you, as a sort of hydro-gravity-powered massage!

It's impossible to list every stopping place and name every waterfall on the way, but what follows are some highlights.

After Hookipa, you'll pass the minuscule towns of **Huelo** and **Kailua.** The entrance to the **Waikomoi Ridge Trail and Nature Walk** isn't very well marked, but it's definitely worth a stop. Look for a bunch of picnic tables in a clearing above the road and a metal gate. You can pull over and park here. The short trail travels into a bamboo grove. If you remain quiet, you can hear Mother Nature singing as the wind whistles among these tall, hollow trees.

Just past Waikomoi, you'll see **Puahokamoa and Haipuaena Falls,** two consecutive waterfalls streaming down the mountain. You can park a bit beyond the falls at **Kaumahina State Wayside Park.** You'll see Puahokamoa first, and a short trek from the road leads to its pool base, at the bottom of a large cliff. If you walk upstream for a few minutes, you'll find Haipuaena Falls and another pool.

The first "town" on the road is **Keanae,** a small agricultural community and a good place to rest your engine and stretch your legs. The scenic vistas from here are delightful, with native rain forests growing in wild contrast with neatly sculpted taro farms. Stop for a picnic at **Puaa Kaa State Wayside Park.** There are grills here for a do-it-yourself barbecue. Various trails lead from here to small waterfalls and idyllic pools, but don't let kids wander off. The earth is damp, and it's easy to slip and slide into potentially hazardous rocks.

The next town is **Nahiku,** identifiable by its small church, serving the local congregation here since 1867, and its most famous resident, musician George Harrison. If you happen to be driving this road during the summer, look for a pod of dolphins swimming offshore. Locals say that the graceful animals perform spontaneous shows of acrobatics—like a real-life version of Sea Life Park on Oahu.

Once you've reached the town of **Hana,** you'll be amazed at the sense of "civilization" you feel even at this isolated spot. After such a long drive through wild, lush greenery, you'll be happy to see some buildings, homes, and stores. But don't expect too much; Hana epitomizes life in a small town, where residents all know each other and life moves real slow. Both the local attitudes and the lush scenery create an atmosphere that's captivating and alluring. Famed aviator Charles Lindbergh became so entranced with Hana, his last wish was to be buried here. His gravesite is near the **Hoomau Stone Church.**

Be sure to visit **Hasegawa General Store.** Even if you don't need any supplies, this local institution is surely something to see. It stocks everything from clothing to fishing lures to camera equipment—it's truly an all-in-one spot.

At **Hana Cultural Center,** visitors are treated to wonderful examples of Hawaiian quilts. Anyone who has ever attempted to create a quilt will appreciate the intricacies and time involved in the Hawaiian styles. The center also has a great collection of shells, stone implements used in precontact times, and tapa cloths. There are ancient Hawaiian brooms made from coconut fronds and clothing made from mulberry bark. The center is a small, one-room museum that imparts a feeling of visiting someone's home. Guests can get really close to all the exhibits—there are no formal glass display cases here.

The center is on Uakea Road and is open daily 10:00 A.M. to 4:00 P.M. Admission is by a $2 donation. For information, call 248–8622.

At **Hana Gardenland Nursery,** you can purchase fresh flowers at great prices. The nursery will ship merchandise to the Mainland, so you can have the smells and sights of Hana wafting through your living room upon your return. For $5.00, you can take a self-guided tour that identifies all the plants you've been seeing and smelling on the drive here. The nursery is open daily, 9:00 A.M. to 5:00 P.M.; call 248–8975.

Even if you've seen enough plant life on the drive to Hana, it's still worth it to visit **Kahanu Gardens** to see Hawaii's largest heiau, **Piilanihale,** built in 1400 A.D. Piilani was one of the greatest rulers of Maui—he was the island's king for more than forty years. The huge walls of the heiau are more than 50 feet high. The 120-acre gardens are part of the National Tropical Botanical Garden network and surround the heiau like a fragrant lei. Within the garden confines is an extensive variety of imported and domestic plants, including a large section of medicinal plants. It's fascinating to learn how the Hawaiians used plants, flowers, and herbs to heal. The gardens and heiau are open daily except Monday, from 10:00 A.M. to 2:00 P.M. For more information, call 248–8912.

The town of Hana is so small it's impossible to miss the **Hana Airport.** Yes, you can skip that beautiful drive and fly here directly from Kahului. Aloha Island Air (248–8328 or 800–323–3345) offers five flights daily.

A bit farther down the road is 120-acre **Waianapanapa State Park,** a great place for snorkeling and swimming—on a black-sand beach. With black-as-night lava jutting out into the deep blue sea, the sights here are breathtaking. But enter the water only on calm days; when the surf is strong, the sandy shore drifts away quickly. The park is great for picnicking and exploring nearby caves.

There is a well-marked trail leading to **Waianapanapa Caves;** two small indentations that look like oversize bathtubs. An old Hawaiian legend tells of Popoalaea, a beautiful princess who ran away from Kakae, her mean husband, and hid in these caves. When Kakae found her, he was so angry that he viciously killed her right here. Hawaiians say the waters periodically turn bright red in memory of the ancient bloodshed. Scientists, however, have reported that the red tinge in the water is caused by several thousand tiny red shrimp that drift this way during various weather and wind patterns.

If you want to go beyond Hana to the **Oheo Stream, Seven Pools,** and **Kipahulu,** it's best to spend a night at the **Hotel Hana-Maui** (rooms at the hotel start at $395 per night; 248–8211). You can do it all in one day, but it's a bit much, and you may be navigating the curves in the dark on the way home.

If you haven't had your fill of the road, a slightly longer drive leads to the picturesque **Oheo Stream and Seven Pools,** about 12 miles from Hana. The stream spills over the mountain, forming a series of pools that eventually open up at the ocean. You can walk and swim in each of the naturally formed pools, and the scenery is spectacular. Parts of the area are very slippery, so keep a tight rein on wandering children. Also, keep an eye on the sky for sudden rainstorms. This area is prone to flash floods, during which the stream rises quickly and can trap people on the cliffs. Most people swim in the pool just under the bridge—only the truly rugged and fit hikers should attempt to climb up the mountain.

The Hotel Hana-Maui offers **horseback rides** throughout the area for $35 an hour. Children must be at least seven years old. It's recommended that you make a reservation ahead of time because hotel guests are given first priority; 248–8211.

For the real adventure-seekers, **Hawaii Helicopters** (877–3900) offers a bird's-eye view of Maui's east coast. Flights start at $129 per person, and a variety of packages are available. Children must be at least two years old and must be able to sit in their own seat.

After a long trek through paradise it's time to stretch your legs. The perfect lunch stop is the **Hana Inn.** The patio seating is close enough to the great outdoors that you feel the spirit of the tropics as you dine. Lunch fare includes upscale entrees of fine quality; however, prices also are upscale. Call 248–8211. $$$.

SOUTHWEST MAUI

Back in Lahaina, if you head east on Honoapi'ilani Highway, you'll soon come to the town of **Olowalu,** which features a good swimming and snorkeling beach. The waters are so abundant with colorful fish that many commercial snorkel tours from Kaanapali to the west and Maalaea to the east anchor offshore from Olowalu.

Views from here are expansive; you can see Molokai, Lanai, Kahoolawe, and the tip of the Big Island to the far south.

Heading down Route 31, the first stop in Kihei is **Maalaea Bay,** which along with Lahaina is a major embarkation point for whale-watching and snorkeling tours. Additionally, on any given day, you'll see dozens of windsurfers decorating the water with their colorful sails. This windy bay is an ideal spot for them to ply their boards across the water. The strong winds don't make it a great place for general swimming, but don't fear, the beaches improve farther down the road in Kihei and Wailea.

Almost 100 condominiums grace the shore at the town of **Kihei,** about a thirty-five minutes' drive from Lahaina. Although overbuilt, it's not as crowded as Lahaina, and the variety of condos means good values for vacationers. The string of beaches that make up this 6-mile section of the coast are ideal, offering everything from beachcombing to snorkeling, windsurfing, and bodysurfing.

The following are a small sampling of the different companies operating from Maalaea or headquartered in nearby Kihei. There are several rental facilities for snorkeling, surfing, kayaking, boogieboarding, or bicycling. Just as in Lahaina, it's best to walk around the harbor to find the ideal excursion for your budget and family.

✹ The **Pacific Whale Foundation,** at Kealia Beach Plaza in Kihei, is a nonprofit organization dedicated to whale research and protection. The foundation offers educational tours via cruises and snorkel trips. For more information, call 879–8811.

✹ *Navatek II* is a specially designed "swath vessel," meaning it features two submerged hulls that act like remote-controlled submarines to provide a smooth, stable trip. The Navateks are known for the calmest rides, and the ships handle the waves with wonderful dexterity. From Maui, one Navatek cruise travels to Lanai and serves breakfast and lunch, another cruise is a sunset dinner trip, and there's a whale-watching tour from January through mid-April. All outings depart from Maalaea Harbor.

✹ For about $14.00 a week, or $2.50 a day, **Snorkel Bob's** rents snorkel gear (plus a fish identification card) and boogieboards. There are three outlets on Maui, and others scattered throughout the islands. You can rent from one Snorkel Bob's, drive around and snorkel to your heart's content, and return the equipment at any other Snorkel Bob's location. In Kihei, Snorkel Bob's is at 1913 S. Kihei Road, 879–8225; in Lahaina, 161 Lahainaluna Road, 661–4421; in Napili, past the Napili Shores Condominium, 669–9603.

✹ **SeaEscape U-Drive Boat Rental** lets you take a small Zodiac (a mototrized rubber boat) out on your own. They'll give you directions to the best snorkel and dive spots around. A 16-foot boat with a twenty-five-horsepower engine costs about $75 per hour. Larger boats are available, too. At 1979 S. Kihei Road; 879–3721.

✹ **Maui Dive Shop** has several locations on the island and offers a wide range of equipment, lessons, and rentals. In Kihei, it's at Azeka Place; 879–3388.

* The **Ocean Activities Central Reservation Center** is a sort of booking service from which you can sign up for a variety of fun-filled activities throughout the island and purchase any kind of equipment you'll need. The center is at 1847 South Kihei Road No. 203; 879–4485.

* Also at the Rainbow Mall, **South Pacific Kayaks** offers a half-day introductory trip for $55, which includes lunch and lots of chances for great snorkeling. More advanced trips are also available. There's a 20 percent discount for kids twelve and under. You can rent a single kayak ($20 per day) or a double kayak ($40 per day) and venture out on your own if you're not interested in the tours. For more information, call 875–4848.

* **Four Winds,** 879–8188, offers SNUBA tours for kids to Molokini Crater. No, that's not a typographical error—SNUBA is a new sport that lets you explore the underwater world without becoming a full-fledged certified scuba diver. In SNUBA, the tank is strapped to a small inflatable raft that floats on the surface above the diver. As the diver swims around, the raft follows. SNUBA-ers breathe compressed air through a regulator, and the views awaiting them are much more detailed, colorful, and expansive than the views afforded to snorkelers. Kids must be at least ten years old. The trip itself costs $69 for adults, $40 for kids three through twelve; the SNUBA activity is an additional $40, regardless of age. The ride includes a full Continental breakfast, an open bar, and a barbecue lunch.

Buzz's Wharf is a fine spot to visit for lunch and dinner. It's located at the head of Maalaea Harbor, and its upstairs dining room gives sweeping views of Southwest Maui and Kahoolawe. Fishing and tour boats parade in and out of the harbor. Buzz's offers great steaks, fine seafood, and good salads with excellent service. On Honoapi'ilani Hwy.; 244–5426.

You can't miss **Kalama Beach County Park** in the middle of town. Although the beach itself isn't ranked among the island's best, and it often disappears in the winter, it's a great place for a family picnic. (Beaches often lose their sand in the winter, when strong currents pull it out to sea, but the sand returns in the summer.) The thirty-six acres include barbecue pits, pavilions, tables, basketball courts, volleyball nets, a soccer field, and a baseball diamond. Local families frequent the area, and the views of Haleakala looming behind you and Kahoolawe sparkling offshore are beautiful.

Signs point you toward the three-part series of **Kamaole Beach Parks,** blessed by wide expanses of sand and picnic tables. Bodysurfing and swimming are great along this whole stretch of coast. Between beaches I and II, a coral reef is home to many colorful fish, making conditions wonderful for snorkeling. There is a miniature playground, for the mini-sized kids in your family, at beach III.

Erik's Seafood Broiler is a newer branch of the justifiably famous Erik's in Kahana Villas on the west end of the island. This restaurant follows the same format, with a wide selection of fresh local fish, served baked, broiled, poached, or sautéed. At 2463 S. Kihei Blvd., in the Kamaole Shopping Center; 879–8400. $$.

Royal Thai Cuisine offers great spring rolls, crispy noodles, spicy curry, delicately flavored seafood, and the usuals like Evil Prince Chicken, Cashew Chicken, and Red Curry Vegetarian Platter. Rate it high on your list of must-try places; you won't be disappointed. At Azeka Shopping Center; 874–0813. $$.

The **Wailea** area is comprised of beautiful resort properties fronting five pretty, crescent-shaped beaches: Keawakapu, Mokapu, Ulua, Wailea, and Polo. All have great facilities and are relatively calm. Additionally, all have public access, so if you're just visiting the area and not staying in one of the hotels, you can still enjoy the beach.

The complimentary Wailea Shuttle runs daily 6:30 A.M. to 10:30 P.M. between the major hotels, golf courses, tennis courts, and Wailea Shopping Village.

Just offshore from all Wailea beaches sits **Molokini,** which looks like a tiny, half-moon-shaped islet but really is a submerged cinder cone. It's also a marine preserve and one of the best snorkeling spots in all Hawaii. There are a variety of commercial outfits that will take you here; some offer picnic lunches, and most offer snorkeling instruction and equipment rental. It's best to pick an early-morning cruise, when the waters are still clear. Too many snorkelers kicking around tends to create murky, sandy water.

If it's whale season (November through April), keep one eye peeled on the horizon, because Makena is a popular whale-sighting locale. In fact, if you swim a little bit away from the shore and keep your head underwater for a few seconds, you may even hear the shrieklike songs of the whales.

To get to **Keawakapu,** the first Wailea beach, keep going on South Kihei Road until it dead-ends. Although there are no amenities here, such as restrooms or picnic tables, there is plenty of parking and the sandy beach is wonderful—calm and great for swimming.

Mokapu and Ulua Beaches are off Wailea Alanui Drive, the main street in the resort. Turn right immediately past the Aston Wailea Resort. Signs point you to the beaches, where there are showers and restrooms. Being so close to the resort means these beaches are well tended, and they're definitely worth a stop. The two beaches are adjacent to each other, separated by a lava promontory where there is great snorkeling. The ocean is sheltered by this rocky point and therefore offers great swimming.

Hula Moons Bar is a pool- and ocean-facing terrace restaurant in the Aston Wailea Hotel that mixes 1930s ambience with good food and comes out a winner all around. If it's a nice evening, dine outside under the stars. This restaurant features a super do-it-yourself salad bar, great steaks, fine fresh fish, a kids' menu, and sweet serenades by local entertainers. $$. **Hula Terrace,** just outside the.Hula Moons, shares the same menu and is open for lunch as well as dinner. **Lanai Terrace,** the main dining room for the Aston Wailea Hotel, is open for breakfast and dinner. A breakfast buffet includes whatever you could possibly want and pastries that are minutes-fresh from the hotel bakery. A variety of dinner entrees are available, but some the best buys are the "Theme Night" specials— Pasta Extravaganza, Fajita Festival, Stir-Fry Chef's Table, Bavarian Night, and Paniolo Prime Rib—and there's also a children's menu. At 3700 Wailea Alanui; 879–1922. $$.

Wailea Beach is less than a mile from the **Wailea Town Center,** a small shopping area with boutiques, restaurants, and a general store. The turnoff is on the right, on a well-marked access road. The facilities are fine and the sandy beach offers great conditions for swimming, but the absence of rocks makes snorkeling fairly futile here.

Children find the sand at Wailea beach ideal for building grand castles. (Courtesy Wailea Destination Association)

Bistro Molokini, an open-air Italian-style cafe in the center of the Grand Wailea Resort and Spa, offers mouth-watering pizzas made on the spot in a wood-burning pizza oven, plus sandwiches, salads, pupus, and ocean- and pool-front views. One of several restaurants in the Grand Wailea, the Bistro serves lunch and dinner. $$. Also at the Grand Wailea, **Humuhumunukunukuapua'a** is named for Hawaii's state fish. The restaurant is freestanding amid waterfalls and its own lagoon. It features a thatched roof, wood floors and railings, and a tropical, open-air design. Bronze statues of mermaids and Hawaiian fishermen add to the Polynesian atmosphere. Seafood is a specialty here, prepared in the style of Pacific Rim cuisine. A nighttime visit to "Humu" transports you back to old Hawaii, Tahiti, or Fiji. At 3850 Wailea Alanui; 875–1234. $$$.

At the neighboring Four Seasons Resort, **Pacific Grill** is a fine place for breakfast, lunch, or dinner overlooking the pool area and ocean. Buffets are spectacular, service sublime. The Pacific Rim cuisine includes grills, pastas, sandwiches, and salads, with both buffet and menu service. The typical luncheon buffet has a marvelous selection of soups, greens, chicken, and seafood; the dessert buffet shows a selection of six cheesecakes (yes, you can sample each!). At Four Seasons Resort, 3900 Wailea Alanui; 874–8000. $$$.

There's never a crowd at pristine **Polo Beach.** Swimming is safe and the snorkeling is illuminating. The water is brimming with colorful fish near the rocks that separate Polo from Wailea. To get here, keep on Wailea Alanui Drive and follow the sign marked POLO BEACH.

Many of the resort properties in this area cater to families by offering special rates and programs for children. At the **Kea Lani Hotel** there's a special family package that includes a three-night stay, rental car, and enrollment in Keiki Lani, a children's program for ages five to twelve. The program includes fun and educational activities such as hula and lei-making lessons, hiking, and swimming.

Caffe Ciao, Kea Lani Hotel's alternative eatery, is patterned after a Sicilian delicatessen. Along with shelves full of take-out munchies, Ciao has breakfast, lunch, and dinner specialties that you can eat on the spot, take to outside tables, or carry back to your suite. Pizza and pasta appear frequently on the menu. Fresh-baked specialties washed down with espresso, cappuccino, or other heavy-duty coffees will help parents launch any morning enterprise. $. **Kea Lani, The Restaurant** is the main dining room of the Kea Lani Hotel. Situated to catch the evening sunset with your choice of inside or outside tables, it also has big closable doors to block out excess wind or the stray rain shower. Open for breakfast and dinner, it features entertainment nightly and typically friendly Maui service. Cuisine is basically Continental with only a few Hawaiian overtones. $$$. **Polo Beach Grille & Bar** is Kea Lani Hotel's poolside bar and restaurant and has a kids' menu, excellent sandwiches, and a super view of the ocean or the pool. All sandwiches are served with fresh Maui-made chips. $.

Kea Lani Hotel is located at 4100 Wailea Alanui Dr.; 875–4100.

At the road's end, sits the Maui Prince Resort and **Makena Beach.** Makena actually consists of **Big Beach** and **Little Beach.** With children, it's a good idea to stick to the first, Big Beach, as the other is frequently a "clothes optional" hangout for locals. Big Beach is quite picturesque, and the waters are optimum for snorkeling, bodysurfing, and swimming.

At Maui's Four Seasons Resort, creative keiki enjoy arts and crafts activities. (Courtesy Four Seasons Resort Maui)

Truly a garden cafe, the Maui Prince Hotel's **Cafe Kiowai** sits on the edge of a koi-filled lagoon with a pastoral view of the lush grounds. Delightful breakfasts, lunch, light evening fare, and special children's dishes are available from the full menu. $$. **Prince Court,** also in the Maui Prince, has some of the finest dining on the island. The Court offers adventures in Hawaiian Regional Cuisine. A meal here will be long remembered. Families are especially welcome for Sunday brunch. $$$$. At the Maui Prince, 5400 Makena Alanui, Makena Resort; 874–1111.

Sunsets are especially beautiful from Makena. The expansive vistas include Kahoolawe, Lanai, and the West Maui Mountains, which have the appearance of an entirely separate island.

Be sure to bring some water and snacks along, since the closest facilities are back at the Maui Prince Hotel. The beach is easy to find, with well-marked signs. Don't leave *anything* in your car.

On the way to Makena, look for **Keawalai Congregational Church,** built in 1832. Services are still held here every Sunday at 9:30 A.M.

At the end of the road, a sign points to **Ahihi-Kinau Natural Area Reserve.** The scuba diving and snorkeling here are among the best in all of Maui. Although the beach is narrow, the waters are crystal clear and there are lots of tide pools to explore.

La Perouse Bay is just beyond Ahihi-Kinau Reserve. In 1786 Jean-Francois La Perouse became the first Westerner to land on Maui, and this bay was where he disembarked. It's a popular snorkeling site, but the beaches are fairly small.

A bit beyond the bay are the remains of the **King's Trail.** This 5.5-mile trail goes from La Perouse Bay over Maui's last lava flow, which dates to 1790. Beyond La Perouse the road gets quite rough and is not recommended for cars, but it's an easy hike. The trail leads over the same path used by the king's tax collectors in Old Hawaii. At one point the path heads inland, past old stone foundations and walls—signs of an earlier civilization. Little offshoots of the main trail lead down to the ocean, where you'll be treated to a wonderfully scenic view of Cape Hanamanioa and the Coast Guard lighthouse.

For a horseback tour of the area, contact **Makena Stables** at 879–0244. Guides well-versed in local plants and legends will take you on the slopes of Haleakala, over the old lava flows to pristine views. The horses are well kept and the folks are friendly. Kids must be at least twelve to participate. Depending on the route, prices range from $99 to $130 per person.

UPCOUNTRY

You'll hear the term "Upcountry" often on Maui. There are no real boundaries setting off this region, but locals use the name to refer to the towns and villages surrounding Haleakala. By this definition, the area is huge, reaching from Ulupalakua Ranch in the south to Kipahulu Park in the east and Makawao in the north.

A series of picturesque, lush green towns surround Haleakala like a fragrant lei. The soil in these areas is rich and heavily cultivated; farms and nurseries dot the landscape, and herds of cows and horses munch contentedly in acres of tall grass.

Undulating roads meander through hills and valleys carpeted in velvety green, looking decidedly untropical, almost like the backroads of England instead of a South Pacific island.

There are different routes leading to Upcountry. The Haleakala Highway, Route 37, leads through Pukalani and Keokea and ends at the 30,000 acres of Ulupalakua Ranch. About midway, Route 377 branches off the Haleakala Highway and heads into Kula, home to several nurseries and protea farms. Or, Baldwin Avenue, off the Hana Highway, leads to Makawao and Olinda.

You'll arrive in **Pukalani** when Route 37 intersects with Route 377. This is the largest town in the area, and a good place to stock up on gas and supplies if you're heading up to Haleakala. No doubt the kids will notice the tall golden arches of McDonald's.

At **Maui Enchanting Gardens,** you can walk among exotic plant species from all over the world as well as native Hawaiian plants. The gardens are just outside of Pukalani, off Route 37 and are open daily, 9:00 A.M. to 5:00 P.M. Admission is $4.00 for adults and $2.50 for children ages six to twelve; children five and under are free. For more information, call 878–2531.

Don't miss a visit to the charming cowboy town of **Makawao.** You'll notice fine dining establishments sitting side-by-side with hitching posts and saddleries. The town was settled by *paniolo* (cowboys) who moved here in the late 1800s to work in the local ranches. Many of the stores are family-run businesses that have been handed down for generations. The Oskie Rice Arena here is the site of the state's largest rodeo, usually held in July, and during the polo season the arena hosts weekend tournaments. Makawao is known statewide for its annual Fourth of July parade, and if you happen to be on Maui then, don't miss it.

It's worth waking up early just to drive up to Makawao and savor a tasty cream bun from **Komoda Store and Bakery.** A local favorite for more than fifty years, the cream buns are usually sold out by mid-morning. Komoda is at 3674 Baldwin Avenue; 572–7261.

The **Hui Noʻeau Visual Arts Center** is an active artists' haven that brings a bit of sophisticated culture to an otherwise cowpoke town. The center is actually a nine-acre estate that used to be called Kaluanui. Within the two-story Mediterranean-style home are beautiful displays of local artists' works. The center also offers art classes and lectures, studio space, kilns, and pottery wheels. Visiting artists often host free lectures. The center is at 2841 Baldwin Avenue and is open Monday through Friday, 10:00 A.M. to 4:00 P.M.; 572–6560.

An outfit called **Pony Express** offers trail rides across the Haleakala Ranch. One-hour and two-hour rides cost $35 and $60, respectively. The Crater Ride lasts from 9:30 A.M. to 2:30 P.M., includes lunch, and delves deep into the volcano. Kids must be at least ten to participate. Call 667–2200 for more information.

Farther up Baldwin Avenue sits the little town of **Olinda,** home to Seabury Hall. For most of the year, this private boarding school, although picturesque, is not notable enough to merit a visit. In May, however, locals come from throughout the islands to the annual arts and crafts fair, complete with food, entertainment, and games. For more information and exact dates, call 572–7235.

Picturesque **Kula** is the heart of Upcountry, and a drive through this town offers the best of the region's sites. You'll see farm after farm of colorful crops, including potatoes, pineapples, grapes, lettuce, strawberries, sweet Maui onions, and cabbages. Nurseries are everywhere as well, growing beautiful protea, carnations, roses, and more.

Getting to Kula involves the same roads that lead to Haleakala. From Pukalani, take the Haleakala Highway (Route 37), turn on Route 377, and then again on Route 378, which is a curving road that leads up to the crater. Kula is a great resting spot before venturing up the mountain.

Just after Route 377 branches off from Route 37, well-marked signs identify the way to **Kula Botanical Gardens,** a picturesque picnic spot. There are five acres of plants and trees, all identified with signs and easy directions for a self-guided tour. The gardens are open daily, 7:00 A.M. to 4:00 P.M. Admission is $3.00 for adults and just 50 cents for children under age thirteen. For more information, call 878–1715.

The **Keiki Zoo Maui** is at 370 Kekaulike Avenue in Kula. For Mainlanders used to zoos with extensive collections of wild animals, this site may seem like kids' stuff. But that's exactly what it is. Kids love it here because most of the facility is a petting zoo, designed especially for children. (*Keiki* means child.) It's an interactive zoo, where children can hug, kiss, and cuddle with the animals. A few of the animals present are Woolite and Lambchop (sheep), Louie (llama), Harley (hog), and Rosie (Shetland pony).

The zoo is very small, so admission ($4.00) and guided tours are by appointment only. For more information, call 878–2189.

Breathtakingly high on the road to the summit of Haleakala, the **Kula Lodge** offers good food plus picture windows that provide a view of the whole northern half of the island. Stop in on the return from a sunrise visit to the summit for mouthwatering omelets or Belgian waffles loaded with raspberries. On Haleakala Hwy., Kula; 878–1535. $$.

All upcountry roads lead to **Haleakala Crater,** a trip that all Maui visitors should include on their itinerary. Its naturally sculpted features and vast dimensions rank right up there with the Grand Canyon and Painted Desert in Arizona. Although some 22,000 feet of the mountain sits below sea level, it is the world's largest dormant volcano. It last erupted in 1790, and scientists, while reluctant to label it extinct, don't believe it's going to blow again within the next few hundred years.

Not only is Haleakala Crater remarkably beautiful, it's also home to two native Hawaiian species that exist only here and on the Big Island: the brilliant-when-blooming silversword plant and Hawaii's state bird, the nene goose. (Recently, nene populations have been bred successfully in captivity on the Big Island, at Volcanoes National Park.) The silversword plant is very rare. It can take up to twenty years to bloom, and when the flowers do open up, they shine gloriously for a short while, from June through October, then die. Please appreciate the silversword plants from a distance.

The 27,500 acres of Haleakala were designated a National Park in 1961 to help preserve the unique plants and animals here and to provide a safe, educational environment for visitors.

The drive up the mountain is almost as breathtaking as the views from the final destination at the top. Ever-changing vistas await at each curve in the road, and each new view is like opening another window. You'll see forests of introduced and indigenous trees, including flowering jacaranda, eucalyptus, and cactus, and you'll pass through virtually untouched tropical rain forests, dry forests, and desertlike environments.

Don't feel pressured to explore the entire park in one visit—that's impossible. The park encompasses some 27,500 acres and more than 30 miles of hiking trails. But the most exquisite feature is the crater. It's 7.5 miles long, 2.5 miles wide, and an unbelievable 3,000 feet deep. At the crater floor, what looks like a small mountain range is really a series of cinder cones, ranging in height from 600 to 1,000 feet.

Hosmer Grove is the first stopping point along the curvaceous Route 378. It's actually a forestry project that's leftover from the 1800s. In the hope of finding a marketable wood for the region, certain trees, such as pine, cedar, sugi, and juniper, were planted here. It's a scenic place to stop and stretch your legs, but don't think you've gotten anywhere close to seeing the best the park has to offer.

The **Park Headquarters** is just a few minutes past Hosmer Grove on Route 378, at the 7,000-foot elevation level. The facility is open daily, 7:30 A.M. to 4:00 P.M., and is the place where visitors must pay the $4.00 admission price to get into the park. There is a free map available at headquarters that will explain the degree of difficulty for each trail, so you can pick the route best suited to your family's abilities.

There's a small trail to the left of the headquarters—take it. It leads to two spectacular overlooks: **Leleiwi** and **Kalahaku.** Of the two, Kalahaku is the better, because you get a good view of rare silversword plants from here. You can follow the signs for the **Silversword Loop Trail**; it's less than 0.1 mile and will offer up-close views of these beautiful plants.

Note: On any hiking trail, it's important to stay on the well-worn paths. With a slight misstep or detour, a hiker could unknowingly crush the roots of an endangered plant, not only killing the plant, but eventually killing the insects that feed off of the plant. Please explore with caution and be aware that the ecosystem here is very fragile.

Several companies offer guided hikes throughout the park. **Hike Maui,** operated by naturalist extraordinaire Ken Schmitt, features a veritable menu of hiking options designed to accommodate different ages and skill levels. Many of his hikes include a picnic lunch, and all of them offer a great chance to learn about the biological, environmental, and geographical particulars of the area. In addition to Haleakala, Schmitt also leads hikes in the remote areas of Hana, La Perouse Bay, Polipoli Springs, and Iao Valley. Don't miss a chance to join his living classroom—it's educational, fun, and beautiful all at the same time. For more information, call 879–5270.

The park's **Visitors Center** is at the end of the road, about 10 miles beyond the headquarters. The center is open from sunrise to 3:00 P.M. and features informative displays that explain the nearby natural wonders. Every hour, the staff rangers provide a short, interesting lecture about the geological wonders of Haleakala. The rangers also host a variety of hikes, during which they take time to explain certain outstanding features of the flora, fauna, or landscape. For more information, call the center at 572–9306.

You can tour this area by air, foot, car, horse, and bicycle—all are great and offer fantastic scenery. But **watching the sun rise** as a new day dawns is free and by far the most spectacular sight in all of Maui, ranking up there with the best sights in the entire state.

The best place to watch the sun rise is at the Puu Ulaula observatory, a glass-enclosed structure at the very top of the mountain. If you're deterred by the thought of dragging the kids out of a warm bed at 4:00 in the morning and driving up 20,000 feet to below-freezing temperatures, don't be. Although you'll need warm clothes, the experience is guaranteed to be unforgettable. Besides, you can let the kids sleep in the car on the way up, and sightsee on the way down, after the sun has risen. You'll no doubt see a few dozen cars parked and waiting, the people huddled together inside for warmth. As the sun emerges, so do the people, and the chorus of "oohs" and "aahs" begins.

You're above the cloud cover here, so you get to watch the sun eke its way through the puffy clouds. Streaks of light flash across the sky, as the sun cooks the cloud color to a rosy, blush pink, then a burnt orange, and then a fiery red as it rises. Soon, it begins to reflect off the natural formations surrounding the crater, and the whole landscape adopts this pinkish-orangish-reddish hue. It's breathtakingly beautiful.

Pretty soon, the sun is officially up, and the weather warms significantly. Sunscreen is important and should definitely be applied liberally. Even if you're not hot, at this high altitude you're quite close to the sun. Beware of blistering lips and noses! Additionally, the oxygen level drops a bit up here, and precautions are advised for anyone prone to respiratory or cardiovascular problems.

From Kahului, the ride up to the visitors center will take about one and a half hours, excluding any stops for gas or food. If you're staying in Kaanapali or Wailea, tack on an additional forty minutes. Because you'd hate to wake up that early and miss the sunrise, plan on being there a half-hour before. You can look in the daily newspaper for specific times, or listen to the recording provided by the National Weather Service at 871–5054.

You're certain to spot groups of people riding bicycles down the mountain (much smarter than attempting to pedal *up*). For families with older children, this offers a way to absorb the beauty of the mountain with minimal physical activity. For more information, contact **Maui Mountain Cruisers,** 296 Alamaha Street, Z–1, Kahului, HI 96732; (800) 232–6284. The sunrise tours cost $115 per person, leave at 2:15 A.M., and return by noon. The midday rides cost $100 per rider, leave at 6:30 A.M., and return by 2:00 P.M. Children must be at least 4 feet, 10 inches tall and over twelve years old, and pregnant women are prohibited from participating. Both rides offer a Continental breakfast and full lunch. Hotel pickups are available.

Pony Express Tours features a variety of four-legged trips through the crater. A full day costs $150, a partial day costs $120, and lunch is provided.

The company will also take riders on one-, two-, and three-hour rides ($35, $60, and $85 respectively). Children must be at least ten years old and pregnant women are not allowed to participate. For more information, call 667–2200.

For guided overnight camping, **Charley's Trailride and Pack Trips** will organize cabins and meals. The rates vary according to how extensive a trip you'd like and the number of riders in your group. For more information, call 248–8209. Children must be at least six years old.

Thompson Ranch Riding Stables specializes in families and will take children as young as five years old, as long as they're accompanied by an adult, for scenic rides on the slopes of Haleakala. Kids under five can go if they ride on a parent's lap. The one-and-a-half-hour ride costs $45, the two-hour sunset ride costs $50, and a two-hour picnic ride costs $55. For more information, contact Thompson Stables, Thompson Rd., Kula, HI 96790; 878–1910.

You may notice a few white dome structures at the very top of the mountain. This area is off-limits to visitors. It's known as **Science City** and encompasses solar tracking stations and U.S. Air Force solar observatories and laser-ranging tracking stations.

If you have a four-wheel-drive vehicle, by all means venture to **Polipoli Springs State Recreation Area.** A variety of short hiking trails here lead through remote wilderness and offer some of the best views in all of Maui. To get there, take Highway 377 (Kekaulike Avenue) to Waipoli Road. You'll reach the Kula Forest Reserve about 10 miles outside of Kula, and from there Polipoli Springs will be easy to find.

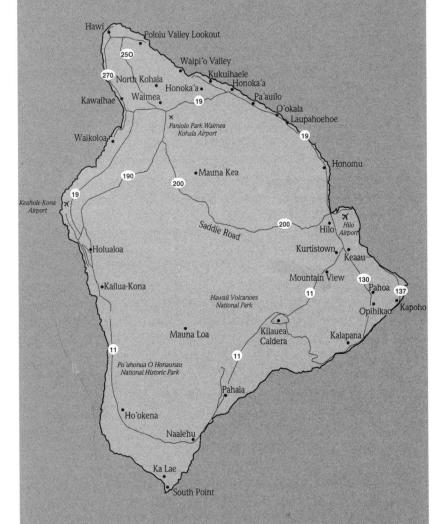

Hawi

Pololu Valley Lookout

250

Waipiʻo Valley

270 North Kohala

Kukuihaele

Honokaʻa

Honokaʻa

Kawaihae   Waimea

Paʻauilo

19

Oʻokala

Laupahoehoe

Paniolo Park Waimea
Kohala Airport

19

Waikoloa

Honomu

190

Mauna Kea

200

Keahole-Kona
Airport

19

Saddle Road

200

Hilo

Hilo
Airport

Holualoa

Kurtistown

Keaau

Kailua-Kona

Mountain View

130

Pahoa

137

11

Kapoho

Hawaii Volcanoes
National Park

Opihikao

Mauna Loa

Kilauea
Caldera

Kalapana

11

Puʻuhonua O Honaunau
National Historic Park

11

Pahala

Hoʻokena

Naalehu

Ka Lae

South Point

The Big Island

The Big Island

Hawaii, commonly referred to as the Big Island, is appropriately named as it's the biggest of the six major Hawaiian Islands and accounts for 63 percent of the state's total landmass. It's 4,038 square miles and, as long as lava continues to spew out of Kilauea, still growing. About 120,000 people live on the Big Island (it's the second-most populated island after Oahu), but it has the lowest population density—barely twenty-five people per square mile. It's almost twice the size of all the other Hawaiian Islands put together.

Of all the islands, the Big Island is the most ecologically diverse, with natural environments ranging from the desert plains of Ka'u to the rain forests above Hilo, to snowcapped Mauna Kea. Small towns, passed over by time, contrast with high-tech scientific communities housing world-renowned telescopes and observatories. Steaming molten lava pours from the earth's center and flows to the sea, creating fresh new land that's still too hot to walk upon, while just a few miles away, rain forests thrive in lush valleys.

Within its 300 miles of coastline, the Big Island offers spectacularly colored beaches, from snowy-white sands of Hapuna to the black and green sands of the southeastern coast.

The Big Island can be divided into two parts: the Kona side and the Hilo side, worlds apart in personality. The Kona side bustles with activity. The weather there is sunny and dry, and the beaches are wonderful, full of color-ful marine life, and ideal for snorkeling. The Hilo side is quiet, often rainy, and lush with flower farms, gardens, and hidden black-sand coves. Tiny one-street towns dot the coastline, rich in history and picturesque sights.

Here are a few fascinating facts about the Big Island:

* Captain James Cook, the British explorer most often credited with discovering the Hawaiian Islands and exposing them to Western civilization, was killed here, at Kealakekua Bay.

* South Point, Ka Lae, is the southernmost point in the whole United States.

* The Big Island is the worldwide leader in harvesting macadamia nuts and orchids.

* Mauna Kea is the tallest mountain in the world (measured from its base at the ocean floor).

* Mauna Kea's cross-island sister peak, Mauna Loa, is the densest mountain in the world. It's 60 miles long and 30 miles wide and is made of more than 10,000 cubic miles of lava—it weighs more than the entire Sierra Nevada range in California.

* Parker Ranch, at 225,000 acres, is the largest privately owned ranch in the United States.

* The Big Island's highest peak, Mauna Kea, is topped with snow every winter and is home to a ski resort, while just a few miles away, at the Kona Coast, the average temperature in January, the coldest month, is 63 degrees Fahrenheit.

* King Kamehameha the Great was born and raised on the Big Island.

* The Big Island is home to Kilauea, the world's most active and largest volcano.

* Wao Kele O Puna is the only remaining lowland rain forest in the United States.

* The island's peaks are home to the world's biggest telescope and more scientific observatories in one place than anywhere else in the world, representing nine different nations.

The Big Island is so vast, many residents have not explored every nook and cranny. It's impossible to do in just one visit. There are two airports serving both sides of the island: Kona and Hilo. Whichever one you choose, a rental car is essential because the island begs to be explored and sights are spread quite far apart. The Kona Airport accepts some direct flights from the Mainland; otherwise you have to first land in Honolulu and hop on a commuter flight.

The island is dominated in the center by its two humongous peaks, Mauna Kea and Mauna Loa. The Saddle Road, Route 200, cuts across the Island, but you can also drive almost completely around on Routes 19 and 11. The Island is so large, however, that it doesn't make sense to drive a Circle Island Tour. It's more feasible and rewarding to explore one side at a time. This chapter begins in Kona and continues north to Kohala and the tip of the island at Hawi. Then it will look at the Hilo side, from where you can venture north up the Hamakua coast to Waipio Valley and south to Kilauea Volcano and South Point.

KONA

Most of the entire 90-mile coastline comprising the Kona District is low and flat, while the mountains just east of town feature forests, ranches, and residential homesteads. Kona can usually be separated into two regions: north and south, with the border being the town of Kailua-Kona. It doesn't matter which way you go, but for purposes of easy orientation, this guide will cover Kailua-Kona, then proceed south to Ka Lae, then north to Kapa'au.

Some say **Kailua-Kona** is what Waikiki looked like forty years ago. The hotels are plentiful but not built too close together. Although the Big Island's major visitor hub, it still has a small-town appeal and is the sort of place where restaurant workers "talk story" with fishermen and hoteliers.

Most sites, restaurants, hotels, and attractions are located within a close proximity to Alii Drive, the main drag. If you don't rent a car, the **Alii Shuttle** runs daily along the strip, from 7:45 A.M. to 10:00 P.M. It costs just $1.00 each way and stops at most major hotels. The Kona Historical Society offers **walking tours** at 9:30 A.M., Tuesday through Saturday. Tours cost $10 per person, regardless of age. For more information, call 323–3222.

To get to Kailua-Kona, take the Queen Kaahumanu Highway, Route 11, south of the airport, and turn right on Palani Road. Palani goes straight to the ocean and leads to Kailua Bay and Alii Drive.

Just south of the airport, before you get into town, you'll pass the **OTEC Natural Energy Labs.** It's worth a small side trip to tour this fascinating facility. Here, cold water is pumped from thousands of feet below the ocean surface, mixed with warm water, and used to generate electricity and provide a suitable environment for aquaculture. Strawberries, lobsters, kelp, and abalone are being cultivated here. Free guided tours are given every Thursday at 10:00 A.M. Reservations are strongly recommended; 329–7341.

Kailua Pier will be the first structure you notice upon arriving in Kailua-Kona. It's bordered by a long seawall that's a great spot to sit and watch the traffic. The pier really comes alive every October when thousands of participants churn up the water at the start of the Ironman Triathlon. The pier is also the embarkation point for many oceangoing tours, including snorkeling, whale-watching, fishing, and submarine excursions.

King Kam Beach, also known as Kamakahonu Beach, is very gentle and therefore ideal for children. It's right near the pier and the King Kamehameha Kona Beach Hotel. Here, from a little shack on the beach, you can rent kayaks, paddleboats, boogieboards, and snorkeling gear.

On the north end of Kailua Bay sits the completely restored **Ahuena Heiau,** where King Kamehameha the Great retreated to spend his remaining days after conquering all the islands. The nearby **King Kamehameha Kona Beach Hotel** (329–2911) offers free guided tours of the heiau grounds Monday to Thursday at 1:30 P.M. Although you must get permission from the security guards to enter the grounds, you needn't visit as part of a tour. Admission is free, and the heiau is open daily 9:00 A.M. to 4:00 P.M.

Within the heiau grounds is a temple dedicated to the god of fertility, Lono. The oracle tower, or *anuu,* is the tallest part of the heiau and is where the high-ranking priest would meditate and receive messages from the gods.

If you happen to be in the area from 10:00 A.M. to 2:00 P.M., the hotel also offers free entertainment provided by the local senior citizens, known as *kupuna*. It's quite heartwarming to watch them strum the ukulele and dance hula in the old Hawaiian style.

For a full-scale luau while in Kona, the hotel hosts a longstanding luau that is well reputed among locals. Performances are held every Sunday, Tuesday, Wednesday, and Thursday at 5:30 P.M. Admission is $45 for adults, $15 for children ages six to twelve.

The **Royal Kona Resort,** also located in Kailua-Kona, hosts a "Drums of Polynesia" luau every Monday, Friday, and Saturday evening. Adults cost $36, children under twelve cost $20; 329–3111. Up the coast in Kohala, most of the larger resorts offer their own Polynesian revue.

Even if you're not staying at the **Kona Surf Resort,** do visit and take a free tour of the picturesque fourteen acres. The grounds consist of gardens, ponds, several thousand flowers, shrubs, and fruits—it's a delight for the senses. Guided tours are given Sunday, Tuesday, and Thursday at 3:00 P.M. For more information, call 322–3411.

Just south of Kailua Pier, the opposite direction of Ahuena Heiau, you can't miss **Mokuaikaua Church,** the tallest structure in town. The land was given by King Liholoho to the first Congregationalist missionaries who arrived on the *Thaddeus* in 1820. The church was built from coral blocks in 1838 and is the oldest church on the island.

The church is across the street from the ocean, at the south end of Kailua Pier. It's open daily, and volunteer docents are on hand from noon to 1:30 P.M. to offer a bit of local history.

Across the street and a few yards south of the church sits **Hulihee Palace,** also built in 1838. It's a two-story building commissioned by John Kuakini, Hawaii's first governor. It was used as a summer retreat for ruling monarchs until 1916. Tours offer a chance to see the period furniture and learn about the lifestyles of Hawaii's monarchs. While Iolani Palace on Oahu was the formal headquarters for kings and queens, Hulihee was a place they came to for relaxation and recreation.

The palace is open Monday to Friday, 9:00 A.M. to 4:00 P.M., weekends 10:00 A.M. to 4:00 P.M. Admission is $4.00 for adults, $1.00 for children ages twelve to eighteen, 50 cents for children under twelve. For more information, call 329–1877.

Waterfront Row on Alii Drive is a mini shopping center with gift stores, boutiques, and restaurants. Be sure to check out "Granders Wall of Fame." Kona is known as the billfish capital of the world because the local waters are chock-full of marlin. At the Granders Wall, people who have caught fish weighing more than 1,000 pounds earn themselves a place on the wall with a picture of their catch.

The beaches in Kona central aren't great for swimming; better conditions are found in North Kohala at the luxury resorts. However, continuing south, past the strip of hotels and condominiums, **White Sands Beach** is a popular local place in the summer. It's also referred to as "Magic's" or "Disappearing Sands" because winter storms often consume the beach. Boogieboarders flock here on swell days. Nearby is the **Ohana Congregational Church,** built in 1855 and still hosting services every Sunday morning.

Kahaluu Bay is just south of Magic's and some locals claim its designation as a nature preserve makes it the best snorkeling beach on the whole island. It's great for beginners because many of the snorkeling sites are close to shore, where it's shallow and protected. Be sure to warn your kids to stay within the bay because the currents are strong outside. There are lots of turtles to see, but not to touch; they are an endangered species.

Farther south on Alii Drive, you'll see the **Little Blue Church,** more commonly known today as St. Peter's Catholic Church. Within a short walking distance are the ruins of **Kuemanu Heiau, Kapuanoni Heiau, Hapai Alii Heiau,** and **Keeku Heiau.** Although these historic sites are not restored, they still present a great deal of the spiritual importance of this area.

It's almost sacrilegious to visit Kona and not take advantage of the clear, beautiful ocean surrounding it. Many of the hotels can arrange for a snorkeling, scuba diving, or fishing excursion, and many offer snorkeling equipment, either complimentary or for a small price. If you're staying in a condominium, however, or if you decide to venture into the ocean when you're driving around, the following Kona-based businesses rent snorkel and scuba gear.

✳ **Dive Makai,** 329–2025, will rent equipment if you're participating in its charter trips, which leave daily from Kailua Pier.

✳ **Jack's Diving Locker,** at 75–5819 Alii Drive, 329–7585, about a mile from the King Kamehameha Beach Hotel, is open daily 8:00 A.M. to 9:00 P.M.

❋ **King Kamehameha Divers,** 329–5662, organizes dive charters and whale-watching trips and also rents boogieboards. Located in the King Kamehameha Beach Hotel.

❋ **Big Island Divers,** in the Kaahumanu Plaza, 329–6068, rents equipment and arranges charters, mostly for scuba divers.

❋ **Snorkel Bob's,** next to the Royal Kona Resort off Alii Drive, 329–0770, rents snorkeling equipment and boogieboards. Open 8:00 A.M. to 5:00 P.M. daily.

❋ **SNUBA,** off Kailua Pier, 326–7446. SNUBA is a new sport that lets you explore the underwater world without becoming a full-fledged certified scuba diver. In SNUBA, the tank is strapped to a small inflatable raft that floats on the surface above the diver. As the diver swims around, the raft follows. SNUBA-ers breathe compressed air through a

Snorkeling excursions aboard the Fair Wind II *are full of fun and adventure.* (Courtesy *Fair Wind II)*

regulator, and the views awaiting them are much more detailed, colorful, and expansive than the views afforded to snorkelers. Prices are $55 for a beach dive, $45 for a boat dive. Open seven days a week.

If you're interested in a guided scuba/snorkel/SNUBA excursion, check out the following companies. Note: Again, most of these trips can be booked through your hotel activities desk.

* **The Fair Wind,** 322–2788, sails on two cruises daily from Keauhou Bay. The morning cruise lasts from 9:00 A.M. to 1:30 P.M. and includes a Continental breakfast, barbecue lunch, and snorkeling or SNUBA-ing at Kealakekua Bay. Admission is $69 for adults, $38 for children ages six to seventeen, free for kids under six. The afternoon cruise, from 2:00 to 5:30 P.M., also goes to Kealakekua Bay for underwater fun, and lots of snacks are offered. Prices are $44 for adults, and $29 for children. Kids will love the water slide onboard this boat.

* **Kamanu Charters,** 329–2021, hosts snorkeling and sailing cruises that cost $43 for adults, $26 for children twelve and under.

* **Ocean Sports,** 885–5555, offers a morning snorkel and lunch cruise costing $54 for adults, $31 for children twelve and under, and an evening sunset cruise for $45 and $31, respectively.

* **The Body Glove,** 327–7122, charges $54 for adults, $24 for kids ages five to seventeen; kids under five are free. Kids enjoy the 15-foot water slide, high dive, and scores of water toys. It's primarily a snorkeling cruise, and it leaves from Pawai Bay.

* **Sea Quest,** 329–7238, has six-person rafts that leave from Keauhou Bay, at the south end of Alii Drive. Trips cost $55 for four hours and $42 for three hours. The boat stops at two different snorkeling spots.

For a glimpse into the colorful underwater world without getting wet, submarines and semi-submersibles may suit your family. Consider an expedition adventure on the **Kona Atlantis Submarine.** The craft dives to 100 feet, where passengers gaze out windows and watch a scuba team interact with the colorful creatures of the deep. The extended coastal cruise has views and narration of Kona's historic sights. Tickets are $79 for adults, $39 for children twelve and under; call 329–6626. (Kids must be at least 3 feet tall.) There's also a night dive that lets you see the changes that occur when the sun drops—prime time for viewing sharks.

The *Nautilus II,* 326–2003, is similar to the Atlantis expeditions, except it is a semi-submersible craft, meaning the upper deck remains open to the air and wind while the air-conditioned lower deck offers a below-the-surface view, about 5 feet under. Tickets are $39.95 for adults, $24.95 for children ages four to twelve. There are four cruises daily, at 9:30, 10:30, and 11:30 A.M. and 1:30 P.M.

There are some wonderful restaurants in Kona; here are a few favorites.

* **Buns in the Sun.** In Lanihau Shopping Center, "Buns" features a great selection of bakery goods and sandwiches; 326–2774. $.

* **Drysdale's Two.** Set up like a "Cheers" type of sports bar, Two features big-screen televisions in every corner for watching sports events, movies, and so on. Along with an incredible number of tropical drinks, the restaurant serves very good sandwiches and suppers. On the west side of Keauhou Center, Alii Dr. and Keauhou Hwy.; 322–0070. $.

* **Kona Ranch House.** Built and decorated in the style of an elegant, early-1900s ranch house, this restaurant is handy to downtown Kailua-Kona, has plenty of parking, and features a big menu that ranges from ranch beef to light entrees to children's meals. Open 6:30 A.M. to 9:00 P.M. Behind the Shell station at the corner of Kuakini Hwy. and Palani Rd.; 329–7061. $$.

* **Kona Beach Restaurant.** The flagship restaurant for the King Kamehameha Hotel, this eatery features upscale prices and outstanding service to complement an interesting menu. At 75–5660 Palani Rd.; 329–2911. $$$.

* **Paddlers.** The King Kamehameha Hotel's breakfast and lunch restaurant is open 11:00 A.M. to 3:00 P.M. and serves up plenty of the good stuff in that time. All the favorites are here, but the banana bread is a special breakfast treat. At 75–5660 Palani Rd.; 329–2911. $.

✺ **Ocean View Inn.** Get here early in the morning (it opens at 6:30 A.M.) so you can get a window-side table. Then you can watch the charter boats loading up, cruise ships unloading passengers, and all the other activities of the awakening town. The food is good, simple fare, the decor is unpretentious, and no one has ever left hungry! On Alii Drive across from the pier; 329–9998. $.

Heading south from Kailua-Kona, Alii Drive leads toward the mountain, joins Highway 11, and passes through small towns of Honalo, Kealakekua, Captain Cook, Honaunau, and Keokea en route to the southern coast of the island and Milolii. Before heading down the coast, however, take a detour on Hualalai Road, Route 182, which leads to Route 180 and the charming town of Holualoa.

Route 182 leads straight up the mountain to Route 180, where you'll run into **Holualoa.** This is a small town that's recently become a haven for art galleries and has two coffee shops. The views from here are expansively scenic, encompassing all of Kailua-Kona and the harbor. It's much cooler here, compared to the coastal towns surrounding Kona. The vegetation is lush with coffee trees, macadamia nut groves, and banana, mango, and papaya trees.

Continuing south on Route 11, another group of historical sites surround **Keauhou Bay.** A free map explaining the different attractions is available, even to nonguests, from the front desk at Keauhou Beach Hotel, 322–3441.

A monument marks the **birthplace of Kamehameha III,** where the monarch was born in 1814. Nearby is a *holua,* a grassy hill that was used as a makeshift water slide during rainstorms. Hawaiians of yesteryear would slide down the hill on wooden sleds.

A few miles from Keauhou is the little town of **Honalo,** really nothing more than a junction for Routes 180 and 11. The **Daifukuji Buddhist Temple** is an interesting attraction located here. It's free and open daily 9:00 A.M. to 4:30 P.M.

Next you'll pass through the South Kona towns of **Kealakekua** and **Captain Cook.** The first attraction worth stopping at is the **Kona Historical Society Museum,** off Route 11 (follow the sign for Kona Meat Company

Market). Here, exhibits show what life was like in Kona in the early part of this century. There are artifacts, manuscripts, and lots of old photographs depicting the Kona community.

The museum is located in the old Greenwell Store, built in 1860 by H. L. Greenwell, a local entrepreneur. It's on the National and Hawaiian Register of Historic Places. The museum is open weekdays 9:00 A.M. to 3:00 P.M.; donation requested. On Tuesday and Thursday mornings at 9:00 A.M., the museum sponsors a tour of the Uchida Coffee Farm, which offers the chance to see a working farm that's been producing coffee since the 1930s. (Reservations required.) For more information, call 323–3222 Monday to Friday, 8:00 A.M. to 4:00 P.M.

The museum also sponsors a variety of jeep tours of the surrounding countryside for $55 per person, and a $20 historical boat tour, usually in late January, that travels south from Kailua-Kona along the coast. There's really no fixed schedule, but it's certainly worth investigating. It's a wonderful opportunity to explore the area with knowledgeable guides.

For tours of the four-legged persuasion, in the outskirts of Kealakekua, **King's Trail Rides,** off Highway 11 at mile marker 111, offers one-and-a-half-hour trail rides for $50, two-hour rides for $60, and a five-hour trip (including a long break for picnic lunch) for $79. The rides travel through the 20,000-acre Kealakekua Ranch. There are no discounts for children, who must be older than seven and have previous riding experience. For more information, call 323–2388.

In Captain Cook, Napoopoo Road branches off Route 11 and leads to the **Royal Kona Coffee Mill.** The mill has been fashioned into a museum of sorts, with displays portraying life in the old-fashioned coffee plantations. There also are free coffee samples and a souvenir shop. The mill is open daily, 8:00 A.M. to 5:00 P.M., and admission is free. For more information, call 328–2511.

Polynesian Village is a new visitor attraction right below the coffee mill that offers daily activities. Visitors are greeted with a flower lei and can participate in cultural arts and crafts, a traditional imu ceremony in which a pig is cooked in an underground oven, and a luau luncheon followed by a hula show. The luau goes from 10:00 A.M. to 1:00 P.M. Tuesday, Thursday, and Saturday. The village is open Monday through Saturday, 9:00 A.M. to

4:00 P.M. Admission to the luau and show is $39.95 for adults, $15 for children ages six to twelve, free for children under six. For more information, call 328–2222.

The twelve-acre **Amy Greenwell Ethnobotanical Garden** is also in Captain Cook, off Highway 11. This is a wonderful place to walk around; the gardens focus on education, conservation, and research of traditional Hawaiian plants and land use. The facility is open Monday to Friday, 7:00 A.M. to 3:30 P.M., and donations are requested in lieu of admission. For more information, call 323–3318.

Don't miss a chance to have a meal at the **Aloha Cafe.** Just look for the old Aloha Theater on the Captain Cook Highway—the Cafe is in the lobby. It offers great sandwiches and soups, fresh homemade cookies and brownies for dessert, and a relaxed, interesting ambience. Open for lunch and dinner; 322–3383. $.

Highway 11 continues to **Kealakekua Bay,** a wonderful underwater playground and one of the best snorkeling sites on the island. Dozens of commercial charters flock here on picnic/snorkel/sail trips. While the bay can get crowded, there's still plenty of room for travelers who venture here on their own. For those independents, access to the bay is via **Napoopoo Beach Park,** where there are restrooms, showers, and picnic tables.

Not only is Kealakekua Bay regarded as a prime snorkeling locale, it's also an important historical site. If you do drive, notice the **Hikiau Heiau** at the parking lot. This heiau is dedicated to the fertility god, Lono, whom Hawaiians of olden days believed would be resurrected and return to this bay. The well-preserved heiau is carved into the steep cliff, where the priests were afforded an expansive view of the ocean so that they might spot Lono's arrival. The cliffs above the heiau are reported to contain numerous gravesites of ancient chiefs.

History played havoc with the Hawaiians' belief in Lono's return, in a particularly ironic way. In January 1779, Captain James Cook sailed his ships, *Resolution* and *Discovery,* into the tranquil waters of Kealakekua Bay. It just so happened that the locals were in the midst of their Makahiki celebration, an annual festival dedicated to rejoicing and thanking the gods for a fruitful harvest. Imagine their surprise when these two majestic ships appeared, full of never-before-seen Caucasian men.

It's understandable that the Hawaiians mistook Captain Cook for a personification of their sacred Lono. (Some Hawaiian scholars dispute this claim.) They showered the surprised captain and crew with accolades and gifts. Unfortunately for Cook, a variety of miscommunications and cultural insults ensued within a few weeks, and the Hawaiians no longer believed he was a benevolent god. A fierce battle followed, and Cook was killed at this very bay.

In 1874, a 27-foot marble pillar was built in the northern end of the bay as a memorial to Cook and his courageous forays into uncharted oceans.

Route 11 continues to the town of Honaunau, known mostly for its seaside attraction, the **Pu'uhonua O Honaunau National Historical Park,** or Ancient Place of Refuge. To get there, pass Honaunau and, at Keokea, follow Route 160 as it veers toward the ocean. You can also take the coastal road that leads south for about 4 miles from Kealakekua Bay. If you're traveling on Route 160, notice the quaint, castlelike **St. Benedict's Painted Church.**

The 180-acre Pu'uhonua, or Place of Refuge, is one of the most important historical sites in all the islands. Some archaeologists claim this sacred temple was used in the mid-1500s, while others say it was used at least 200 years earlier. Places of refuge were an integral part of old Hawaiian culture. Within these areas, absolution was granted to opposing armies, *kapu* (taboo) breakers, or anyone guilty of disobeying common law. If the miscreants could reach a pu'uhonua before being caught, they were safe within its boundaries. Kahuna lived here for the sole purpose of granting salvation to the inhabitants; they alone had the power to cleanse the avengers' *mana,* or spirit. This temple at Honaunau is the largest of its kind in all Hawaii.

The temple was completely restored and earned national park status in 1961. During the restoration, local artists studied old records and drawings from ancient voyaging ships to give the site as much authenticity as possible. They used traditional techniques and tools to carve the renditions of the gods from large *ohia* logs.

The park, 328–2326, is open Monday to Thursday, 7:30 A.M. to 5:30 P.M., Friday 7:30 A.M. to 11:00 P.M., and weekends and holidays,

7:30 A.M. to 5:00 P.M. The $2.00 admission is certainly a worthwhile price to pay to visit such an inspirational site. Children ages sixteen and under are admitted free. The visitor center has maps and brochures detailing a self-guided tour.

Continuing south, after Keokea, the next towns are **Kealia** and **Hookena,** the latter being a charming coastal town with a wonderful beach. To get to Hookena, follow the well-marked road leading off Highway 11 just a few miles south of the Pu'uhonua O Honaunau exit. The beach park offers picnic tables and showers, and the long black-sand beach is ideal for swimming and bodysurfing.

The rest of this area is known as South Point, but since most people head to South Point after visiting the volcano, and most people go to the volcano from the Hilo side of the island, the South Point section is covered in detail in the Hilo section of this chapter.

NORTH KONA

Just a few yards north of Kailua-Kona and the King Kamehameha Kona Beach Hotel is the site of the old Kona Airport, which has been turned into a beach park called **Old Kona Airport State Recreation Area.** Facilities here include picnic tables, showers, restrooms, and lots of parking. The beach is somewhat rocky and therefore not great for swimming, but the snorkeling is good. Beware of rough waters during high surf.

Kona Coast State Park at Mahaiula Bay is a newly opened beach park that also offers picnic tables and restrooms. Swimming is safe here, during calm weather. It's about 2 miles north of the airport, off Route 19, between mile markers 91 and 90. The dirt road is a bit rugged, but passable, and it's only about 1.5 miles to the beach. On the way, look for a well-defined path that leads to the right. A five-minute walk will take you to scenic and secluded Mahaiula Bay.

Honokohau Harbor is between Kailua-Kona and the airport and is the departure point for the majority of deep-sea fishing excursions. If a fishing expedition is too daunting with young children, at least visit the weigh station at the harbor—it's free and often exciting to watch. When the fishing boats come back, the large catches are hoisted off the boat, measured, and photographed.

The **Harbor Hut Restaurant,** easily found at the harbor, has excellent food and lots for the kids to look at during lunch.

Kona is ranked among the world's best sites for deep-sea fishing, particularly for marlin. There are a few different ways to go about trolling for that "big one." Usually, boats are available for either a full-day or half-day trip, and can be rented as a private or shared charter. Rates vary from $85 for a half-day on a shared charter to $400 for a full day on a private charter. The gear is usually included in the price, and no licenses are required.

There are a few booking agencies that will arrange a fishing trip according to your family's size and budget: **Charter Services,** 334–1881; **Kona Activities Center,** 329–3171; **Kona Charter Skippers Assoc.,** 329–3600; and **Jack's Kona Charters,** 325–7558.

Also at the harbor is the headquarters for **Captain Zodiac,** which provides oceangoing tours and snorkeling along the Kona Coast, combined with a light picnic lunch. The advantage of traveling in a Zodiac is that its small size enables it to explore the nooks and crannies, including sea caves. A Zodiac is a tough, virtually unsinkable motorized rubber boat that holds up to sixteen people. The adventure lasts five hours and costs $62 for adults, $52 for children ages two to twelve, under age two are prohibited. For more information, call 329–3199.

For year-round whale-watching, check out **Dan McSweeney's Whale-Watching Adventure,** which also departs from Honokohau Harbor. The humpback season runs from November through April, but during the rest of the year you can always find other types of whales in Hawaii's waters, such as false killers and pygmy and sperm whales. Visitors are guaranteed a sighting, or else they're invited to come back for free next time. On every trip, Captain Dan McSweeney takes a photo of a whale and all passengers get a souvenir copy. Admission is $39.50 for adults, $29.50 for children ages eleven and under. For more information, call 322–0028.

KOHALA

The **Kohala coastline** north of the Keahole Airport is divided into North and South Kohala. South Kohala features the best and the most beautiful swimming beaches on the island, and North Kohala stretches to Hawi, the tip of the island.

Traveling north on the Queen Kaahumanu Highway, Highway 19, you'll get a sense of why Hawaii is known as the Big Island. There are no structures at all, just black, barren lava. Driving through this desolate lava desert, beware of the "Kona Nightingales," wild donkeys that were originally brought to this area to carry saddlebags full of coffee. They have bred out of control and now roam the area freely, including the highway. They have become quite a road hazard, especially at night.

Notice the Hawaiian-style graffiti that borders each side of the road, where local families or couples spell out their love and devotion with light-colored rocks that contrast sharply with the dark lava. Feel free to pull over and create your own sign.

You may notice the presence of vog and laze—two atmospheric conditions that are by-products of volcanic eruptions. Vog is a volcanic fog that is caused by sulfur particles and sometimes makes the sky look more like Southern California than Hawaii. Laze occurs when lava flows into the ocean and reacts with the salt water, creating hydrogen chloride gas. The gas dissolves in water droplets and forms hydrochloric acid, which can cause stinging eyes and sore throats. These unpleasant conditions usually are blown out to sea with normal trade winds.

The string of hotels and resorts situated on this coastline begins about 30 miles from the airport. Here are some of the finest ultra-deluxe resort properties in all Hawaii. From the first property, Kona Village Resort at Kaupulehu, to the last, Mauna Kea Beach Hotel at Kauna'oa Beach, there is really no designated town, in the sense of a post office and main street. It's almost as if each resort occupies its own little town. The first official town is Kawaihae, a few miles north of the Mauna Kea Beach Resort.

The coastline has a lot more to offer than nice hotels. There are a series of fishponds, petroglyph fields, tidepools, and rarely visited archaeological sites. The area is full of historical and natural wonders, and nonguests are encouraged to tour the grounds of each hotel. Most of the hotel activity desks distribute free maps and brochures listing walking tours and important stops. All of the properties are on well-marked roads leading down to the ocean from Highway 19.

Even if you're not staying at the **Kona Village Resort,** take the road down from Highway 19 to walk around the property. Hotel rooms are

Children learn how to weave lauhala in the traditional way at Kona Village Resort. (Courtesy Kona Village Resort)

authentic *hales,* or grass huts. There are no televisions or telephones—this resort is for people who really want to get away from it all. You can take a free tour of the resort and its surrounding historical sites daily at 11:00 A.M. The resort hosts an authentic luau, complete with an imu ceremony, every Friday. Nonguests are welcome to attend, but reservations are required (call 325–5555). Admission is $63 for adults, $35 for children ages six to twelve, $21 for ages two to five.

Mauna Kea Stables offers **guided trail rides** throughout the nearby Parker Ranch. You needn't be a hotel guest to participate, but reservations must be made at the hotel. Children must be at least eight years old. Rates are $35 for one hour and $60 for two hours, and increase with the length of the tour. For more information, call the Mauna Kea Beach Hotel at 882–7222.

Anaehoomalu Bay is part of the grounds of the Royal Waikoloan and Hilton Waikoloa Hotels and a great place to watch windsurfers. The beach is open to the public, and while the sand may be a bit rough, it's still wonderful for swimming, snorkeling, scuba, and windsurfing.

A few minutes' walk north along the bay leads to well-formed tidepools and **ancient fishponds.** Hawaiians of old constructed fishponds with gaps so that young mullet could swim in and feed in the protected area, but once they ate a lot and grew to a certain size, they could no longer swim back through the gaps to freedom in the open ocean. These particular fishponds were solely for the local chiefs of this area.

There are well-marked trails surrounding the bay that lead to petroglyph fields and the lava path known as the **King's Highway.** The king's tax collectors would follow this path to collect payment in the form of fresh fish from oceanside dwellers.

A truly wonderful attraction at the **Hilton Waikoloa Resort** is the **dolphin pool,** where people can actually swim and play with Atlantic bottlenose dolphins. Before any animal-rights activists begin to worry, the dolphins live in a specially built saltwater pond that's sixty-five times larger than federal regulations deem necessary. The dolphins come from Florida, where in their natural habitat they swim in lagoons and bays not more than 20 feet deep. Here, their pond is 350 feet long and 22 feet deep in the center, and contains 2.5 million gallons of seawater.

The program was started by two well-respected veterinarians and the experience is designed to be educational and safe—both for humans and dolphins. You don't get to sit astride the dolphins and ride them like a horse and there are no acrobatic tricks performed. Instead, chosen participants are given a short lecture on marine life and then they stand in the shallow part of the pool. If the dolphins want to be touched, they stop; if not, they glide right by. Guests of the resort and nonguests who want to participate are chosen via a lottery system. For more information about the Dolphin Quest at Hilton Waikoloa, call 885–1234.

Heading inland on Waikoloa Road, 7 miles up, the little town of **Waikoloa** contains a small shopping center with a grocery store, a few boutiques, and restaurants, mostly serving residents in the local community. A few rental condominiums are also here. There is free entertainment at the King's Shops every Thursday, 6:00 to 8:00 P.M., where local musicians perform contemporary Hawaiian music. King's Shops also offers a food pavilion with a good choice of food your kids will appreciate.

Swimming with the dolphins will be a highlight of any child's vacation. (Courtesy Hilton Waikoloa Village)

The **Waikoloa Village Stables,** 883–9335, is nearby and offers a number of trail rides. It also hosts a few rodeos and Wild West shows. Shows are held every Thursday from 6:00 to 9:00 P.M., and attending one will be a big hit with your kids. The first hour features a variety of barn games, complete with rides on a mechanical bull. The second hour is a full-scale paniolo barbecue, and the final hour is an interactive rodeo, in which four events are performed by cast members and four are performed by audience members. Even young children can participate. Prices are $78 for adults, $39 for kids five to twelve, and free for kids under five.

The rest of the week, rides are available by appointment only and groups must have at least eight people. The trail ride lasts for a half-hour, and the rest of the time is spent on fun activities, such as barrel and relay races. Prices vary according to group size.

Nearby is a small heliport that's home base for two helicopter companies. Their close proximity makes for competitive prices. **Kenai Helicopters,** 885–5833, flies to rain forests, over the volcano, and up the Hamakua Coast. Prices range from $145 to $297. **Hawaii Helicopters,** (800) 994–9099, flies over the volcano, into Waipio Valley, and along the Kohala Coast. Prices range from $129 to $279 from the heliport, $129 to $169 from Hilo Airport.

Waikoloa road will intersect with Route 190, which leads up to Waimea and is covered later in this chapter. Back on the highway, the **Mauna Lani Resort Area,** comprised of the Mauna Lani Bay Hotel and Bungalows and Sheraton's Orchid at Mauna Lani, fronts the **Puako Bay and petroglyph field.** There is a 1.5-mile well-marked path that leads through the field and a *kiawe* forest. It's a short hike, and, although the heat can be stifling, it's very easy and suitable for young children. (Be sure to wear hiking shoes and bring some water along—hot lava radiates heat like a lit barbecue pit.) It's a fascinating experience to walk among the 3,000-plus etchings on the rocks in this 233-acre park. These are considered some of the oldest, finest, and most extensive petroglyph examples in all Hawaii. Look for circles outlining a small hole. Families placed their infants' umbilical cords in these holes to forever connect them to the land, *aina,* and ensure a long and healthy life.

Holoholokai Beach Park is part of the grounds of the Orchid at Mauna Lani, and it's open from 6:30 A.M. to 7:00 P.M. Although quite scenic, the beach offers limited water access because it's full of rocks. The picnic tables and beautiful surroundings provide an ideal spot for a shady respite and wonderful tide pool exploring.

The Orchid at Mauna Lani has four restaurants: The **Dining Room** (for dinners only) features Hawaiian regional cuisine and is a little too formal for young children. $$$. The **Grill Restaurant and Lounge** features fresh seafood and grill specialties with a special kid's menu. $$$$. The **Cafe Restaurant and Lounge** offers Pacific Rim favorites such as steamed opakapaka laulau, plus music and hula. $$. The **Ocean Bar and Grill** has traditional island favorites such as smoked-chicken pizza, Oriental chicken salad, and Puna goat cheese salad. $$. One North Kaniku Dr.; 885–2000.

Hapuna Bay and Mauna Kea Beach are on grounds shared by two resorts: the **Mauna Kea Beach Resort** and **Hapuna Prince Resort.** The beach is one of the prettiest in all Hawaii; it's long, sandy, crescent-shaped, shallow, calm, and great for children during summer months. Families with young children gravitate toward the north end, where a small cove provides year-round calm waters. In winter, however, Hapuna's rough waters can be dangerous, so use caution when entering the water.

In **Kawaihae,** Highway 19 intersects with Route 270, which continues up the coast to North Kohala, while Highway 19 heads inland to Waimea. The main attraction in Kawaihae is the **Pu'ukohola Heiau National Historic Site,** encompassing a whopping seventy-seven acres. The area is comprised of the **Mailekini Heiau** and the nearby **John Young House**.

John Young was an English seaman who settled in Hawaii and became a close friend and advisor to Kamehameha the Great. It was Young who taught the Hawaiians how to use muskets and cannons, which helped Kamehameha in his quest to conquer all the islands.

The site is maintained by the National Park Service and admission is free. It's open daily, 7:30 A.M. to 4:00 P.M.; 882–7218. A free map at the visitor center highlights specific points of interest.

Kohala Divers, off Route 270 in Kawaihae Shopping Center, rents snorkeling equipment and hosts cruises, mostly for scuba divers but occasionally for snorkelers, too. It's open daily 8:00 A.M. to 5:00 P.M.; 882–7774.

Spencer Beach County Park is a great place to snorkel, swim, and picnic. There are restrooms, showers, picnic tables, tennis courts, and even electricity for campers. An offshore reef around Kawaihae Bay protects the waters and helps keep them calm, providing great swimming conditions for kids. The reef also is home to many colorful species of fish, making for great snorkeling. It's just a few miles north of Pu'ukohola Heiau, off Highway 19. There are trails that lead from this beach park up to the heiau.

NORTH KOHALA, HAWI, AND KAPA'AU

Highway 270, known as the Akoni Pule Highway, continues up the coast for what is among the prettiest drives in all Hawaii. You'll pass through North Kohala's two major towns, **Hawi** and **Kapa'au,** and the road ends at Pololu Valley. The road leads into an area that's damper than dry, desert-like Kona; trees with hanging mossy vines stand vigil at the roadside next to boldly colored flowers, palms, and banana trees. Time and modern lifestyles haven't changed secluded North Kohala too much, as witnessed by the old homes and stores still functioning for the small group of people that call Kohala home.

An alternative road, Route 250, cuts inland from Waimea to Hawi and also offers expansive views. It meanders through miles of green grass, an occasional cactus, and small old-fashioned shacks. About halfway to Hawi, the **Von Holt Memorial Park** is a great spot for a picnic. As you get closer to Hawi, you'll find huge panoramic vistas of rolling hills and sparkling seas.

Lapakahi State Park is a must-visit attraction, full of historical significance. This ancient fishing village has been restored and reconstructed to look just as it did before Westerners arrived. It's a living museum, with exhibits you can actually touch and feel, that lets you learn firsthand about local history.

The different stations are numbered and include canoe sheds, a salt-making area, and a fishing shrine dedicated to Ku'ula, god of fishing. Children will love learning how to play *ulumaika* and *konane,* Hawaiian games similar, respectively, to bowling and checkers.

Lapakahi is about 12 miles north of Kawaihae, well marked from Highway 270. The park is open daily, 8:00 A.M. to 4:00 P.M.; 889–5566. The **Koai'e Cove Marine Life Conservation District** is next to Lapakahi and offers good snorkeling, weather permitting. It's rough and isolated here, so only expert swimmers should enter the water.

During the heyday of the sugar industry, **Mahukona** was a busy port from which the Kohala Sugar Company shipped its harvest. Today, all that's left are abandoned warehouses and buildings. During the summer months, the bay and pier are good for swimming and snorkeling, but stay out of the water during the winter.

Mahukona is a few minutes' drive past Lapakahi, and **Kapaa Beach** is a few minutes beyond Mahukona. Although the beach is rocky at Kapaa, it's a great place for a quiet picnic and expansive views.

Mo'okini Heiau is the oldest, most important heiau in all Hawaii and in 1963 it became the first Hawaiian site to be included in the National Register of Historic Sites. There are genealogical charts that can trace the origins of this place to 480 A.D. and the High Priest Kuamo'o Mo'okini. It was designed and constructed only for the *ali'i* (chiefs), who came here to purify themselves. The temple is shaped as an odd-sized rectangle, 125 by 250 feet. The walls are 30 feet high and 15 feet thick. One legend says the heiau was built in a single night; stones were passed hand to hand by a 14-mile chain of 18,000 men that stretched here from Pololu Valley to the east. Today, the site's caretaker, Kahuna Nui Leimomi Mo'okini Lum, is a direct descendant of the first Mo'okini priest.

The heiau was the point of convergence for religious life in Kohala. Kamehameha the Great was born in approximately 1758 right near the heiau, and historians believe he was taken here for his birth rites, returning as a young man to worship here and gather spiritual strength before he rebuilt Pu'ukohola Heiau in Kawaihae.

To get to Mo'okini Heiau from Highway 270, turn left toward Upolu Airport at mile marker 20. This one-lane road will end at the runway.

JULIE'S TOP FAMILY ATTRACTIONS ON THE BIG ISLAND

1. Exploring the rain forests at Hawaii Tropical Botanical Gardens
2. Delving into Thurston and Kaumana Lava Caves
3. Visiting the ancient structures at Pu'uhonua O Honaunau Historical Park
4. Snorkeling at Kealakekua Bay
5. Horseback riding at Parker Ranch, in Waimea
6. Watching the lava flow from Kilauea into the sea
7. Swimming with the dolphins at Hilton Waikoloa
8. Traveling to the depths of Waipio Valley
9. Hiking to the floor of Pololu Valley
10. Watching macadamia nuts being processed at the factory in Honokaa

Turn left and continue on a rough, bumpy dirt road for about 2 miles to the isolated site. Look for a tall transmission tower that marks the road to the heiau. If you come to a closed gate, it's just a five-minute walk up to the temple.

Just a few minutes' walk beyond Mo'okini Heiau, a small plaque marks the spot where Kamehameha the Great was born, **Kamehameha Akahi Aina Hanau.** Kamehameha the Great was raised in North Kohala and it was here that he began his mission to unite the islands under one rule.

Highway 270 eventually curves around the tip of the Big Island and leads to a junction with Highway 250 at **Hawi,** a former booming sugar town that's relatively deserted today. Local residents are trying to revive the area, and there's been slow growth of new stores, restaurants, and art galleries. There's a charming old-fashioned theater in town that still runs movies.

You can get free maps, information, and a chance to "talk story" with the old-timers at the Kohala Visitor Center in the center of town.

Just beyond Hawi is the sleepy town of **Kapa'au,** best known for its huge **statue of King Kamehameha.** The statue was commissioned by King Kalakaua in 1878, and the *kahuna* (priests) of the time felt it was best to situate it in the community where he was born. If you happen to be visiting the Big Island on June 11, Kamehameha Day, be sure to drive up to Kapa'au to see the thousands of leis that are draped on this statue.

You may have noticed a similar statue in downtown Honolulu, on Oahu. This is because the two statues were created by the same person. The original, as soon as it was completed, was sent to Paris to be bronzed. The freight ship carrying the statue back from Paris to Honolulu sank, and everyone thought the nine-ton statue was lost forever. So, with the insurance money, King Kalakaua commissioned a new statue, which arrived in Honolulu in 1883. Soon after, a British ship arrived in Honolulu carrying the original statue, which had somehow been salvaged and unceremoniously dumped in a Port Stanley junkyard in the Falkland Islands.

Kamehameha County Park is in Kapa'au, down a well-marked side road, and it's definitely worth a stop if your children are itching to be active. The park has a 25-yard pool, basketball and tennis courts, a driving range, weight rooms, and a little kiddie area—all free and open to the public.

If you're heading all the way to the end of the road at **Pololu Valley** (and if you've come this far, you might as well go all the way to Pololu), Kapa'au will be the last chance to stock up on food, gas, and supplies.

Kalahikiola Congregational Church is a few minutes' drive beyond Kapa'au. A sign points down a formal driveway, framed on both sides by pines and well-manicured stands of macadamia and palm trees. It leads to the picturesque church, built in 1841 by the Reverend Elias Bond and his wife, Ellen.

On the way to the church, you'll pass the weatherbeaten buildings of the old Bond Estate. It's currently being renovated and therefore is closed to the public. Descendants of Reverend Bond are tending to the renovation and expect it to be open for tours in the near future.

Just before the end of the road, about 2 miles beyond Kapa'au, there's a small fruit stand where a side road veers left, toward the ocean and **Keokea Beach County Park,** a very secluded and picturesque spot popular with North Kohala residents. The rocky shoreline is open to the ocean, but be careful of strong currents if you decide to venture in, and definitely stay out of the water in the winter. The park facilities include restrooms, picnic tables, showers, and a pavilion. It's a truly beautiful spot to picnic.

The road ends at **Pololu Valley Lookout,** where you can see the astounding beauty of the Hamakua Coast. A series of trails here transcend five lush, relatively uninhabited valleys to Waipio, the most well-known. By all means, do take the short trail to the bottom of the valley, where a beautiful black-sand beach awaits you. The trail takes about fifteen minutes and can be slippery if recent rains have fallen. But, slippery or not, this is one of the prettiest hikes in all Hawaii.

The beach is a series of sand dunes that offer safe swimming only during the summer months.

WAIMEA

Waimea is inland of South Kohala, a great *paniolo* (cowboy) town and the center of Parker Ranch, which encompasses 200,000 acres of Mauna Kea's western slopes and is the largest privately owned ranch in the United States. It was started in the 1800s by John Parker. Today, 50,000 head of cattle and about 1,000 horses are raised here. This is picturesque country; the rolling green grassy hills contrast sharply with the desolate black lava fields of Kona.

Waimea is one of the few remaining towns in Hawaii that have maintained their old-fashioned paniolo heritage, the other most famous one being Makawao on Maui. Various rodeos and Wild West shows are held in Waimea year-round. Kids will love the Anuenue Playground in the center of town. It was constructed by local residents and is the pride of the community. It's very unusual and certain to please kids of all ages.

There are a few different routes leading to Waimea. If you're coming from Kailua-Kona, the quickest way is via Route 190, the Hawaii Belt Road, also known as Mamalahoa Highway. If you're coming from Kohala, the Kawaihae Road heads inland from Kawaihae straight to Waimea. From Hilo, you can either travel up the Hamakua Coast on Highway 19 and head inland at Honokaa, or take the Saddle Road, Route 200, across the island and up to Waimea.

In Waimea, the **Kamuela Museum** is the largest privately owned museum in all the islands. The museum houses rare stone idols, some of the first Hawaiian bibles, and a collection of furniture handed down from various members of the old monarchy. There are antiques from all over the world and a wonderful set of old photographs depicting life on Parker Ranch from back in the 1800s to modern times.

The museum is located on Route 19, just west of the junction with Route 250. It's open daily, 8:00 A.M. to 5:00 P.M. Admission is $5.00 for adults; children under twelve get in for $2.00. For information, call 885–4724.

You may not expect to find artworks by Degas or Renoir here in the midst of cattle country, but a visit to **Puuopelu** will prove you wrong. Richard Smart, heir to the Parker Ranch, was a longtime supporter and collector of fine art. He opened this museum before he died in 1992. It features the works of more than 100 artists, some internationally acclaimed, some local superstars.

This ultra-classy establishment is worth a visit. It's open daily 10:00 A.M. to 5:00 P.M. Admission is $7.50 for adults, $3.75 for children ages four to eleven. (Cheaper prices are available by combining a tour with the Parker Ranch Visitor Center—see below.) It's located a few minutes south of central Waimea, along Route 190.

A visit to the **Parker Ranch Visitor Center and Museum** will give you a complete history and overview of the Parker Ranch and Waimea town. There are two museums and a wonderful slide show that demonstrates how today's ranch hands hold fast and proud to their important place in history. The center (885–7655) is comprised of both the Mansion (Puuopelu, with its original homestead artifacts) and the Visitor Center Museum (with a video and an entire exhibit of the family history). It's open daily, 9:00 A.M. to 5:00 P.M. Admission to the museum only is $5.00 for adults, $3.75 for children ages four to eleven. Admission to the homesite is $7.50 for adults, $2.75 for children. To tour both facilities, admission is $10.00 for adults, $7.50 for children.

HILO

Hilo has the dubious distinction of being one of the rainiest cities in the United States, with more than 135 inches of annual rainfall. But don't let the rainy weather deter you from visiting. All that moisture has helped foster a beautiful, green, lush community full of waterfalls, gardens, and nurseries. In fact, Hilo is the orchid capital of the world and the only major town on the Big Island's windward coast.

The majority of Big Island visitors blindly head for Kona, missing the old-fashioned charms and natural scenery in Hilo. While Kona is growing, fast-paced, and modern, Hilo has remained mostly unchanged. A few New Age eateries, coffee houses, and art galleries have sprouted up in recent years, but for all intents Hilo is a small-town, slow-moving residential community.

Every spring, however, the town jumps to its feet with a feverish beat when the "Superbowl" of hula competitions, the **Merrie Monarch Festival,** is held here. During the festival, hotels are 100 percent occupied, and restaurants can't prepare the food fast enough. Obtaining tickets is difficult, so unless you've planned ahead, don't expect to be admitted just because you happen to be in town. In fact, unless you're lucky enough to be attending the festival, it's better to plan a Hilo visit for another time. To get tickets, you must write to Merrie Monarch Festival, c/o Hawaii Naniloa Hotel, 93 Banyan Drive, Hilo, HI 96720, well in advance of your trip.

Most of the buildings in downtown Hilo are two-story, with raised wooden sidewalks and charming old-fashioned facades. Downtown boasts various gardens, natural phenomena, museums, and lots of riverbank fishing.

Armed with a detailed map from the Hilo Main Street Program, you can take a free, self-guided **walking tour** that highlights the important historic sites and also leads you down streets and lanes that demonstrate

Hilo's architectural diversity. Hilo Main Street offices are at 252 Kamehameha Avenue (935–8850), open 8:30 A.M. to 5:00 P.M., Monday through Friday. The free pamphlet, "Discover Downtown Hilo," also is available at most local shops, restaurants, and hotels.

The young and the old will be awed by a walk down historic **Banyan Drive.** Each majestic tree is named after a famous politician, movie star, athletic hero, or other celebrity and was dedicated when its namesake visited Hilo. Some of the more famous trees were planted by Richard Nixon, Franklin D. Roosevelt, Babe Ruth, and Amelia Earhart. The series of banyans forms a green canopy that's quite picturesque. The road follows the edge of Waiakea Peninsula, which occupies the east end of Hilo Bay.

Although the long expanse of black sand at **Hilo Bayfront Park** makes this an interesting site, the swimming isn't great here. Fishing and picnicking, however, are top-notch.

At the end of Banyan Drive, **Reeds Bay Beach Park** is another idyllic picnic spot. Swimming is safe here, although the water is often pretty chilly.

Just offshore of Hilo Bay, **Coconut Island** is a tiny speck of land that used to be a place of refuge, or *pu'uhonua,* in precontact Hawaii and has since been turned into a picturesque park. Once you've crossed the footbridge that connects Waiakea Peninsula to Coconut Island, you'll feel as if you've entered a Japanese meditative garden. There are pagodas, stone lanterns, *torii* gates, and a meandering series of streams shadowed by little crescent-shaped stone bridges. It's a wonderful place to enjoy a picnic and the panoramic views of Hilo.

There is a cozy little natural pool here, complete with a diving tower, that offers a sheltered area ideal for small children.

Liliuokalani Gardens are named after Hawaii's last reigning monarch. These formal Oriental-style gardens are at the west end of Banyan Drive. It's a quiet, scenic place good for a meditative stroll, but it may not be exciting enough for energized children.

For early risers, the **Suisan Fish Market** is definitely an experience not to be missed. Local fishermen gather around 7:30 A.M. with an extensive variety of fresh fish caught in local waters. The fish are placed on piles of ice on the ground, while restaurateurs, local moms, and resort chefs stroll by and inspect the goods. The auction features a wide array of local dialects, and you're certain to look at last night's *mahimahi* in a new light. The fish market is at the corner of Banyan Drive and Lihiwai Street.

Heading east of Hilo Bay on Kalanianaole Avenue, you'll soon pass Kuhio Bay and Puhi Bay. Head straight to **Onekahakaha Beach Park,** where a wonderful large sandy pool is sheltered by the reef and is great for children. Local families often come here for picnics and to explore the nearby tide pools. Don't swim too far out, however, because the currents can be strong here. Just past Onekahakaha is **James Kealoha Park,** frequented by snorkelers and people fishing. The tiny island just offshore is called "Scout Island," as it's a frequent camping spot for local Boy Scouts.

Leleiwi Beach Park is a great black-sand beach that's really a series of small coves, perfect for swimming and snorkeling during calm-weather days. Beware, however, of heavy storms that can create strong currents. The waters are shallow and clear, and a nearby retaining seawall helps keep the ocean calm. The park facilities include pavilions and restrooms. The park is at the eastern tip of the island and is quite picturesque and peaceful.

Snorkelers will definitely want to walk past Leleiwi to **Richardson Ocean Park,** another black-sand beach and the most popular snorkeling area on this side of the Big Island.

If there are any scuba or snorkeling fans in your family, the **Nautilus Dive Center** is one of few dive shops on the Hilo side of the island that not only rent equipment but will take visitors on guided cruises. It's at 382 Kamehameha Avenue; 935–6939. Here you also can pick up a free map detailing nearby dive sites.

Lehia Park sits at the end of the road. If you're visiting in the winter, don't bother coming all the way out here; the sandy beach disappears and the waters are rough. In the summer, however, the series of pools are safe. To get there follow the dirt road after the pavement ends and you'll run right into the park.

At **Wailoa State Park,** you'll want to stop by the **Wailoa Information Center** (933–4360) for all sorts of free information on local sights and activities. There are also historical exhibits and artworks by local artists that rotate every month. The center is open Monday through Friday, 9:00 A.M. to 4:00 P.M., and Saturday, 9:00 A.M. to 3:00 P.M.

The **East Hawaii Cultural Center** displays revolving exhibits by local and international artists. If you're on the Big Island in July, by all means come to the center for the annual Shakespeare in the Park Festival. Local performers design, direct, and stage various plays, performed under the banyan tree. The center is at 141 Kalakaua Street; 961–5711. It's open Monday through Saturday, 9:00 A.M. to 4:00 P.M.

In front of the **Hilo Library,** off Waianuenue Avenue, sit two large stones. The bigger of the two is called the **Naha Stone**; the smaller, **Pinao.** In Old Hawaii, royal infants were placed upon the Naha stone; if they remained silent and did not cry, they were true *ali'i,* members of the Naha clan. If they cried, they did not earn the Naha status.

The Naha Stone is also important because legend dictated that the man who could pick it up and move it would be the one great king of all the islands. Kamehameha the Great, as a young man, astonished the town by moving the colossal stone, thus fulfilling the prophecy, and became Hawaii's most powerful ruler of all time.

View life in Hawaii in the 1800s at the **Lyman Mission House Museum,** an old missionary home that's been converted into a living museum with wonderful artifacts such as old canoe paddles and stone implements. The home, built in 1839, is the oldest frame building on the whole island. Guided tours by docents offer a glimpse into the local history. Displays include period furniture and missionary artifacts.

The museum is at 276 Haili Street, on the opposite side of Waianuenue Avenue from the library. It's open Monday through Saturday, 9:00 A.M. to 5:00 P.M., and Sunday, 1:00 to 4:00 P.M. Admission is $4.50 for adults, $2.50 for children under seventeen. For information, call 935–5021.

Heading inland on Waianuenue Avenue, you'll soon come to **Wailuku River State Park** and **Rainbow Falls.** The park is well marked and easy to find. The falls are colorful and beautiful as they cascade over boulders into a large pool and spray rainbow-colored plumes of water in the air.

Continue inland on Waianuenue a few miles past Hilo Hospital and look for a sign for **Pe'epe'e Falls** and the **Boiling Pots,** where it's said that Mother Nature likes to enjoy a Jacuzzi bath. A small path leads to an overlook where you'll see a series of naturally formed holes. The water in some of these holes actually bubbles as if it were a man-made Jacuzzi. The scenic falls are just upriver from here.

Hilo is like one big flower bouquet; fragrant blooms grow everywhere. Some nurseries have become living galleries where visitors can stroll along paths surrounded by delicate tropical petals. The **Hilo Arboretum** is a nineteen-acre garden established in 1920. It's filled with most of the different types of trees (native and introduced) that thrive throughout the state. You can take a self-guided tour with a free map that's available at the office.

The arboretum is well maintained by the Department of Natural Resources' Division of Forestry. Admission is free, and it's open weekdays, 7:45 A.M. to 4:30 P.M. For information, call 933–4221.

The tour through the **Hilo Tropical Gardens** is also self-guided, and the plants are identified. You'll see anthuriums, pineapples, plumeria, birds of paradise, lipstick trees, papayas, orchids, and coconuts. There's a gift store at which you can buy everything from fresh leis to packaged plants to send home. The gardens are open Monday through Saturday, 9:00 A.M. to 5:30 P.M., and Sunday, noon to 5:00 P.M. They are located at 1477 Kalanianaole Avenue; 935–4957. Admission is $3.00; children under twelve get in free.

At the east end of town, off Route 11, the **Nani Mau Gardens** are the largest, most renowned in town. Guided tours lead you along wide pathways, bordered on both sides by flowering trees, shrubs, and vines. The special features of all plants are explained in detail. Nani Mau is open daily, 8:00 A.M. to 5:00 P.M., and is located at 421 Makalika Street; 959–3541. Admission is $7.50 for adults, $4.50 for children ages six to eighteen; children under six are admitted free.

The **Panaewa Rain Forest Zoo** is the only tropical rain forest zoo in the U.S. It's a few miles south of Hilo proper, continuing on Route 11 toward Hawaii Volcanoes National Park. Here live an international assortment of animals including an extra-large anteater from Costa Rica, pygmy hippos from Africa, and a wide assortment of birds. The zoo hosts many endangered animals indigenous to Hawaii, such as the Laysan albatross, Hawaiian coot, *pueo* (owl), and Hawaiian gallinule. There are some iguanas, mongooses, lemurs, and an aviary section with exotic and colorful birds. It doubles as a botanical garden, and much of the growing plant life is labeled. Most kids are drawn to the center of the facility, where tigers roam in a large fenced-in area with a pond.

The zoo is at 25 Aupuni Street and is open daily, 9:00 A.M. to 4:00 P.M. Free admission; 959–7224.

No doubt the macadamia is Hawaii's most famous nut. Visit the **Mauna Loa Macadamia Nut Mill** for the opportunity to see how the machines crack the tough hull and harvest this tasty treat. You can watch a free video that fully explains the process and then take a self-guided tour among the orchards. Especially wonderful are the macadamia treats at the snack shop. The mill is easy to find; just look for the signs for Macadamia Road off Route 11, just 6 miles outside of Hilo. It's free and open daily 8:30 A.M. to 5:00 P.M.; 966–9301.

There are plenty of restaurants in town, and this is by no means an attempt to list them all—just some of the many that are good for families.

❋ **Broke the Mouth Plate Lunch Shop.** This inexpensive, local-style snack bar features locally grown products and vegetarian fare including pasta, manapua, spring rolls, salads, and plate lunches. Open Tuesday to Saturday, 9:00 A.M. to 2:00 P.M. At 55 Mamo Street across from the Hilo Farmers' Market on Kamehameha Ave.; 934–7670. $.

❋ **Harrington's.** Overlooking scenic Hilo Bay, Harrington's has to be the best dinner restaurant on the east side of the island. Fish, steaks, chicken, and veal are specialties of the house; there's a kids' menu. Reservations are advised. At 135 Kalanianaole St.; 961–4966. $$$.

❋ **Restaurant Osaka.** Lunch and dinner menus feature many local favorites and Japanese-American selections. At 762 Kanoelehua Ave.; 961–6699. $$.

❋ **Sun Sun Lau.** Family-style Cantonese fare served in steaming, generous quantities. At 1055 Kinoole St.; 935–2808. $.

Directional note: From Hilo, there are three different directions in which to explore the Big Island. Heading south, the Hawaii Belt Road (Route 11) leads to Hawaii Volcanoes National Park and South Point. Northern Route 19 travels up the Hamakua Coast to Waipio Valley. Inland, the Saddle Road (Route 200) skirts Mauna Kea, crosses the island, and lands you in Kona. All three routes offer stunning sights and unusual environments, and all are worth taking. For purposes of easy orientation, this guide will first follow the southern route, then the northern route, then the inland route on the Saddle Road.

Going south on Route 11, the **Hawaii Belt Road,** leads to Hawaii Volcanoes National Park. The first small town you'll arrive at is **Keaau,** where Route 130 branches off toward Pahoa and continues along the coast. There are several worthwhile sights and detours along Route 130, and if your mission is to head straight to Hawaii Volcanoes National Park, where you'll need at least a full day to explore, it's quicker to stay on the Belt Road. But if you have an extra day during a Hilo visit, Route 130 offers enough diversions to occupy the better part of it. This is a longer, more scenic route, and it presents some spectacular beaches and views. You can walk right up to places where lava has run over the road, creating huge cauliflower-like chunks of land where highways and homes once stood.

If you take Route 130, you'll travel directly south to **Pahoa.** Here, you can veer east on Route 132 to **Lava Tree State Park.**

At one time, Pahoa's claim to fame was that it housed the largest sawmill in the United States. The town and sawmill were destroyed in a 1955 fire, but local residents have been trying to rebuild and restore. It's a quaint town that's currently enjoying a renaissance of sorts. Locals are trying to join the nationwide Main Street USA program, which will help designate historic sites and bring new vitality to old buildings.

It's fun to stroll along the streets, framed on both sides by old-fashioned false-front shops, mostly housing produce and flower stands.

Lava Tree State Park is an unusual geological formation that's definitely worth a detour. It was formed in 1790 when a quick-moving lava flow slammed into an ohia forest. The lava crept up the tree trunks, but the interiors of the trunks were too moist and cool to become engulfed in flames as one would expect. Instead, the lava cooled and solidified, covering up all the land that held the roots of the ohia trees. What's left is the site you see today. Huge trees stand like ominous statues, looking like fearsome guards forbidding you to enter. The hike here takes about a half-hour and is well suited for children.

A picturesque lighthouse sits at **Cape Kumukahi,** the eastern tip of the island, at the end of Route 132. This area is notable because in 1960, when the last big lava flow destroyed the surroundings, the cape and lighthouse were spared. Local superstition explains the phenomenon with the following story: Madame Pele, the Hawaiian goddess of the volcanoes, came to this area disguised as an old woman. She traveled door to door, asking for food and shelter, but the local townsfolk refused to take her in. The only person who did help was the keeper at the lighthouse, his goodwill thereby securing his safety.

Route 137 leads south from Cape Kumukahi and passes a series of fishponds. **Isaac Hale Beach Park** is less than 10 miles away, at Pohoiki Bay, formerly the commercial wharf for Puna Sugar Company. This is the only boat launching site for the entire southern coast and is therefore usually quite busy with private and commercial boaters. If you can avoid the seagoing traffic, this is a great scuba site, especially in the summer when the ocean is calm. A short walk on a well-worn path east of the beach leads to naturally formed hot springs that bubble like Jacuzzis.

MacKenzie State Recreation Area is a thirteen-acre park that may not be suitable for young children. It's framed on both sides by rugged fingers of lava, and the currents here have been known to pluck unsuspecting people who were walking on the lava and carry them out to sea. It's a popular fishing site, but swimming is unsafe. It is located in a grove of ironwood trees planted by forest ranger A. J. MacKenzie.

Routes 130 and 137 end at the two towns of **Kaimu** and **Kalapana,** once-thriving residential areas since destroyed by Madame Pele and her flowing lava. You can drive right up to the barricades, where the fresh lava is still steaming. There is a sign that warns adventurous explorers from continuing on foot, and this warning should be strictly heeded. Not only are there spontaneous brush fires and toxic levels of methane gas, you may hit on a patch of thin crust, slide right into a moving river of molten lava, and never be seen again!

The lava has been advancing almost continually since 1983. More than 600,000 cubic yards of lava have been pouring from the volcano daily, hitting the sea like a slow-moving fireball. While it's added more than 500 new acres of land to the Big Island, it's annihilated almost 20,000 acres, including homes, schools, and ancient heiau (religious temples), and caused more than $25 million in property damages. (For more about the volcano's devastation, see the section "Hawaii Volcanoes National Park," below.)

An old church sits on the side of the road, looking awfully out of place in this black landscape. This is the **Star of the Sea Catholic Church,** also known as the Painted Church, which was in danger from an advancing lava flow. Local people joined forces to move the church out of the way but have not been able to find a new home for the structure. So it sits at the side of the road, the lone surviving structure of a community lost to nature.

Back at Keaau, if you don't take the longer Route 130, but stay on the Belt Road, you'll travel through the higher elevations and the communities of Kurtistown, Mountain View, Glenwood, and Volcano.

HAWAII VOLCANOES NATIONAL PARK

Don't miss a chance to experience the awesome powers of Madame Pele at **Hawaii Volcanoes National Park,** home of the most active volcano on our planet. Here your family can see new earth being formed as lava spits, chortles, and blasts from deep inside the earth's core. Whether you simply motor around the Crater Rim Drive, or hike into the inner sanctum of the park, the experience is an amazing blend of science and legend and is guaranteed to be unforgettable.

There is a $5.00 per car entrance fee, and all visitors are given a brochure and map upon arriving. You can call ahead for an eruption update, at 967–7977. A recording will direct you to the site of the latest activity. But the moving flow is just one of many attractions in the park. Extensive trails lead to steaming vents, fern forests, and ancient petroglyphs, and even *into* old lava tubes. The best idea is to save visiting the flow for the end of the day, when you can watch the glowing lava hiss its way into the sea, creating a cloud of steam that turns an eerie purple color at sunset.

There is a danger inherent in visiting here that's important to be aware of. No, it's not the chance of getting swept away by an approaching lava flow, rather the risk of running over the endangered native nene goose. The nene are quite tame and often approach visitors and congregate in parking lots. They're short and brown, often blending in with the landscape and easy to miss if you're driving fast, so keep one eye peeled for the nene.

There are heavy fumes present in the air that may present problems for pregnant women, elderly people, and small children, but occurrences of respiratory problems aren't too frequent as long as people use common sense and know their limits.

The lava flow moves slowly in predictable paths, and visitors often seek the most active areas instead of avoiding them. Don't be afraid to follow the signs to the flow.

Since January 3, 1983, when a huge explosion sent lava 1,500 feet into the air, Madame Pele has been spewing her wrath from Kilauea. A total of 181 homes have been completely covered; 8 miles of public highway is gone, as well as several private roads; and scientists say there's no end in sight. Those who believe in superstitions say that Pele may be appeased after several bottles of gin are offered to her in the most reverent seriousness. So don't think the many empty bottles of gin scattered throughout the park were left behind by careless party people. But after thousands of bottles have been poured into the crater, it seems she's still thirsty.

Your first stop should be at the **Visitor Center,** where you can pick up a variety of maps and brochures and plan your exploring strategy. The center is open 7:45 A.M. to 5:00 P.M. daily; 967–7311.

Crater Rim Drive is a scenic 11-mile road that circles the summit of Kilauea, passing sulfur banks, recent flows, craters, and steam vents. Many of the most popular sites in the park are situated along this drive.

Although the **Hawaii Volcano Observatory** is closed to the public, there is an accessible lookout here that offers a gaping view into the **Halemaumau Crater.** Plaques situated throughout the area offer information about the history and geological particulars of the park. Near the observatory, the short **Halemaumau Trail** travels for just a quarter of a mile around the rim of the crater.

Jaggar Museum is a wonderful facility that presents a multimedia display of the specific volcanology of the area. There are great photos, topographical maps, and videos here. The exhibits are constantly changed as updated information is provided. The museum is free and open 8:30 A.M. to 5:00 P.M. daily; 967–7643.

Look for signs pointing to the **Devastation Trail.** This paved path, well suited for children, travels for a half-mile through an ohia forest that was damaged by the lava but continues to hold fast to the landscape. The stark trunks and leafless stems contrast sharply with the black, desolate landscape, and this is among the most photographed sites in the park.

The **Thurston Lava Tube** is an amazing, 450-foot-long cave. The plant life surrounding the cave's entrance is vibrantly green and lush, its very existence a testimony to the tenacity of regenerating plant life. If you bring flashlights, you can walk far into the cave; for the first 500 feet the cave is illuminated with electric lights and is quite spacious. The remainder of the cave is about 15 feet in height and width. Be sure to wear good, closed-toe shoes, as the lava is rocky and uneven in many sections—guaranteed to stub a sandal-footed toe! Explore with the utmost of caution, because getting lost in these caves means getting lost in a place that never sees the light of day. If your flashlight batteries were to expire, you would have to wait for another explorer to rescue you, whereas if you got lost on a hiking trail as the sun was setting, you'd simply have to wait until sunrise to find your way out.

Volcano House Inn is the first hotel ever built in the islands. The Volcano House overlooks Halemaumau Crater and has been welcoming guests since 1866. It's definitely worth a stop to walk through the lodge, even if you're not spending the night. The inn is open for breakfast, 7:00 to 10:30 A.M.; lunch, 11:00 A.M. to 2:00 P.M.; and dinner, 5:30 to 8:30 P.M. $$.

The **Volcano Art Center** is the original Volcano House Inn, which was converted into an art center in 1974. It's an educational center that functions as a mini-museum. Displays feature artwork created by local artists. It's free and open daily, 9:00 A.M. to 5:00 P.M.; 967–7511.

The **Chain of Craters Road** branches off the Crater Rim Drive and leads to the most recent lava flow that has seeped over the highway. It takes about a half-hour to reach the end, where a makeshift visitors station is staffed with rangers who offer the latest eruption scoop.

On the way to the end of the road, look for the sign KAU PUNA TRAIL. The **Puu Loa Petroglyph Field** is on the other side of the road. The trail to the field is marked with little *ahu,* or triangular-shaped piles of stone.

You can walk on a wooden path around the field, but do stay on the path to protect the petroglyphs. The ancient markings are fascinating and offer a glimpse of what life was like for ancient Hawaiians. Etchings of warriors, canoes, and families are easily discernible.

Look for an etched circle with a hole in the center. These are known as *puu loa.* Fathers would place the umbilical cords of newborns into these holes as an offering to the gods and to ask for a long life for their child.

Touring Hawaii Volcanoes National Park is possible by car, by foot, and by air. No doubt, you'll see a few helicopters flying overhead as you're driving around. Some visitors swear these mechanical birds offer the best (albeit expensive) sightseeing. They fly directly to the most active areas, over pools of bubbling lava and streams of red-hot flows—places impossible to reach by hiking, biking, or driving. Some pilots dip so low to the ground, your face becomes flushed with the heat.

In recent years, however, the helicopter industry on all Hawaiian islands has been mired in controversy. Safety and maintenance standards became suspect after a few fatal crashes. Additionally, hikers and naturalists object to the annoying whir of the engines disturbing otherwise pristine environments. But ask anyone who's ever soared in the skies above the volcano, Waipio Valley, Maui's lush valleys, or Kauai's rugged Na Pali Coast, and they'll say the experience is incomparably incredible.

The following list of companies offering **helicopter rides** is by no means inclusive. Some offer hotel pickups, some land for lunch, some offer a souvenir videotape, and some offer piped-in narration through stereo headphones. These companies come and go frequently, so it's best to shop around. Also, be sure to schedule a flight as early as possible. Late-afternoon trips often are plagued with fog and soot and prohibit optimum visibility. The **Activity Information Center,** 329–7701, is a central ticketing agency for several helicopter flight-seeing companies. It may cost more to book through the center, but the staff can answer a lot of different questions and can recommend the best tour for your budget and family. Additionally, the helicopter companies based on the Kona side of the island, also feature volcano tours.

* **Volcano Helitours,** 967–7578. The only company that's based within the park. Open Monday through Friday, 9:00 A.M. to 3:00 P.M.
* **'Io Aviation,** 935–3031.
* **Mauna Kea Helicopters,** 885–6400. Flies out of Waimea Airport.

KA'U

Beyond Hawaii Volcanoes National Park, the Belt Road continues to the Ka'u District, and the area known as **South Point.** The sights along this section of the Belt Road are among the most ecologically diverse in Hawaii, as green pastures butt up to desolate black lava fields. Most of the area can be reached by a normal car, but some of the secluded coastal spots are accessible only with a four-wheel-drive vehicle.

Shortly after passing through **Pahala Town,** look for **Punalu'u Beach County Park,** which is well-known for its expansive black-sand beach. There are restrooms, phones, showers, and a pavilion. Swimming is safe only during calm weather.

Punalu'u Beach Park is home to many green sea turtles and the legendary turtle princess Kauila. Please be aware that the turtles are endangered and prone to heart attacks when struck with fear. It's okay to view them from a distance, but you should never approach one up close.

Beyond Punalu'u the coastal drive is lush and beautiful. **Whittington Beach County Park** is about 5 miles past Punalu'u, but it's a little difficult to find because it's not very well marked. The turnoff comes before you cross a bridge and head up a hill toward Na'alehu. The beach offers full amenities, including restrooms, phones, and drinking water. Nearby **Honuapo Bay** used to be a busy port for transporting sugar, and the surrounding area is home to many old ruins from that era.

The next town is **Na'alehu,** the southernmost town in the entire United States, and the largest town in this area. It's a good place to refurbish your supply of gas and snacks if you're heading all the way up to Kona.

There's also a fruit stand here that's a favorite place to stock up on fresh banana bread.

About 6 miles beyond Na'alehu, the Hawaii Belt Road leaves the coastline and cuts inland toward Kona and the western side of the island. After the tiny town of **Waiohinu,** look for a turnoff labeled South Point Road. This road leads straight south for 12 miles, ending at **Ka Lae,** South Point, which is the southernmost point of the United States. Its latitude is equivalent to 500 miles south of Miami, Florida. Many scholars believe that this is where the migrating Polynesians first landed, as early as 150 A.D.; others claim it wasn't until 750 A.D.

Don't be alarmed if you see a sign claiming the land is controlled by the Hawaiian Homeland Agency and trespassing is not allowed. This means that you shouldn't park your car randomly on the side of the road and explore the surrounding area on foot. But you have complete right-of-way if you're traveling on the road, and it's heavily frequented by tourists. Veer right when the road splits; there's a parking lot at the end of the road. The views are captivating, and you'll be able to say you walked on the southernmost tip of the United States.

East of Ka Lae, a 3-mile trail leads to **Pohakuloa** and **Green Sand Beach.** Yes . . . *green* sand. The green is a dull olive shade, not a vibrant grassy color. It's formed by olivine present in the lava. Olivine is a semi-precious stone, and here it has been weathered into sandlike pieces. The trail leading to the beach is beautiful, but be sure to bring plenty of water and venture this way only if the weather is sunny and dry.

Although you can't see it, 23 miles southeast from the Big Island, another volcano is erupting. Called Loihi, it's spewing lava from 3,000 feet below the ocean surface. Scientists estimate that within the next 100 to 100,000 years, a new island will be born.

THE SADDLE ROAD

The **Saddle Road,** Route 200, goes directly from central Hilo across the middle of the island for 87 miles until it ends at the Mamalahoa Highway near Kona. Most car rental companies try to forbid clients from venturing this way because it's pretty rocky for a few miles and there are many potholes. Also, it's very isolated; if you were to break down, there would be virtually nowhere to go for help. But, it certainly is passable and offers some of the best views on the Big Island. Don't let the car rental companies discourage you from exploring.

Mauna Kea towers at an elevation of 13,796 feet to the north, and Mauna Loa, at 13,679 feet, looms to the south. A road branches off from the Saddle Road and travels all the way to the top of Mauna Kea, where astronomical observatories house an international collection of scientists who gaze into the heavens and study the stars.

Just a few minutes' drive from Hilo on 200, the way to **Kaumana Cave** is well marked. (Another, bigger lava cave is Thurston, mentioned earlier in the section on Hawaii Volcanoes National Park, page 146 .) Lava caves, also known as tubes, are formed when the flowing lava turns into a molten river. Similar to the top layer of water crusting into ice on a freezing Mainland lake, the top layer of lava hardens. Underneath, the lava continues flowing, creating a tube. When the volcano ceases erupting and the lava stops flowing, the lava eventually drains out of the tube. Sometimes the lava on the top of the tube is too heavy to be unsupported and the tube crushes into itself, but other tubes remain intact and offer an amazing look at the underground environment—navigable of course only after the tube is significantly cooled off.

This cave has had plenty of time to cool since it was formed in 1881. A staircase leads down a hole that looks as if you're entering a wild forest. Flowers and ferns bloom everywhere, creating a misty, ethereal green.

You can walk only about 50 yards into the cave without a flashlight. If you bring flashlights, you'll see quiltworks of color, owing to white, yellow, and orange mineral deposits. Be sure to wear good, closed-toe shoes, as the lava is rocky and uneven in many sections, and explore with caution.

Continuing along the Saddle Road, you'll see certain areas lush with green life that look markedly out of place in the dry lava-scape. These are called *kipukas* and are formed when the lava simply goes around an area instead of covering it, creating an isolated little mini-ecosystem. You can explore the kipukas, but be considerate of the fragile environment; many rare and endangered birds flit about.

MAUNA KEA

The Saddle Road continues to skirt around the edges of **Mauna Kea** and climbs to the summit at 13,796 feet. A few well-marked side roads also lead to the summit. As the serpentine road winds its way up the mountain, you'll rise above the cloud cover and feel as if you've left ordinary civilization behind. The landscape becomes barren; instead of the greenery of Hilo, you'll see a series of reddish volcanic cones.

While the sun may be beating down on the resorts of Kona, the temperature up here is always cold, so dress warmly. In the winter, it snows atop Mauna Kea, and skiers flock to the mountain. If you don't have a four-wheel-drive vehicle, it's best not to attempt to reach the very top of the mountain. Not only is the road often closed due to snow, it's a windy, steep incline that would claim easy victory in a battle with ordinary rental cars. If you're going to venture up here, be prepared for temperatures less than 20 degrees Fahrenheit, and wind that blows up to 70 miles per hour. It's really, really cold. Additionally, altitude sickness is a serious predicament for young children, the elderly, or pregnant women. In fact, because of the remoteness of the area and the inherent dangers of high altitudes, children under age sixteen are prohibited from venturing all the way to the top (but not many people want to, anyway). If health and age circumstances deem it all right for members of your family to venture all the way up, however, it's recommended to use a four-wheel-drive vehicle and to spend about an hour at the Onizuka Center, at 9,300 feet, to acclimate to the altitude change.

A safe, fun place to visit is the **Onizuka Center for International Astronomy.** Ellison Onizuka was a local Hilo boy with big dreams that landed him a spot as a crew member of the ill-fated space shuttle *Challenger.* The center is dedicated to his memory.

The entrance to the center is well marked off the Saddle Road. The center hours are Monday, 8:00 A.M. to noon; Friday, 1:00 to 5:00 P.M.; and Saturday and Sunday, 9:00 A.M. to 10:00 P.M. Children under the age of sixteen and pregnant women are not admitted, due to the inherent dangers of the altitude. The center is about the altitude limit for young children, pregnant women, elderly, and people with respiratory problems. There are free stargazing programs, Friday to Sunday 7:00 to 10:00 P.M.

You must have a four-wheel-drive vehicle to get up here. Call 961–2180 for a recording detailing hours, various programs, and summit information.

Lake Waiau, at 13,020 feet, is the third-highest lake in America and is almost at the summit.

At the top of the mountain, astronomers from all over the world work in a variety of different observatories. They can only stay here for four-day stints because the high altitude can cause brain malfunctions over a long period of time. These scientists are privy to exploring the heavens above 40 percent of the earth's atmosphere—the lack of light pollution and dust make this the best observatory site in the world. The W. H. Keck telescope, the largest in the world, sits atop Mauna Kea. It has thirty-six mirrors and is 33 feet in diameter.

Although the University of Hawaii manages the entire summit, teams from France, Canada, Japan, Great Britain, and the Netherlands have permanent outposts here. Visitors can tour the complex, but reservations are necessary. For more information, call the Hilo-based Mauna Kea Support Services, 935–3371.

Summit Tours, offers a six-hour, $80 trip in a four-wheel-drive with an experienced mountain guide who also serves a picnic lunch. Tours leave Parker Ranch Shopping Center in Kamuela and are conducted Tuesday, Thursday, Saturday, and Sunday. Children under age sixteen and pregnant women are not admitted on the tours. For more information, call 775–7121.

Paradise Safaris, 322–2366, offers air-conditioned, four-wheel-drive trips throughout the Big Island but specializes in the journey to Mauna Kea. Not only does the ride include plenty of stories and great facts, the guides bring warm jackets along for cold visitors to borrow. The rides cost $110 per person, and children must be over age thirteen.

There's even a **ski resort** atop Mauna Kea, where skiing is good from late November to late May. Only the truly physically fit should attempt it, however, as the air is extremely thin at 13,796 feet. There always is a group of hardy snow bunnies braving the slopes, and recently snowboarding has become the hottest rage. For more information, call Ski Guides Hawaii, 885–4188.

HAMAKUA COAST

Route 19, leading north of Hilo to the **Hamakua Coast,** heads through some of the prettiest scenery in all Hawaii. Gorgeous rain-carved, velvety-green valleys lush with tropical foliage contrast with black-as-night craggy lava promontories and foaming white-water from pounding waves. For many years, the Hamakua Coast was dominated by sugar plantations, and although those are now gone, the handful of towns formed to accommodate local workers still exist, virtually unchanged by time.

The Hamakua area encompasses Highway 19 and the entire northeast coast of the Big Island, from Waipio 50 miles to the north on Highway 19, to Hilo in the east. Although traveling on Route 19 affords many breathtaking views, the best vistas are inaccessible by car and best seen by soaring above ground in a flight-seeing helicopter.

Small country roads occasionally veer off Highway 19, leading to one-lane towns where a few dozen people comprise a whole community and life is so slow-paced that pets lounge lazily in the middle of the road and families don't even lock their doors at night.

Even if your kids aren't excited at the proposal of venturing to yet another beautiful garden, you should insist on including **Hawaii Tropical Botanical Gardens** on your itinerary. Here, you'll get to explore a true tropical rain forest up close. (Bring mosquito repellent!)

In fact, getting there is half the fun. A few minutes' drive from Hilo, you'll hit **Papaikou Town.** Look for a "Scenic Drive" sign leading to a right turnoff. This road is literally carved through a jungle; it quickly becomes narrow and winding, and you'll travel over a series of small bridges as you head toward the coast.

After you pay admission at the registration center, a shuttle van transports you down to the gardens at **Onomea Bay.** There you can pick up self-guided maps that show a variety of trails that are well maintained and easily navigable. The Ocean Trail leads to the sea, where violently foaming waves crash into the jagged coastline. Even the sounds are impressive as the water sloshes in and out of submerged lava tubes.

The gardens were started when a transplant from San Francisco, California, wanted to do his part to save the endangered Hawaiian rain forests, so he purchased this land and set about caretaking and preserving it. It's said that the gardens house the world's largest selection of tropical plant species.

The gardens are open Monday through Friday, 8:30 A.M. to 4:30 P.M. The last van leaves for Onomea at 4:30 P.M. Admission is $15; children ages sixteen and younger are free. Facilities include restrooms and drinking fountains. For more information, call 964–5233.

The Scenic Drive reconnects to Route 19 at the small sugar town of Pepeekeo. Just a few minutes' drive past Pepeekeo is **Honomu.** With a little imagination, it's easy to picture the saloons, hotel, and bordello that used to be the focal points of entertainment in this now-forgotten town. The small town of Honomu prospered when sugar plantations dominated the coastline, but today it has become a mere shell of its former grandeur. The town is a worthwhile stop; you can walk down the main street, with its old-fashioned storefronts and raised sidewalks, and gather a sense of the charming atmosphere.

Be sure to visit **Ishigo's General Store,** one of the few real plantation stores still operating. Ishigo's has been around since 1910, and today's owner, Hideo Ishigo, is a descendant of the original owner. Ishigo's is open weekdays, 7:00 A.M. to 4:30 P.M.; Sundays until 2:30 P.M.; closed Saturdays. For information, call 963–6128.

Route 220 leads from Honomu to **Akaka Falls State Park.** There is an easy, well-maintained, short loop trail at Akaka Falls. The trail is suitable for children of all ages, and the majestic sights beyond each turn will delight everyone. You'll pass through groves of orchids, ferns, and bamboo, and over small gurgling streams. The falls tumble 445 feet into a beautiful jungle pond.

The park is free and there are picnic tables and restrooms on site. To get there, take Route 220 inland from Highway 19 at Honomu. The falls are a short but scenic drive from Honomu, and there are signs directing drivers where to turn.

A few minutes past Honomu on Highway 19, a sign points to **Kolekole Beach County Park.** The small road wiggles a short way down to a beautiful black-sand beach. The park is popular with local families, and facilities include pavilions, showers, barbecue grills, restrooms, picnic tables, and electricity for camping. This is a wonderful, well-equipped, and scenic picnic site, but the ocean can be quite treacherous here, so please use extreme caution.

At one time many farmers and fishermen lived in **Laupahoehoe Valley,** and there was a boat landing here that bustled with activity. Today, it's nothing more than a beach park that's frequented by local fishermen. There are showers, electricity for camping, and picnic tables. Swimming isn't advised here because the ocean is too rough, but you may see some brave surfers catching a ride offshore.

You won't be able to miss the brightly painted **Local Cafe,** a great lunch stop. This clean, country-style cafe in an old gas station has a menu featuring pizza, plate lunches, burgers and sandwiches, homemade ice cream, fresh pies, and more. It's open Monday through Friday, 7:30 A.M. to 7:30 P.M.; Saturday, 10:00 A.M. to 7:30 P.M.; and Sunday, 10:00 A.M. to 5:00 P.M. $.

Kalopa State Recreation Area is an inland park that offers a great chance to walk among lush native forest plants and trees. There are well-maintained hiking trails that will appeal to a variety of ages and abilities, and many of the plants are identified. It's about 12 miles beyond Laupahoehoe, before Honokaa.

Although there's just one main street, **Honokaa** is the largest town on the Hamakua Coast, with a population of about 2,000. The town features a few craft shops, boutique-type stores, restaurants, gas stations, and a general store.

Be sure to stop at **Jolene's Kau Kau Corner** at the corner of Mamane and Lehua Streets. This renovated old shop is clean and bright and offers a wide range of local-style plate lunch specials such as teriyaki beef and chicken, plus burgers, sandwiches, and snack items. $.

The profitable macadamia nut industry began in Honokaa when John MacAdams harvested the first batch of these tasty treats in 1892. In the coastal section of town, near the boat landing, is the **Hawaiian Macadamia Plantation Factory** (775-7201). You can take a self-guided tour and learn the history behind Hawaii's most famous nut. The factory is open daily, 9:00 A.M. to 5:00 P.M., and admission is free. The on-site gift store and deli feature a variety of macadamia-flavored items, including delicious ice cream.

Here, Highway 19 bears left toward Waimea and Highway 240 continues up the coast to Waipio Valley. Because this chapter already covered Waimea, it will now focus on the remainder of the Hamakua Coast.

Highway 240 ends at **Kukuihaele,** a charming one-street town that boasts a few gas stations, restaurants, and galleries. The **Last Chance General Store,** open daily 9:00 A.M. to 6:00 P.M., is a good place to stop for snacks and supplies, and just beyond, the lookout point over Waipio Valley is a truly beautiful spot for picnicking.

At road's end is the 1,000-foot overlook to **Waipio Valley,** a place so lush, green, and picturesque that no words can do it justice—it begs exploring. From the overlook, you can see the terraced taro patches and gardens. Although today's inhabitants include just a few families, Waipio used to be home to thousands of Hawaiians who lived off this fertile land, and it was the largest cultivated valley in all Hawaii. Today, only about fifty people live here, and the land has changed very little in the last hundred years. It mostly consists of taro farms, but there are a few horses and cattle as well. In the heart of the valley, passionfruit, bananas, coffee, avocados, coconuts, grapefruit, and a large variety of other fruits and vegetables thrive.

Waipio is the largest valley on the Big Island: 6 miles deep and 1 mile wide. In its interior, majestic Hi'ilawe Falls tumble 3,000 feet, among the highest falls in all Hawaii.

Unless you have a four-wheel-drive vehicle, don't try to navigate the road down to the valley—your car will never make it. Hikers in excellent physical shape will enjoy the hike, but remember that going down is the easy part—the hill is mighty steep.

Waipio Valley Wagon Tours takes about twelve people at a time on a surrey-type horse-drawn wagon. The two-hour tours leave four times daily, at 9:00 and 10:30 A.M. and 12:30 and 2:00 P.M. Adult fare is $35; the fare for children under 12 is $17.50. Children age two and under are free. For more information, call 775–9518.

Waipio Naalapa Trail Rides offers forty-minute four-legged forays into the valley. Along the ride, guides relate the fascinating history and legends of this region. The horses, which are descendants of the original herd given to the chiefs in the 1700s by Captain George Vancouver, transport you to picturesque swimming holes, waterfalls, and a heiau. The rides cost $65, last two-and-a-half hours, and are offered twice daily, at 9:30 A.M. and 1:00 P.M. Children under twelve are not allowed. For more information, call 775–0419.

The **Waipio Valley Shuttle** offers valley tours in comfortable air-conditioned vans. For children too young to handle a long trail ride, this is a good way to see the valley sites. The tours cost $35 for adults, $15 for kids four to twelve, and last one-and-a-half hours; 775–7121. The tour desk for booking some tours is in Honokaa, at 775–7291.

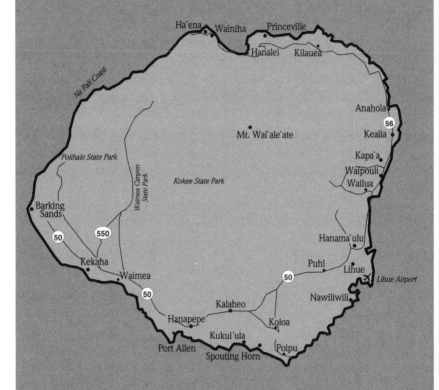

Ha`ena • Waniha • Princeville
Hanalei • Kilauea
Na Pali Coast
Anahola
Mt. Wai`ale`ate
Kealia
Polihale State Park
Kapa`a
Waipouli
Wailua
Kokee State Park
Barking
Sands
Hanama`ulu
Kekaha
Puhl
Lihue
Waimea
Lihue Airport
Nawiliwili
Kalaheo
Hanapepe
Koloa
Kukui`ula
Port Allen
Poipu
Spouting Horn

Waimea Canyon State Park

50
550
50
50
56

Kauai

Kauai

auai is the northernmost, oldest, and first-populated island in the Hawaiian chain. Its age has made it a grand natural spectacle—over time, wind and rain have sculpted great cliffs and valleys lush with picturesque foliage and tumbling waterfalls. Nicknamed "the Garden Isle," Kauai is known worldwide for its awe-inspiring beauty. Mt. Waialeale in the island's center is the wettest place on earth, with more than 450 inches of rainfall every year. The mountains have been carved to form deep crevices, from which waterfalls drop to isolated pools, and the damp fertile soil is home to many colorful flowers and fruits. These pools have formed a series of streams, which in turn have created Hawaii's only navigable river. Of all the islands, Kauai is home to the most beaches per mile of coastline and the most miles of hiking trails.

From the craggy Na Pali Coast, rising 4,000 feet above the foamy waves, to the kaleidoscopic Waimea Canyon, Kauai is blissfully beautiful. Apparently Hollywood producers agree, for film crews habitually arrive, creating internationally famous flicks. The island has been used in *South Pacific* (1958), *Blue Hawaii* (1961), *Lord of the Flies* (1989), and *Jurassic Park* (1992).

Some historians believe the first Polynesian explorers to settle on these islands made landfall on Kauai around 200 A.D., about 500 years before the rest of the islands were populated.

Kauaians have a distinctive spirit. This is the only island that King

Kamehameha could not conquer. During his conquest to unite the islands under one rule, Kamehameha could never get Kauai's King Kaumualii to concede. (The rough Kauai channel that separates Kauai and Niihau from the other islands claimed many of Kamehameha's soldiers and canoes and probably had a lot to do with Kamehameha's inclination to back off.) It wasn't until Kaumualii's death in 1810 that Kamehameha's dream was finally realized, for Kaumualii had agreed to let Kamehameha have Kauai upon his death.

That spirit is still present in modern times. Kauai has been inundated with two ferocious hurricanes in the last fifteen years. In 1982 Hurricane Iwa swept through the Hawaiian chain, hitting Kauai the hardest and leaving millions of dollars of damage in its wake. But the people rebuilt their homes, hotels and restaurants reopened, and life went back to normal. Then, in 1992, Hurricane Iniki slammed Kauai with a level-four force that brought winds blowing more than 160 miles per hour. This time, damage was estimated to be in the billions, and a few hotels, restaurants, and businesses remain closed, waiting for insurance settlements. But the majority of the island has been repaired, and the hardy residents of Kauai, in the spirit of King Kaumualii, prosper.

Kauai ties with the Big Island as the third most-visited island, after Oahu and Maui. At present, there are no direct flights from the Mainland into Lihue or Princeville, the two airports on Kauai. Most commuter flights land at Lihue, with just a few landing at Princeville. Lihue is serviced by Aloha, 484–1111; Hawaiian, 838–1555; and Mahalo Airlines, 833–5555. Although the bigger resort properties offer airport pickup, a rental car is essential here—Kauai's beauty begs to be explored. The island is about 33 miles long and 25 miles wide, but you can't drive completely around because much of the northern coast is inaccessible by car.

Most of the resort and hotel properties are in Poipu and Lihue, with a few scattered in Kapaa, Hanalei, and Princeville. Kauai is relatively under-developed, compared to Oahu, Maui, and even the Big Island. The resorts here are built conservatively—instead of crowded condominiums and strings of hotels on a single street, the construction has been designed to be unobtrusive, to blend in with the beautiful landscape. Developers chose not to build sprawling, Disneyland-type accommodations, foregoing opulence for nature's grandeur. They must have known that no matter how beautiful a resort is, it can't compare with the lush, picturesque surroundings.

Unlike the other islands, it's very easy to self-navigate your way around Kauai. The main highway travels from Waimea in the southwest in a large U shape to Hanalei in the north. A few smaller roads branch off the main highway. This chapter begins in Lihue, the site of the main airport and the biggest city on the island. Then it goes south to Poipu and west to the end of the line at Waimea, then up the road to Waimea Canyon and Kokee State Park. The latter part of the chapter focuses on the towns north of Lihue: from Wailua to Hanalei and the magnificent Na Pali Coast.

LIHUE

Although Lihue is the biggest city on the island, the place still exudes a small-town feel and appeal. The majority of the island's shops and restaurants are here.

The **Kauai Museum** is a charming site, right in central Lihue, that reveals Kauai's distinctive wildlife and cultural, geological, and social history. The displays focus on Hawaiiana and the missionary era. There are great examples of ancient Polynesian canoes, musical instruments, and feather capes.

The museum is actually comprised of two buildings. Visitors enter in the two-story Wilcox Building; the Rice Building is the site of the permanent exhibit "Story of Kauai." Both are named after prominent Kauai missionary families.

The museum is at 4428 Rice Street; 245–6931. It's open Monday through Friday, 9:00 A.M. to 4:00 P.M., and Saturdays from 9:00 A.M. to 1:00 P.M. Admission is $5.00 for adults, $1.00 for children ages six to seventeen, and free for children under six. The first Saturday of every month is family day and admission is free.

The **Grove Farm Homestead** is a wonderful place to visit and learn about the enormous impact of the sugar industry on Kauai. The Grove Farm, under the helm of missionary son George Wilcox, was once the most profitable plantation in all the islands. Wilcox engineered a series of aqueducts that let water flow around the surrounding eighty acres and produced large harvests. The plantation flourished from 1864 until the 1930s, when Wilcox died. Today, the museumlike grounds are maintained by his descendants.

The facility is open Monday, Wednesday, and Thursday. Guided two-hour walking tours pass through the various buildings and grounds, left much the same as they were during the farm's working days. You'll see antique furniture made from Hawaiian koa wood, walk among gardens and fields where workers once toiled, and stroll through old homes and cottages that housed the staff. Tours leave at 10:00 A.M. and 1:00 P.M.; they cost $5.00 for adults, $2.00 for children under twelve, and are available by reservation only. The trip involves a great deal of walking and may not be suitable for younger children. For more information, call 245–3202.

Don't miss a chance for a family meal at **Hamura Saimin,** a local institution that's been making its own noodles for generations. Saimin is a Japanese soup that comes with different variations of fish, meat, or vegetables but always includes long, spaghetti-like noodles. The food is cheap and the local ambience priceless. It's at 2956 Kress Street; 245–3271. $.

The beautifully elaborate 16,000-square-foot mansion at Kilohana Plantation was built in 1935 and still exudes an aura of grand class. It was built by Gaylord Wilcox to suit his wife Ethel's expectations of a Hollywood-type manor.

Today the home has been authentically restored, and various rooms have been converted into a small sampling of galleries and shops. The old living room looks like a museum with its period furniture, artifacts, and collectibles.

An optional hour-long horse-and-carriage tour pulled by Clydesdale horses is available, or you can simply park and walk around the grounds on your own for free. Tours leave each hour between 11:00 A.M. and 2:00 P.M. on Tuesday, Thursday, and Saturday and cost $18 for adults, $10 for children under twelve. The horses pull tourist-filled wagons on other routes as well, through Lihue valley or sugar cane fields. Rates vary depending on the tour. Reservations required; 246–9529.

Inside Kilohana, **Gaylord's Restaurant** is a wonderfully scenic place for a meal and offers great Continental food at reasonable prices. It's in the Manor's original dining room, and some of the original furniture remains.

Gaylord's menu features fresh fish and steaks and local-style specials. (Try Wally's special salad, named for current owner Wally Wallace.) Off Kilohana Hwy., next to Kauai Community College, 1 mile from Lihue; 245–9593. $$.

To get to Kilohana from Lihue, take the Kaumualii Highway (Highway 50) west toward Puhi for just a few minutes. The plantation is in front of the mountain, and well-marked signs point the way.

If you're on the island during the months of February, April, July, and November, be sure to call the **Kauai Community Players** to see if they're holding any performances. Shows are offered just four times a year, and it's best to call ahead because sometimes the "on" months vary. This nonprofit community group has been producing well-known plays for more than twenty years, and it's definitely worth attending a performance for a great slice of Kauai life. The plays are usually held in the Lihue Parish Hall, on Nawiliwili road near the Kukui Grove Shopping Center. Admission is $7.00 for adults, $5.00 for students. For more information, call 245–3408.

In Lihue, you can rent snorkeling equipment from **Snorkel Bob,** 4480 Ahukini Road, 245–9433, open 8:00 A.M. to 5:00 P.M. daily. When you rent from Snorkel Bob, and you're traveling to other islands, you can drop off at other Snorkel Bob locations. There's another store on Kauai, in Koloa, at 742–2206.

Even if you're not staying at the **Kauai Marriott,** do stop by and walk around the property. It's the former site of the Westin Kauai that was destroyed by Hurricane Iniki in 1992, and much of what made the Westin legendary has been renovated and reinstated. There are man-made lagoons dotted with tiny picturesque islands. The resort features the largest swimming pool in the state, and a multimillion-dollar art collection is scattered thoughtfully, unobtrusively, throughout the gardens, lobby, and grounds. The Marriott and its surrounding attractions are a five-minute drive from the airport and are easy to find, with well-marked signs pointing the way.

Kalapaki Beach, fronting the Marriott, is one of the most scenic in all Hawaii. Its gentle waves make it a perfect playground for beginning surfers, windsurfers, boogieboarders, or just plain swimers. There's a shack on the beach from which you can rent surfing, snorkeling, windsurfing, and sailing equipment, or arrange for lessons. For more information, call 246–6333.

Oceanfront **Duke's Canoe Club Restaurant** is adjacent to the Marriott and is a favorite eatery and watering hole for locals and visitors, with a special kids' menu. The view is grand and spacious, and the famous mud pie is a dessert institution on the island; 246–9599. $$.

Just a short way beyond Kalapaki sits the Alakoko Pond, more commonly known as the **Menehune Fishpond.** It's one of the most famous archaeological sites on Kauai and was supposedly built by the menehune, Hawaii's mythological little people (similar to Ireland's leprechauns). Some historians believe the menehune actually existed, that they were the lost tribe of what may have been the first Polynesians to land on these islands. Living in isolation for many years, some scientists claim, they could have evolved with different physical characteristics. Whether their existence is a fact or a myth, they live forever in Hawaiian legends. According to the tales, the menehune work only at night, anonymously performing kind deeds or building great structures, but never allowing themselves to be seen in daylight.

The legend about the Alakoko Fishpond says there once were a royal prince and princess who asked the menehune to build this large pond for them so they could raise mullet. The menehune agreed, with the stipulation that the couple not try to see them or disturb their work. In one night, the menehune formed a line to create a human chain and passed the stones needed to separate the pond from Huleia Stream for 25 miles. They used the stones to construct a wall that's 5 feet high and 900 feet long, creating a dam that trapped the fish inside.

The royal couple could not stifle their curiosity, and climbed to the top of a nearby mountain to check the progress. The menehune spotted them, left the pond unfinished, and as punishment turned the couple into two stone pillars, still seen today, standing vigil on the mountainside overlooking the pond.

To find the pond, follow Rice Street out of Lihue until it turns into Route 51. Turn on Nawiliwili Road and head toward the ocean. Turn left on Niumalu Road, following it to Hulemalu Road. A lookout offers scenic views of Nawiliwili Harbor, the Hoary Head Mountain Range, and Huleia Stream is off Hulemalu Road. Many adventurers enjoy kayaking up Huleia Stream for a closer view of the fishpond. (Kayak rental information appears on page 166.)

POIPU

Continuing west from Lihue on the Kaumualii Highway, Route 50, look for Maluhia Road, Route 52, which veers left and heads toward the ocean and **Koloa Town.** Maluhia Road is commonly referred to as the "Tunnel of Trees" because of the large trees growing on either side of the road; their uppermost branches and leaves at one time joined overhead, to create a picturesque living green tunnel. Hurricane Iniki, however, wreaked havoc on this area in 1992. Although the trees are slowly returning to their original splendor, they remain bent and almost barren.

As you arrive in town, note the stone chimney and adjacent cement structure. The chimney dates from 1835 and is a remnant of the **Koloa Plantation,** Hawaii's first sugar mill. The structure near the chimney is actually a permanent display dedicated to the birth of the sugar industry, the development of which is chronicled on plaques circling the monument.

The mill opened in 1837, thereby starting an industry that would forever change the people of these islands. As more plantations opened, there was more of a need for workers, and immigrants arrived from Asia, Europe, and the Caribbean.

Not only has sugar been grown in these fertile lands, but Koloa is also home to one of Hawaii's first coffee plantations, started in 1836. Today, the 4,000-acre Koloa Plantation is the largest coffee plantation in the state.

In Koloa, there's a nice sampling of shops, restaurants, and businesses specializing in water-sports rentals and lessons. It's fun to walk through the small town, where most buildings are restored from original plantation structures.

Route 52 leads to the ocean and east to **Poipu.** On the way, you'll see the tall steeple of **Koloa Church,** also known as the White Church, built in 1837. Nearby, St. Raphael's Catholic Church was built in 1841 and was the first Roman Catholic mission in the islands. To get there from Maluhia Road, turn left on Koloa Road, go right on Weleweli Road, then take Hapa Road to the church.

Maluhia Road ends at the coast, where a left turn leads to the string of hotels and condominiums comprising the Poipu Resort area. A right turn leads to Spouting Horn.

Fathom Five Divers, 742–6991, next to Koloa's Chevron Station, offers scuba charters and certification courses and also rents snorkeling gear. It's open 8:30 A.M. to 6:00 P.M. Monday through Saturday, 8:30 A.M. to 4:30 P.M. on Sunday.

Sea Sports Divers, 742–7288, mostly offers scuba excursions but also holds certification classes for scuba wanna-bes. You can also rent boogieboards and snorkeling gear. It's at 2827 Poipu Road.

Captain Andy's Sailing Adventures, 822–7833, offers daytime and sunset catamaran rides along the south shore. Sunset cruises leave from Kukuila Harbor in Poipu and include snacks and drinks. Tickets cost $45 for adults, $30 for children ages five to twelve. Children under five are free. Also, a Na Pali tour leaves from Port Allen Small Boat Harbor daily except Sunday. It costs $95 for adults, $75 for kids five to twelve, includes a Continental breakfast, a complete lunch, snorkeling, and sailing. Children must be at least five to participate in the Na Pali tour.

Located at the Poipu Plaza, **Kauai Sea Sports,** 742–9303, offers rental gear for snorkeling and lessons in scuba diving and snorkeling. Charter trips are available, mostly for scuba divers. Open 8:00 A.M. to 5:00 P.M. daily.

You can rent kayaks and paddle upstream for an up-close view of the pond. **Outfitters Kauai,** in the Poipu Plaza, 742–9667, rents not only kayaks, but bicycles, too, and offers a huge variety of guided tours on both modes of transport. Most popular are the Kokee mountain-bike trip—in which guides explain the native plants, special geographic features, and local legends—and a bicycling/snorkel tour. In addition to normal adult- and child-size bikes, they also rent trailers that hook up to a bike to accommodate a small child. Open Monday to Saturday, 9:00 A.M. to 5:00 P.M.

Those itching with fishing fever should contact **Cast and Catch Freshwater Bass Guides** of Kauai, 322–9707, which hosts charter tours throughout this area.

Kiahuna Plantation Resort is worth exploring—it's home to thirty-five acres of well-kept, colorful gardens, boasting more than 3,000 varieties of flowers, plants, and trees. Many of the plants are identified, and nonguests are permitted to walk among the gardens during the day for free. For more information, call 742–6411.

Poipu Beach County Park, at the end of the road, is a well-tended park that's great for families and is the most popular beach on the south shore. The waters are quite clear here, ideal for close-to-shore snorkeling, as well as swimming and boogieboarding. Great for picnics, too. There are restrooms, showers, a playground, picnic tables, and a pavilion. There also is a naturally formed sheltered pool, surrounded by lava, that's tame enough for toddlers and young, inexperienced swimmers. Poipu is one of the safest beaches on the island.

You can take **surfing lessons** from world champion **Margo Oberg,** 742–8019. Lessons are held in Poipu Beach Park and cost $45 for one-and-a-half hours. The only requirement for children is that they be able to swim.

From Poipu Beach, if you walk east along the rocky coastline, there are a number of tide pools at **Nukumoi Point.** Farther east is **Brennecke's Beach,** a good place to boogieboard and surf, although it's frequented by many local families and may be crowded. Brennecke's **Beach Center,** 742–7505, rents surfboards and boogieboards and can arrange for surfing, snorkel, or scuba lessons from its shack right on the beach.

A young dancer carries on the Hawaiian tradition of hula dancing. (Courtesy Hawaii Visitors Bureau)

Shipwreck Beach, also known as Keoneloa, is just past the Hyatt Regency Poipu Resort. This secluded spot features a long, wide strip of sand and offers good sunbathing spots and swimming. Swim only during calm weather, however, because the beach is fairly deserted.

If you happen to be in this area, the Hyatt Regency Poipu Resort hosts different cultural demonstrations daily, free even if you're not a guest at the hotel. The schedule is as follows: Monday, 10:00 A.M. to noon, poi-pounding demonstration; Tuesday, 9:00 to 11:00 A.M., hula and ukulele lessons; Wednesday, 9:00 to 11:00 A.M., *lauhala* weaving; Thursday, 10:00 A.M. to noon, Hawaiian quilting demonstrations; and Friday, 9:00 A.M. to noon, lei-making lessons.

The Hyatt also features a children's program known as Camp Hyatt. The program includes Hawaiian arts and crafts and lessons about Kauai's history, archaeology, and ecological preservation. The schedules vary daily but usually include a nature trek along the sand dunes near Shipwreck Beach, a visit with the wildlife manager, kite flying, snorkeling, face painting, and tennis. The program costs $45 per child, includes lunch, and runs from 9:15 A.M. to 4:00 P.M.; 742–1234. Participants get a "Camp Hyatt" T-shirt.

The **Ilima Terrace** is the Hyatt Regency Kauai's spot for breakfast, lunch, and dinner. The menu, complete with kids' specialties, includes Hawaiian, Asian, and American fare. The Sunday champagne brunches are colossally wonderful; be sure to make a reservation. It's popular with Poipu locals. $$. Also at the Hyatt Regency, **Dondero's** offers regional Italian cuisine in an elegant setting of inlaid marble floor and ornately patterned tile work. Try the tasty Involtini Alla Saltimbocca, rolled veal with prosciutto and mozzarella. $$$$. At 1571 Poipu Rd.; 742–1234.

A variety of horseback-riding trips are offered by **CJM Country Stables,** situated just beyond Shipwreck Beach, past the golf course. A three-hour ride includes breakfast and costs $71 per person (no special discounts for children). A two-hour trip travels through the surrounding countryside, down to the beach, and costs $56; 742–6096. Children must be at least seven years old.

Mahaulepu Beach sits at the east end of the Hyatt Regency Poipu Resort, just beyond Keoneloa Beach. It's a 2-mile trip, best done by car, from the end of Poipu Road. To get there, turn right at the road's first fork, pass the first turnoff, and look for the McBryde Sugar Plantation's guard booth. You'll have to sign in; hours are 7:00 A.M. to 6:30 P.M. There are some nice tidepools to explore here, but the undertow can be fierce so swim with caution. Mahaulepu is actually three separate beaches: Kawailoa Bay, Ha'ula Beach, and Gillin's Beach.

This area is important to Kauai's history. In 1796 Kamehameha the Great sent 10,000 warriors in outrigger canoes from Oahu, across the channel, intending to land at Mahaulepu. Severe storms sank many of the canoes. The soldiers who did complete the journey were killed by King Kaumualii's warriors as soon as they landed here.

If you turn right on Lawai Road, instead of heading left to Poipu, you'll reach **Baby Beach,** a small protected cove that offers ideal conditions for young children. Soon after, look for **Kuhio Park,** which marks the birthplace of Prince Kuhio, Hawaii's first delegate to Congress. There are a statue and monument here, dedicated to the prince.

It's almost impossible to miss the site of **Spouting Horn.** It's at the end of the road and there's a large parking lot designed to hold several tour buses. As with the Halona Blowhole on eastern Oahu, water spurts up from an open-ended lava tube that extends into the ocean. Depending on surf conditions, the currents can send fountains of water quite high.

Back on the Kaumualii Highway, if you don't detour down to Poipu, the road meanders west and passes through the small sugar towns of Omao, Lawai, and Kalaheo. Along the way are three glorious garden attractions.

In Lawai, the 186-acre **National Tropical Botanical Garden** is the only tropical plant research station in the United States. Here you'll see lily pads the size of swimming pools, along with dozens of rare and endangered plants, including strawberry bananas and wild ginger.

There are more than 6,000 species of tropical plants flourishing in this fertile land. The gardens are organized into sections, such as plants with medicinal value, plants of nutritional importance, endangered species, and herbs and spices.

As the world's rain forests are being destroyed at an alarming rate, this is an important facility where tropical plants are preserved and propagated and the public is educated about the role of each plant within its ecosystem.

JULIE'S TOP FAMILY ADVENTURES ON KAUAI

1. Swimming at Poipu Beach
2. Exploring Waimea Canyon
3. Spending a day at Hanalei Bay
4. Hiking up to the Sleeping Giant
5. Waterskiing Wailua River
6. Learning to Windsurf at Anini Beach
7. Taking a cruise up the Na Pali Coast
8. Touring Kokee State Park
9. Riding on a carriage drawn by Clydesdales through Kilohana Plantation
10. Soaring above ground in an ultralight plane with Birds in Paradise

The research station was founded by congressional charter in 1964 but is supported today through private donations. The National Tropical Botanical Garden also manages two off-site properties: 1,000 acres in Limahuli Valley in northern Kauai, and 100 acres in Hana, Maui.

The interior of the garden is open for guided tours only. The two-hour tours are in open-air sampans and are given Monday through Friday at 9:00 A.M. and 1:00 P.M., Saturday at 9:00 A.M., and Sunday at 1:00 P.M. Tours are led by horticultural specialists and are quite enlightening. Reservations are necessary, so plan ahead. For more information, you can call the visitor center at 742–2623.

The tour also includes the neighboring 100-acre **Allerton Gardens.** The Allerton estate was a favorite summer vacation spot for Queen Emma, wife of Kamehameha IV, in the 1800s. Today it's run by John Allerton, whose father, Robert, bought the property in the 1930s for the purpose of creating a beautiful garden. The father and son team certainly succeeded, and Allerton is a cornucopia of sights and smells.

To get to both gardens from the Kaumualii Highway, turn down Route 530, then take Halima Road toward the right. The visitor center is at the end of the driveway (beyond the DEAD END sign). The tour costs $25 per person.

The twelve-acre **Olu Pua Botanical Gardens** include a fun *kaukau* (to eat) garden that contains edible plants and fruit trees. Also on the grounds are a jungle garden, palm tree garden, and hibiscus garden.

This is a private property, but it's open to visitors from 9:30 A.M. to 2:30 P.M. There are six tours daily, leaving every hour on the half-hour. Guided tours are by reservation only and cost $12 for adults and $6 for kids ages five to twelve; children under five are admitted free. For reservations, call 332–8182.

To get there from the Kaumualii Highway, look for the sign pointing to the gardens just after the junction with Route 540, beyond Kalaheo.

Although it's a little difficult to find, **Kukui O Lono Park** is a nice place to stop for a picnic or just to stretch your legs. The views are expansive and immensely beautiful. The park contains a Japanese-style garden and golf course. To get there from Kalaheo, turn left at the little convenience store called Menehune Food Mart. The road leads uphill for about a mile; pass Puu Road and turn right at the second Puu Road, where you'll find the gates to the park. The gates are open from 6:30 A.M. to 6:30 P.M.

HANAPEPE

Beyond Kalaheo, the highway veers south and leads to Port Allen Harbor, then continues and travels through acre after acre of sugar cane, west to **Hanapepe.** On the way to Hanapepe, look for a small sign leading to Hanapepe Valley Overlook, a must-stop. The views from here encompass the picturesque valley, lush with sugar cane and taro farms.

Just before Hanapepe is the little town of **Ele'ele.** Stop here to sample such goodies as coconut krispies cookies and macadamia shortbread at the **Kauai Kookie Kompany.** The facility is at 1–3959 Kaumualii Highway;

335–3291. It's open Monday through Friday, 8:00 A.M. to 4:00 P.M.

You'll know you're in Hanapepe when you see the sign reading KAUAI'S BIGGEST LITTLE TOWN. The town consists of "Old Hanapepe" and "New Hanapepe." To get to the old part, take Hanapepe Road right at the intersection where Green Garden Restaurant sits. (Green Garden, 335–5422, is somewhat of an institution in town, it's been here so long.) It's a charming one-lane town that looks just as it did a hundred years ago, when sugar dominated the landscape and all the plantation workers lived here. What once were plantation homes are now art galleries, boutiques, and restaurants.

Be sure to stop by the **Omoide Bakery and Delicatessen** on Kaumualii Highway, famous since 1956 for delectable, mouthwatering lilikoi pies. Open Monday, 7:00 A.M. to 3:00 P.M., and Tuesday to Sunday, 7:00 A.M. to 9:00 P.M.; 335–5291.

The beaches in Hanapepe and Waimea, the next town west, not only are quite scenic, but are among the best on the island, blessed with lots of sunny days and cooperative currents making for smooth swimming conditions.

Salt Pond Beach Park is at the west end of town, just beyond the Port Allen runway. Look for large basins carved into the red dirt. For centuries Hawaiian families have created salt from evaporated seawater here. The ancient practice has been continued through the generations, and the product is used for cooking and medicinal purposes. This is the best spot on this side of the island for swimming, windsurfing, and snorkeling. There's even a calm area that's ideal for toddlers. Facilities include picnic tables, restrooms, showers, and a pavilion.

To get there, take Route 543 from Route 50. You'll pass the local humane society, then a refuse dump and a small cemetery, and then a sign points the way to the beach.

For a truly spectacular flight experience, consider soaring above the ground in a motor-powered ultralight plane or on a tandem hang glider. **Birds in Paradise,** 822–5309, leaves from Port Allen airstrip and offers flights ranging from a half-hour to two hours. The trips are not traditional sightseeing excursions; owner Jerry is a licensed flight instructor, and participants are encouraged to take control of the plane. (He performs the difficult elements of taking off and landing.)

Beyond Hanapepe, the highway skirts along the coast and passes through the small sugar towns of Kaumakani, Olokele, and Pakala. Historic Waimea is a few minutes' drive from Pakala.

WAIMEA AND KOKEE

Captain James Cook, on his ocean voyage searching for the Northwest Passage, landed in Waimea in January 1778, forever changing this isolated island environment and the thousands of people who lived in the sheltered society here. A small monument marks the spot where Cook landed. Hawaiian scholars are quick to mention that Cook did not "discover" the islands, since the Polynesians had migrated here centuries before Cook found them.

Cook remained in Waimea just a short time, trading iron and nails for food. When he returned a year later, he landed at Kealakekua Bay, on the Big Island.

In 1820, Kauai's first missionaries arrived in Waimea on the brig *Thaddeus.*

Visitors should stop at the **Waimea Public Library** (338–6848) or at the front office of **Waimea Plantation Cottages,** 338–1625, for a free map that highlights the town's historical hot spots. The town has recently joined the Main Street USA program in an attempt to revive local businesses and promote community-sponsored restoration and historical awareness.

The **Waimea Plantation Cottages,** just north of Waimea, feature authentically restored homes that are relics from the sugar industry. There are forty-six cottages throughout the property, each decorated with period furniture and named for the families that lived in them. On the first and third Wednesday of every month, the property hosts a free coconut presentation at 11:30 A.M. It lasts about forty minutes and explains everything you always wanted to know about coconuts, including a brief history of the 750-tree grove at the resort. Guests are shown how to husk coconuts and offered fresh coconut meat and coconut milk. For more information, call 338–1625.

Upon arriving in town, it may be surprising to see the remains of a Russian fort, here in the middle of almost nowhere. A sign points left to **Fort Elizabeth State Park.** In the early 1800s, George Anton Schaffer, a visiting German doctor, constructed this fort and named it after the Elizabeth, Czar Nicholas's daughter. Schaffer believed the strategic location of these islands in the middle of the Pacific Ocean was an important factor for Russia to consider and wanted to turn the fort into a trading post. (There are a few other Russian forts still standing on Kauai.) Czar Nicholas never agreed with Schaffer, and the fort eventually fell into disrepair.

The fort was designated a National Historic Landmark in 1966; in 1970 it was acquired by the state to be developed into a historic park, but there hasn't been much activity to restore the structure.

On the coast, at Waimea's eastern tip, sits the five-acre **Lucy Wright Beach County Park.** Facilities here include restrooms, showers, picnic tables, and a playground. It's a popular recreational spot for the local community.

In Waimea, you can rent masks, fins, and snorkels as well as surfboards and boogieboards from the **Captain's Cargo Shop,** 338–0333, located right off Kaumualii Highway just after the bridge. At the same spot, **Liko Kauai Cruises** offers Na Pali Coast lunch/sightseeing tours that begin from the west side of the island. The trips are aboard a 38-foot cabin cruiser. The tours last about five hours and cost $85 for adults, $65 for children ages four to fourteen; children under four are free.

Another Na Pali trip leaving from Waimea is aboard the **_Na Pali Explorer,_** the largest craft of its type to be built in the United States. It features a SCARAB racing hull to promote speed, and inflatable tubing to promote stability. The day cruise ventures to Nualolo Kai for snorkeling, and whale-watching in season. It lasts five-and-a-half hours and includes breakfast, lunch, and all-you-can-consume beverages. The tour costs $122 for adults, $64 for children ages five to eleven. The _Explorer_ also goes sunset cruising, costing $69 for adults, $37 for children. For more information, call 335–9909.

In Waimea, look for Kiki a Ola, more commonly known as the **Menehune Ditch,** built by Menehune Chief Ola and his followers. This is among the most impressive structures linked to the famous little people. It's said that the ditch was built in one night, and its unique design and distinctive stonework differ from any other archaeological structures in Hawaii.

From Waimea, the highway continues east to Kekaha and farther on to the end of the road at Mana Point and Barking Sands Pacific Missile Range. At Kekaha, Route 55 leads north to Waimea Canyon State Park. A shortcut to Waimea Canyon is via Waimea Canyon Road, which leads inland from Waimea town, then joins with Route 55 coming from Kekaha.

Kekaha Beach stretches for miles and offers good swimming, surfing, and snorkeling. It butts up against Barking Sands Military Base. Beyond here, the official road ends, but a smaller cane road leads to the absolute end of the line at **Polihale State Park.** This beautiful, secluded wide beach is nearly always sunny, but the swimming conditions aren't optimal because the currents cause a strong undertow. Facilities include restrooms, showers, and a picnic area. Be sure to bring some snacks and water, because Polihale is far away from convenience stores.

The Na Pali Explorer *takes guests on a scenic adventure to Kauai's majestic northeastern coastline.*

This was a sacred area to Hawaiians of old. There's an isolated heiau out here, and this is one of a few spots statewide where the Hawaiians believed the souls of the dead left earth and journeyed to the spiritual world.

Looking northward, views include the razor-sharp crags of the Na Pali Coast. If you're here when the sun is setting behind Niihau Island, you're in for a special treat as the cliffs are transformed into a spectrum of color ranging from forest green to golden brown.

This is the southern end of the Na Pali Coast, the rest of it being inaccessible by car, but it's definitely worth exploring either on foot, by boat, or by air. (See the section "Na Pali Coast" in this chapter.)

WAIMEA CANYON

The spectacular **Waimea Canyon** should definitely be included on the itinerary of any Kauai visitor. It's commonly referred to as the "Grand Canyon of the Pacific," after its similarity to Arizona's natural wonder. The canyon is only 1 mile wide, but it's a whopping 14 miles long. It features a wide variety of trails designed for all levels of hikers.

Officially, Waimea Canyon State Park begins about a mile inland from Waimea, on the Waimea Canyon Road. The park borders the road for the remainder of its winding path, which culminates at Kokee State Park.

Although quite curvy, the road is well maintained as it leads up the mountain, where the landscape changes almost immediately and the temperature drops a few degrees. Along the way, don't miss the chance to park at one of the many scenic points. The views are expansive and get even more glorious as you climb higher.

When you reach an altitude of 3,100 feet, the first stop is **Waimea Canyon Lookout,** where you have a fantastic view of the canyon. At **Pu'ukapele Lookout,** about 3,700 feet up, there's a small rest area with picnic tables. The best views of the canyon are from **Pu'uhinahina Lookout.** A short trail beginning behind the restrooms leads to an even better view, where, if cloud cover permits, you can see Niihau.

The road ends at the 4,345-acre Kokee State Park, where another slew of hiking trails can accommodate any skill level. It gets cold up here, so be sure to bring warm clothes.

Staff at the park headquarters can answer questions about the particular plants and animals in this region and about the conditions of certain trails. Be sure to pick up a free map that details all the trails in the park. The headquarters are open daily, 10:00 A.M. to 4:00 P.M.

Children should be able to navigate initial curves of the **Kukui Trail,** well identified between mile markers 8 and 9. The first part of the trail is known as **Iliau Nature Loop** and is a wonderful, short, self-guided path. Beyond the loop, the trail descends 2,000 feet into the canyon through a series of switchbacks. Figuring that you'll have to climb back up, this may be difficult for young children. Take note of the grade and use good judgment.

A series of other trails branch off Mohihi Camp 10 road, near park headquarters. It's wise to ask for recommendations at the headquarters for the trails that best suit your family's abilities. Everyone should be able to handle the easy 1-mile **Berry Flat Trail** and the half-mile **Puu Ka Ohelo Trail.** Both are loops that take hikers through a picturesque forest.

The **Alakai Swamp Trail** is the most famous trail here, but it should be attempted only by the most experienced hikers—not young children. It rains 450 inches a year here, and scientists say this is the most fragile ecosystem on earth.

Be sure to visit the **Kokee Natural History Museum** for a larger selection of maps of the area's hiking trails. There also are exhibits that explain the distinctive characteristics of the environment up here, as well as displays of native plants, birds, and animals living in the park. The museum is free and is open daily, 10:00 A.M. to 4:00 P.M.; 335–9975.

Believe it or not, for those who really want to get away from it all, there are overnight accommodations up here. The **Kokee Lodge** offers rustic cabins that were built in the 1930s by the Civilian Conservation Corps, or CCC. Nonguests are welcome to eat at the restaurant, which serves dinner on Friday and Saturday, 6:00 to 9:00 P.M., and breakfast and lunch daily, 8:30 A.M. to 3:30 P.M.; 335–6061. $$.

Be sure to follow the road all the way to its end, at **Kalalau** and **Pu'u O Kila** lookouts. From Kalalau you can see deep into Kalalau Valley, the largest and widest valley in the Na Pali cliffs, and you can also see the backside of that ever-beautiful Na Pali Coast. From Pu'u O Kila, you also can see into Kalalau Valley, as well as across the Alakai Swamp to Mount Waialeale, in the center of the island.

Outfitters Kauai, 742–9667, offers informative, exciting Kokee mountain-bike trips, in which guides explain the native plants, special geographic features, and local legends.

Kauai Mountain Tours offers van tours of Kokee, a great alternative for families with children too young to hike. You'll get to see the backwoods of the park from an air-conditioned vehicle. Views include Waimea Canyon, sugi pine forests, waterfalls, and rare birds. The trip costs $84 for adults, $56 for children twelve and under. The tour includes hotel pickup, breakfast, and lunch. For more information, call 245–7224.

WAILUA

Heading north from Lihue on the Kuhio Highway (Route 56), Ma'ala Road (Route 583) turns inland and follows the Wailua River. You'll notice that the fertile landscape is lush with sugar cane as you head toward the green velvety mountains. After a few miles, Route 583 ends at **Wailua Falls,** which drop 80 feet into a large pool. Hawaiians say that the *ali'i* (royalty) would jump from here as an exhibition of their power. There's a trail leading down to the pool, but it's fairly rugged and not recommended for children.

Back on Kuhio Highway, turn toward the ocean on Hanamaulu Road, and go right on Hehi Road, which leads to the wonderful **Hanamaulu Beach County Park.** It's a great place for swimming and picnicking, and it's rarely crowded. There's a sheltered lagoon area, complete with natural pools, that's an ideal playground for small children.

Lydgate State Park is well marked off Kuhio Highway (look for a tall group of palm trees east of the Wailua River), and is a perfect place for children of all ages. There are two large, naturally formed lava pools that make for year-round safe swimming and snorkeling. If you bring some fish food, which should be available at any convenience store, you can try feeding the fish right from the shore. Be sure to warn your kids to stay within the protected waters and off the slippery lava barriers.

On-site are the **Hau'ola O Honaunau** and **Hikina O Kala Heiau.** The first was a place of refuge, where *kapu* (taboo) breakers or soldiers on the losing end of a battle could seek refuge and be forgiven for all wrong-doings. After a kahuna cleansed their souls, the individuals could return to society with a clean bill of spiritual health.

A few miles north of Hanamaulu, you'll pass **Wailua River State Park** and arrive at the oceanside town of Wailua, a place abounding with historic sites and attractions. At one time, there were at least seven heiau from the river to the top of Mt. Waialeale. Religious processions would make the trek to the top, stopping at each heiau along the way.

Just as Route 580 veers inland, look for the **Holo Holo Ku Heiau,** one of Kauai's oldest. While some ancient heiau were places of refuge, this was not. Here those unfortunate criminals of war or kapu breakers were sacrificed to the gods. Look in the corner for the large flat rock that was the altar of the heiau.

A guardrail leads up the hill behind the heiau to a Japanese cemetery, and beyond that, the large rocks were known as **royal birthing stones.** Wives of *ali'i* came here when they were about to deliver their babies, thinking that this area possessed great *mana,* or spirit.

If you look very carefully, with a bit of imagination and an open mind, at the mountains above Wailua, you should see the form of a reclining giant, known as **Nonou, the sleeping giant.**

You can hike up to the sleeping giant on the **Nonou Mountain Trail.** The eastern side of the trail is a bit more difficult than the western side. The eastern side trailhead is just north of the junctions of Routes 56 and 580, at Haleilio Road. Look for a space to park near a water pump about 1.5 miles up Haleilio (at pole 38). The trail starts across from the drainage ditch and proceeds up the mountain for about 1.5 miles. It's a steady climb that concludes at a picnic site, complete with a shade-providing shelter and tables.

From here, you can walk across the giant's face by taking another trail just south of the picnic site. While you're afforded expansive views, how-ever, this section of the trail is difficult and dangerous—suited only for experienced, hardy hikers.

To get to the easier, western side of the trail, turn onto Route 580, then 581, and look for parking at pole 11. There's a little path here that joins the trail. After about one-and-a-half miles, this trail joins the eastern trail and heads up to the picnic site. Bring plenty of water for whichever trail you choose.

Legend says **Poliahu Heiau,** just a few minutes' drive on Route 580, is another structure built by the industrious menehune. Today all that's left is an overgrown enclosure surrounded by walls. Down the ridge from here are the **Royal Bellstones,** rung whenever an *ali'i* gave birth.

The Wailua River is the only navigable stream in all Hawaii. It flows from Mt. Waialeale, the rainiest place on earth (nearly 500 inches a year), through the **Fern Grotto** to the ocean at Wailua Bay. It's also known as one of the best kayaking spots on the island, although even the best kayakers will be able to navigate only about a third of the river. Motorized barges cruise up the river, docking at the Fern Grotto, one of the frequently visited sites on Kauai.

The Fern Grotto is a naturally formed amphitheater, framed completely by hanging ferns that flourish in the misty, moist air. It's a romantic, beautiful spot, the kind of place that typifies a tropical island, and it's a frequent spot for weddings. And whether or not your visit coincides with romantic nuptials, the "Hawaiian Wedding Song" is played here several times a day by local musicians.

Since 1947, **Smith's Motor Boat Service** has ferried visitors to the Fern Grotto. On the way, passengers are serenaded by musicians, singers, dancers, and master storytellers of local legends. Cruises depart daily, every half-hour, from Wailua Marina, 9:00 A.M. to 4:00 P.M. Admission is $15.00 for adults, $7.50 for children ages two to twelve, free for children under two; 821–6892.

Wai'ale'ale Boat Services, 822–4908, also cruises along Wailua River to Fern Grotto, and offers an entertainment program on the way. The cost is $15 for adults, $7.50 for children ages three to twelve.

Kauai Water Ski and Surf, 822–3574, is located in the Kinipopo Shopping Village, 4–356 Kuhio Highway. It's a complete water-sports shop that rents snorkel gear, kayaks, surfboards, and boogieboards and offers waterskiing excursions, complete with boat, driver, equipment, and instruction. They have taught children as young as four years old. Lessons cost $85 an hour, and usually three or four people need only one hour to take turns and get a couple of rides in each. Beginners need more time. Four or five passengers are allowed in the boat at one time, but not everyone needs to be a skier. Open Monday through Friday, 9:00 A.M. to 7:00 P.M.

Right next to the Wailua Marina are twenty-three riverfront acres with unusual birds, rain forest, and gardens. **Smith's Tropical Paradise** is a well-maintained cultural and botanical feast for the senses. You can walk among a striking collection of exotic plants and feel as if you're in the midst of a jungle.

On the grounds are a luau house and a theater; evening entertainment includes dinner, Hawaiian music, and a variety of South Pacific dances. There also are a series of ethnic villages representing different local groups, including Polynesian, Filipino, and Japanese.

The facility is open daily, 8:00 A.M. to 4:00 P.M. Admission is $5.00 for adults and $2.50 for children ages two to twelve. Visitors can ride through the facility on a mini tram for an additional fee of $3.00 for adults,

Head out into the waters off of Kauai in one of Na Pali Adventures' motorized catamarans for a day of adventure and fun. (Photo by William Waterfall, courtesy Hawaii Visitors Bureau)

$2.00 for children. The evening luau and performance is held Mondays, Wednesdays, and Fridays and costs $47 for adults, $27 for children ages seven to thirteen, and $18 for children ages three to six. For just the show, admission costs $12 for adults, $6.00 for children three through twelve. Reservations are necessary; 821–6895.

Continuing inland on Route 580, look for a sign pointing to **Opaeka'a Falls.** Although you can see the falls from the road, it's definitely a place to park the car and walk around. There's an overlook that offers views of Kamokila Hawaiian Village, Wailua River, and pristine Kauai country. Across the highway from the falls overlook are a series of descriptive signs that offer information about **Poliahu Heiau** and the archaeological sites below, along the Wailua River. Some scholars believe Wailua was home to the highest-ranking *ali'i,* who worshiped at a private heiau.

Kamokila Hawaiian Village is reconstructed to appear just as villages did in Old Hawaii. This attraction is about as low-key as they come —there's no fancy gift shop and no hard sell. In fact, it's never even advertised. Visitors may walk around the village's thatched huts, including the traditional separate structures for sleeping and eating, and view the taro patches. There are demonstrations of Hawaiian crafts, such as poi-pounding. The village is open Monday through Saturday, 9:00 A.M. to 4:00 P.M. Admission is $5.00 for adults, $1.50 for children under twelve. You can take a boat ride there for an additional fee. For more information, call 822–1192.

The thirty-acre **Keahua Arboretum** is no doubt one of the best-kept secrets on the island—hardly anyone ventures up here. In the mountains above Wailua, the arboretum features pools that beg to be jumped into and bubbling streams perfect for wading and exploring. The surrounding forests are so green they almost look more like a painting than real life. There's even a rope swing where kids, and kids at heart, can grab hold, take a flying leap, give a Tarzan yell, and plop into the stream. There are a series of trails within the arboretum, or you can walk upstream and explore what will seem like uncharted territory.

To get to Keahua simply follow Route 580 all the way to its end.

KAPAA

Back on the Kuhio Highway heading north, the **Coconut Marketplace** is home to a large concentration of shops and restaurants. The shopping center hosts free hula shows Monday, Wednesday, Friday, and Saturday at 4:30 P.M. The Kauai Visitors Center is here and is a great place to pick up free information about activities island-wide; 245–3882.

Beyond Wailua, the Kuhio Highway leads north to **Kapaa.** On the way, **Waipouli Beach County Park** is on the ocean side of the highway, just north of the Coconut Plantation Marketplace. It's a nice place for swimming (only in calm weather, please) and is connected to Kapaa Beach County Park, which encompasses about fifteen acres and features picnic tables, showers, restrooms, and a pavilion for shade.

You can see virtually the whole town of Kapaa just by driving through it on Kuhio Highway. It is fun to stroll among the colorful shops and eateries; it's a quaint place, serving needs of visitors and locals. There are a host of recreational shops here that offer a variety of rentals and adventures.

For evening entertainment, the **Kauai Coconut Beach Resort** in Kapaa hosts the traditional visitor-oriented luau, complete with an *imu* ceremony, buffet dinner, and hula show. The luau is held Tuesday through Saturday and costs $49 for adults, $28 for children ages six to seventeen; kids under six get in free; 822–3455.

For two-wheel exploring, you can rent a variety of types of bikes at the following Kapaa locations: **Bicycle John's,** 245–7579, has rates starting at $25 a day. It's at 3142 Kuhio Highway and is open weekdays 9:00 A.M. to 5:00 P.M., weekends 10:00 A.M. to 4:00 P.M. **Bicycle Kauai,** 822–3315, starts at $20 a day and also offers customized guided tours, in which the cost is dependent on skill level and the itinerary. It's at 1379 Kuhio Highway and is open Monday to Friday, 9:00 A.M. to 6:00 P.M.; Saturday, 9:00 A.M. to 4:00 P.M.; Sunday, 10:00 A.M. to 1:00 P.M.

Scuba and snorkeling rentals, and a variety of guided excursions, are available at **Aquatic Adventures,** 822–1434. Open daily, 7:30 A.M. to 5:00 P.M.

Also in Kapaa, **Bubbles Below,** 822–3483, and **Wet and Wonderful Ocean Sports,** 822–0211, specialize in scuba rentals, first-time scuba lessons, and diving excursions. Kids must be at least twelve years old.

Kayak Kauai, 822–9179, across from Farmer's Market in Kapaa, offers kayak and bicycle rentals and guided excursions. Open daily, 8:00 A.M. to 5:00 P.M.

Ray's Rentals and Activities, 822–5700, rents scuba-diving equipment, surfboards, kayaks, snorkel gear, boogieboards, bicycles, and Harley Davidson motorcycles. They can also arrange for lessons, maps, and directions. Downtown Kapaa, 4–1345 Kuhio Highway; open 8:00 A.M. to 6:00 P.M.

Continuing on the Kuhio Highway, your next stop should be **Kealia Beach** and the tiny town of Kealia. To get to the beach, look for a sign after mile marker 10, directing you to turn onto a small cane road that leads to the ocean. It's not an official park, so there are no facilities, and swimming isn't recommended for young, inexperienced children, but the wide sandy beach is quite scenic and a good place to check out the talents of local surfers. During the summer, the north end of Kealia Beach is tremendously popular with boogieboarders. If your kids are good swimmers, it's safe to let them try their boogieboarding skills here.

The Kuhio Highway meanders along the picturesque coast to **Anahola.** The drive offers superb sights as each turn reveals a more stunning view of lava arms jutting out into the ocean, being pummeled by a never-ending succession of crashing waves. The grass is green, the sky is blue with puffy white clouds, the ocean sparkles brightly. The whole drive, all the way to Haena, is a must-do, for it feels as if you've left ordinary civilization behind and entered a virtual-reality tropical paradise.

Look for the turnoff called Anahola Road, which leads to the ocean and **Anahola Beach County Park** a few miles north of Kealia. The park features restrooms, picnic tables, showers, and grills. Swimming is best in a little protected cove at the south end.

The road soon curves around and travels the northern end of the island. To visit **Moloa'a Bay,** a secluded, beautiful site, turn right on Koolau Road, which leads to skinny Moloa'a Road. At road's end, you can park and follow the signs to the beach, a wide, picturesque crescent-shaped strip of sand. Swimming is best at the southern end and safe only during calm weather, but the beautiful beach is a delightful spot to relax in Kauai's splendor.

The Kuhio Highway continues to roll through northern Kauai, and the next town worth a stop is **Kilauea,** the northernmost point of the main Hawaiian islands. You'll know you're there when you see the tall white lighthouse, standing incongruously, although picturesquely, on the coast. The lighthouse was built in 1913 and played an important role when ships frequented this area, traveling to and from Asia. Although its light was turned off permanently in 1976, the lighthouse is now preserved as a National Historic Landmark.

Kilauea is a favorite spot of naturalists and ornithologists because it's a stopover site for such migrating seabirds as the Laysan albatross and the red-footed booby. But even ordinary folks will appreciate the great spectacle as the seabirds flit in and out of their nests within the crevices of these cliffs. Kilauea Point is the largest colony of seabirds in the state. Be sure to stop at the visitor center for free information about the birds. The center even lets visitors borrow binoculars for closer inspection of the flying creatures. The center is open weekdays 10:00 A.M. to 4:00 P.M., closed weekends and holidays. It costs adults $2.00 to get in; children under age sixteen are admitted free.

In Kilauea, on the Kilauea Lighthouse Road, the **Kong Lung Company** is worth exploring. It's an old plantation store that's been in business longer than any store in all Hawaii. You'll find a variety of gourmet food and wine and a bunch of interesting artworks, clothing, toys, and general paraphernalia. The store is open Monday through Friday, 10:00 A.M. to 6:00 P.M.; Saturday, 9:00 A.M. to 6:00 P.M.; Sunday, 10:00 A.M. to 5:00 P.M. For information, call 828–1822.

Anini Beach is about 2 miles north of Kilauea, and it's another one of those wholly picturesque North Shore beaches. It's known island-wide as the best place to learn how to windsurf because the winds are gentle but steady, and it's fairly shallow and protected. Additionally, the longest exposed reef on Kauai makes it a great place for snorkeling. The beach features restrooms, picnic tables, grills, and a pavilion.

To get there, turn right on the second Kalihi Wai Road, then turn left at the fork. Anini is at road's end. For windsurfing lessons, contact **Anini Beach Windsurfing,** 826–9463. Kids must be at least 65 pounds, and it costs $65 for a three-hour introductory lesson. Hours vary, but the company is located right on the beach. **Windsurf Kauai,** 828–6838, also headquartered on the beach, offers a three-hour class for $60. Children must be at least seven years old.

NORTH SHORE

Princeville is the largest town on the north shore, and within its 11,000 acres there are a host of great attractions, restaurants, and accommodations, and even a small airport. This area used to be Kauai's oldest ranch, started in 1853 by R. C. Wyllie, a Scottish immigrant. It was renamed Princeville after King Kamehameha IV, Queen Emma, and their son Prince Albert visited in 1860. Wyllie was so taken with young Albert that he renamed the area Princeville in his honor.

At the Princeville Resort, try **Cafe Hanalei** for breakfast, lunch, or dinner. The dinner menu features local specialties such as *yose nabe* and *sashimi.* At 5520 Kahaku Rd.; 826–9644. $$. **La Cascata** offers Italian cuisine for dinner only at the Princeville Hotel. Try the garlic soup with onion and parmesan cheese. $$$. The **Princeville Restaurant & Bar** is part of the Princeville golf complex; the restaurant serves breakfast, lunch, dinner, and Sunday brunch. Menu items are named with golfers in mind. A "Bogey" is a beef burger with a choice of cheddar, grilled onions, and bacon, while a "Birdie" is a teriyaki chicken breast topped with grilled onions. $$. At 5–3900 Kuhio Hwy.; 826–5050.

Princeville Ranch Stables offers three different horseback-riding adventures. The longest one is a three-hour private ride to a remote waterfall, where riders may spend some time frolicking about in the natural pool. Another is a two-hour trip along the coast to Anini Beach. The easiest ride is a one-and-a-half-hour foray into the Hanalei countryside ($55). For more information and prices, call 826–6777. Kids must be eight or older.

About 920 acres of this lush valley is designated as the **Hanalei National Wildlife Refuge.** Although no visitors are generally permitted in this area, there is restricted access, which permits you to drive along the river to find great fishing, hiking, and scenery. Just after the bridge, take Ohiki Road inland. You'll pass simple, quaint farms set among picturesque wildflowers and taro patches.

Just around the corner from Princeville sit idyllic Hanalei Town and **Hanalei Bay,** so pretty it's hard to believe it's real. To get there, you'll cross a tiny one-lane country bridge over the Hanalei River. The bridge was built in 1912. Inland, a patchwork quilt of green taro fields and groves of papaya and banana flourish, providing fruitful harvests to most of Hawaii.

When you get over the bridge and see Hanalei Bay on the left, you'll definitely want to stop and marvel at this priceless view. In fact, many visitors and residents, myself included, think this is the most beautiful spot in all Hawaii. To the north are the famous "Bali Hai" cliffs that served as the tropical backdrop for the movie *South Pacific.* The bay itself sparkles in a dozen different hues of blue and is wide and calm, inviting all sorts of water-sport enthusiasts including swimmers, sailors, snorkelers, surfers, boogieboarders, and windsurfers. (The bay can get rough with winter storms.) There are showers and restrooms on-site.

Surrounding the bay are the famous Na Pali Cliffs, where centuries of wind and rain have carved deep gulches. If it's rained lately, there will be dozens of waterfalls tumbling over the gulches, creating a magical mist.

Hanalei Town is small but charming. **Tahiti Nui** is a great place to stop for refreshments. Not only is the food good, but the decorations are the ultimate in Hawaiiana kitsch. Lanterns are fashioned from puffer fish, and carved palm-tree trunks are formed into stools. $$$.

Tahiti Nui is famous island-wide for its luau, which isn't the fanciest or most extravagant affair but offers a wonderful homegrown charm. It's held every Wednesday and Friday at 6:30 P.M. Even locals come, and there's a great mix of singing, dancing, and good feelings. Admission is $40 for adults, $17 for children ages six to eleven, free for children under six; 826–6277.

Continuing through town, look to the left for the **Waioli Hui'ia Church.** On Sundays, the church choir sings lilting hymns in Hawaiian. The adjacent **Waioli Mission House Museum** is the former home of missionaries Abner and Lucy Wilcox. There are wonderful artifacts dating from the early 1800s, including dishes and home furnishings. The museum, 245–3202, is currently going through a renovation and is scheduled to reopen by January 1997.

For the best local-style teriyaki burger on the North Shore, stop at **Bubba Burgers** in Hanalei, on Highway 56; 826–7839. $.

The **Hanalei Surf Company,** 826–9000, provides rentals for surfing, boogieboarding, and snorkeling. It's open 9:00 A.M. to 9:00 P.M., seven days a week, and is located at 5–5161 Kuhio Highway.

Pedal and Paddle, 826–9069, is in the Ching Young Village Shopping Center. Here you can rent bicycles, kayaks, and camping gear. During the summer, the store is open from 9:00 A.M. to 6:00 P.M.; it closes at 5:00 P.M. in the winter.

Kayak Kauai, (800) 437–3507, 826–9844, or 822–9179, leads guided bicycle tours through the historic, charming towns of Hanalei and Kapaa. It also leads guided kayak tours, the most popular of which is on the Kilauea River, where you kayak to an isolated waterfall and swim in the pool below. If you want to explore on your own, you can rent a variety of equipment here.

For those who rank Hanalei Bay as Hawaii's all-time most beautiful spot, **Lumahai Beach** is likely a close second. It's just north of Hanalei Bay and offers an inviting stretch of soft white sand, framed by the glorious, majestic Na Pali Cliffs. This is where Mitzi Gaynor "washed that man right out of her hair," in the musical *South Pacific.* One way to get there is by parking just west of Hanalei Bay and walking down the trail to the east end of the beach. Or, you can keep going until just before the bridge that crosses the Lumahai River. Look for a grove of ironwood trees (they look like Mainland pines); the beach is a short walk from here. The ocean currents can be quite fierce in winter, so be cautious when entering the water. But even if the weather is rough, by all means stop here, if only to appreciate one of the most majestically beautiful treasures of Kauai.

Almost at the end of the road, **Haena** is a must-stop—it features an amazing variety of naturally formed **lava caves.** You can explore the Maniniholo Dry Cave and two wet caves, Waikapalae and Waikanaloa. The ocean here is good for swimming and snorkeling, but only during the calm summer months.

Look toward the mountain for the large Maniniholo Dry Cave. You can walk right inside and explore the mysterious hidden spaces. If you're really daring, you can continue exploring through the whole structure, which ends at a small opening at the top of a cliff. Beware, however—the high roof at the cave's entrance lowers considerably as you get farther in.

The name Maniniholo comes from one of the head fishermen of the menehune. According to legend, the menehune were planning to journey to the interior of the island and leave this coastal site. They were catching fish at Haena to sustain them on their journey. They couldn't carry all the fish at one time, so they left half at what is now Maniniholo Dry Cave. Upon returning for their catch, they found that an *akua,* or evil spirit, had stolen their stash. They formed two parties to capture the akua. Half the menehune began digging down from the clifftop and the other half dug from its base. The result is the great cave you see today.

Ke'e Beach is at road's end and is great for swimming in the summer months. It's also known island-wide as one of the best snorkeling spots in all of Kauai. You'll see a variety of colorful marine life, and the offshore coral reef makes snorkeling safe here even when it's choppy other places.

After a short walk west, look for the series of stone platforms marking Lohiau Heiau. It's said that Pele fell in love here with the young prince Lohiau. Who knows, perhaps her affections were spurned, and that's why she's still blowing smoke and lava from Kilauea on the Big Island.

Nearby, along the coastal trail, are two heiau, **Ka Ulu a Paoa** and **Ka Ulu o Laka,** and wonderful coastline views.

The hiking trail through the **Na Pali Coast** to Kalalau Valley begins at Ke'e Beach. This is one of the most famous trails in all Hawaii, offering enchanting views, pristine beaches, and total seclusion. It's also one of the most difficult trails, however. The round-trip trek to Kalalau Valley cannot be completed in one day, and is recommended only for experienced hikers and campers.

You needn't travel all the way to Kalalau to get a sampling of inner Na Pali's beauty. It's 2.5 miles to secluded **Hanakapiai Beach.** You can make this round-trip in one day; allow about four or five hours. But proceed with caution; parts of the trail are very narrow and slippery. This hike is not recommended for kids under eight and should probably be undertaken only in dry weather.

As an alternative to hiking into the interior of Na Pali, a slew of companies offer a different view—from the ocean or the air.

Boats provide fantastic perspectives of the towering jagged cliffs, deep valleys, and sea caves. You'll hear the lilting chorus of dozens of waterfalls as they spray down the steep promontories. You'll see otherwise inaccessible jungles, completely isolated from modern civilization.

Most of the oceangoing excursions leave from Hanalei Bay and stop first at Hanakapiai Beach and next at Nualolo Kai for snorkeling. The captain and crew of most of the tour boats are well versed in local legends and the distinctive wildlife of the area. They are able to identify birds and marine life as they guide you through the Pacific wilderness. Plan on seeing dolphins, sea turtles, and, in season, humpback whales.

The tamest rides are in large catamarans, sailboats, or Boston whalers and usually include a picnic lunch. Zodiacs, which are large, sturdy motorized rubber rafts, offer a slightly rougher ride but can fit into the various seaside caves for more in-depth exploration. About six or eight passengers can fit in a Zodiac boat. In the calm summer months, there are even escorted kayak trips to this picturesque coastline. Tours vary in price and length.

There are dozens of companies eager to share the beauty of Na Pali with visitors. The following list is merely a sampling of the choices.

* **Captain Zodiac Raft Expeditions,** 826–9371, offers Zodiac trips. Children must be at least four years old.

* **Hanalei Sea Tours,** 826–7254, offers Zodiac and catamaran trips along the Na Pali Coast. Children must be at least five years old to ride in the Zodiac and three years old for the catamaran.

* **Na Pali Adventures,** 826–6804, will take children age two and older on a double-hulled, motorized catamaran that's similar in size to a large Zodiac. The unique design of this boat allows it to cut through the water faster and more smoothly than other craft.

* **Whitey's Boat Cruises,** 826–6853, offers rides on a 40-foot sailing boat and 32-foot powerboat. Children under two are free.

* **Captain Andy's Sailing Adventures,** 822–7833, offers snorkeling and sunset cruises.

* **Bluewater Sailing Kauai,** 822–0525, sails out of Hanalei Bay into the open ocean, on a 42-foot sailboat. Kids must be at least five years old.

* **Catamaran Kahanu,** 826–4596, offers trips on a huge catamaran. The four-hour swimming and snorkeling cruise costs $85 for adults,

$65 for children ages four to twelve. A two-hour sunset cruise costs $65 and $45, respectively.

❋ **Paradise Adventure Cruises,** 826–9999, offers trips on Wild Cat catamarans. There's a four-and-a-half-hour snorkeling tour that includes one-and-a-half hours of actual water time and costs $80 for adults and $60 for children ages four to twelve. Another option is a two-hour sunset trip that costs $55 and $40, respectively.

Helicopters offer fantastic aerial views of the coast and Kalalau Valley, but they are not permitted to land. Again, the following list is not inclusive; it's worth the effort to do some of your own investigating for the best deal.

❋ **Air Kauai,** 246–4666

❋ **Ohana Helicopters,** 245–3996

❋ **Hawaii Helicopters,** (800) 367–7095 or 826–6591

❋ **Safari Helicopters,** 246–0136

❋ **Bali Hai Helicopters,** or (800) 325–TOUR, 335–3166, 332–7331

❋ **Jack Harter Helicopters,** 245–3774

❋ **Island Helicopters,** 245–8588

❋ **South Seas Helicopters,** (800) 367–2914 or 245–2222

❋ **Will Squyre Helicopters,** 245–8881

❋ **Safari Aviation Inc.,** (800) 326–3356 or 246–0136

❋ **Interisland Helicopters,** 335–5009

Molokai

Molokai

Molokai is the fifth-largest and the least developed of the main Hawaiian Islands. It also boasts the largest population of native Hawaiians—of the 6,000 residents, more than 2,500 have more than 50 percent Hawaiian ancestry. It's nicknamed the "Friendly Isle," and after one visit, you'll understand why. The environment here is less developed than a typical small town in Anywhere, U.S.A. There are no high-rises, no fast-food chains, and there's just a single traffic light on the whole island.

The beaches are expansive and unspoiled—oftentimes you'll be the only people there. While this means the island offers great natural beauty and solitude, it can be too slow for active teenagers. Additionally, with solitude comes the potential for danger; use caution when entering the ocean at any deserted beach. If the currents become fierce, it will be difficult to get help.

In ancient Hawaii, Molokai differed from the other islands, which were ruled by chiefs who controlled large armies of warriors. On Molokai, the chiefs ruled through chants and religious power. The *mana* (spirit) here was considered to be the strongest and greatest in all Hawaii. It was a powerful spirit, handed down through generations, that lives on today, in the depths of Halawa Valley or in the town of Maunaloa.

The slow-paced island lifestyle comes alive on the third Saturday of every May with the annual **Ka Hula Piko Festival.** The hula festival celebrates Molokai as the birthplace of hula, the ancient art form that has perpetuated the history and lifestyles of native Hawaiians through dances and chants passed down for centuries.

Hawaiian legend says that Laka, the first goddess to dance the hula, first danced at Ka'ana, in Maunaloa in the western part of the island. Laka then traveled from island to island, teaching the words and movements and helping to preserve what is, today, one of the few aspects of Hawaiian culture still intact.

Laka's efforts and grace are celebrated at the festival, and visitors come from all over the world to join in the fun. The week prior to the festival includes a variety of lectures on Hawaiian history and hula, and there are excursions to the island's historic sites that are sung about in many hula chants. The daylong hula festival is staged at picturesque Papohaku Beach Park.

You can fly to Molokai from Oahu or Maui in about twenty minutes on Hawaiian Airlines, Aloha Island Air, Mahalo Airlines, and Air Molokai. There's also a ninety-minute cruise that travels from Maui to Molokai on a large, stable, air-conditioned craft, the *Maui Princess.* For more information, call 661–8397 from Maui or (800) 833–5800 from elsewhere.

There is no public transportation on Molokai, and there are only two rental car companies: Budget, 567–6877, and Dollar, 567–6156. Supplies are limited, so be sure to make a reservation in advance.

The airport is in Ho'olehua, and most of the accommodations are on the western coast, except for Hotel Molokai in Kaunakakai. The island is long and skinny, and the main highway travels from the west end to the east end, with various smaller roads branching out on either side. This chapter begins in the west end, at Kaluakoi, and travels east to Halawa.

WESTERN MOLOKAI, KALUAKOI, AND MOLOKAI RANCH

Before Western contact, when the civilization here was primarily Stone Age, Kaluakoi was regarded as one of the best adze quarries in all the islands. People traveled from the other islands to procure the strong stone of Kaluakoi.

Today Kaluakoi is the site of **Kaluakoi Resort and Golf Course,** 552–2555 or (800) 777–1700, the largest accommodations on the island.

In the lobby, a bulletin board lists all the activities happening at the resort and throughout the island. Available within the resort are lessons in lei-making and hula, as well as bicycle paths and nature walks.

Some of the units are condominiums, completely furnished with full-fledged kitchens: **Kaluakoi Villas,** (800) 525–1470; **Ke Nani Kai Condos,** (800) 888–2791; and **Paniolo Hale,** (800) 367–2984.

Kaluakoi Resort fronts beautiful, spacious **Papohaku Beach,** among the largest in all the islands and considered by many to be one of the best. Its golden sands stretch for 3 miles along the coast; parking, restrooms, and showers are at the northern end.

Swim with caution since there are no lifeguards on duty here, but during the summer months the currents are very mild. In the winter, the ocean churns up monstrous waves and the area is frequented by surfers.

For guided tours on bicycles, catamarans, or kayaks, and for snorkeling and boogieboard rentals, contact **Fun Hogs Hawaii,** 552–2555.

To the north, **Kepuhi Bay** is smaller but just as pretty. Surfers flock here year-round to take advantage of the strong currents. Beyond Kepuhi,

Getting to feed a giraffe at Molokai's Wildlife Safari Park is a big hit with visitors of all ages.
(Courtesy Phil Spalding III)

Kawakiu is the northernmost beach on this side of the island. In calm weather, the beach is good for snorkeling and swimming, but be aware that there are no facilities here and it's usually pretty isolated.

To get to Kawakiu, you can make the forty-five-minute trek up the coastline, but plan on a dry, hot hike. If driving, take the dirt road marked KAWAKIU that veers off Route 460 before the Kaluakoi Resort. The road ends at the beach.

A great deal of the western end of the island is owned by the **Molokai Ranch.** More than 6,000 head of cattle, along with herds of axis deer, roam the 70,000 acres. You'll definitely want to visit the **Wildlife Safari Park,** where exotic animals—including Barbary sheep, eland, oryx, and giraffe—roam at will in a naturalistic setting. Throughout the ranch and park, there are guided **trail rides on horseback** and mountain-biking trails. For more information, call 552–2681. Tours are given Tuesday through Saturday at 8:00 and 10:30 A.M. and 1:30 P.M. They cost $35 for adults, $15 for children ages thirteen to eighteen, and $5 for children ages three to twelve.

CENTRAL MOLOKAI, MAUNALOA TO KUALAPU'U

In ancient Hawaii, Maunaloa Mountain (not to be confused with Mauna Loa Mountain on the Big Island) was the cultural center of the island. It was here that the art of hula was born and soon spread to all the islands as an ancient form of communication. Today, Maunaloa is a quaint, old-fashioned plantation town that's changed little since the large pineapple production companies pulled up stakes and headed for greener pastures in other countries.

If you see a colorful kite flying in the wind, you'll know you've arrived at the **Big Wind Kite Factory.** You'll be amazed at the variety of kites available here, in such a remote small town. The inventory ranges from decorative wind socks to old-fashioned single-line kites and even flashy four-liners that carry enough pull to lift small children in the air! All are created by hand on the premises and are just like the slick sport kites sold in fancy sporting-goods stores. The staff even offer free flying lessons in the park adjacent to the store. The Factory is open Monday through

Saturday, 8:30 A.M. to 5:00 P.M.; Sunday, 10:00 A.M. to 2:00 P.M. For information, call 552–2364.

Just up the hill from the kite factory is **Under the Banyan Tree,** a gift shop situated in a renovated plantation home. Here you'll find souvenirs such as jewelry, books, and gifts. The store is open Monday through Saturday, 9:00 A.M. to 5:00 P.M.; 552–0012.

Also in town is the **Maunaloa General Store,** (552–2868), where you can pick up general sundries, produce, and other food. The store is open Monday through Saturday, 9:00 A.M. to 7:00 P.M.; Sunday, 10:00 A.M. to 2:00 P.M.

In the tiny town of **Ho'olehua** are the airport, a small post office, and a few government offices. It's also home to **Purdy's Natural Macadamia Nut Farm,** where mac nuts have been harvested for more than sixty-five years. Free tours are given of the farm, and there's a gift shop at which you can buy, of course, macadamia nuts and other nut-related products. The farm is open Monday through Saturday, 9:00 A.M.

Colorful creations in all sorts of shapes and sizes are a trademark of The Big Wind Kite Factory on Molokai. (Courtesy Phil Spalding III)

JULIE'S TOP FAMILY ADVENTURES ON MOLOKAI

1. Taking a trip on the Molokai Wagon Ride
2. Visiting Molokai Ranch and Wildlife Park
3. Sampling fresh, hot-from-the-oven Molokai Sweetbread
4. Soaking in the natural pools of Kapuaiwa Coconut Grove
5. Snorkeling at Murphy Beach Park
6. Touring the Purdy Macadamia Nut Farm
7. Flying a colorful kite from the Big Wind Kite Factory
8. Sunning, swimming, and snorkeling at beautiful Papohaku Beach
9. Driving down to Halawa Valley and swimming in the bay
10. Exploring the Molokai Museum and Cultural Center

to 1:00 P.M., and Sunday, 10:00 A.M. to 1:00 P.M. For more information, call 567–6495 or 567–6001.

From Ho'olehua, continuing east on Maunaloa Highway (460), your next stop should be at **Mo'omomi Beach.** Although it's a bit of a struggle to get there because part of the road is severely pitted, it's well worth the drive. Turn left on Route 480, then left again on Farrington Avenue. Soon Farrington ends and the rough dirt road begins. Car rental agencies will warn against venturing here, but with careful driving, it's feasible. You'll come to an intersection of sorts, at which you should bear right and continue to the road's end. Note: Don't leave anything of value in your rental car. Mo'omomi is great for surfing, fishing, and swimming and is very popular with locals. Swimming is desirable and safe only during the summer months; winter storms often bring large rocks to the beach.

From here, a short walk west leads to a series of tiny coves and beaches that offer pristine beauty, isolation, and good snorkeling. Use caution while swimming if there's no one else around, and don't swim too far out, where the currents may be rough.

Look for a large black rock to the right of Moʻomomi Beach. Legend says that in Old Hawaii a woman became impregnated by the gods, which infuriated her jealous husband. He was angry that their child would be a spirit, and he sent her down to this rock while he contemplated their situation. She was so distraught with tears that she went into labor. One of her many tears was actually a tiny fish, which rolled off her cheek and into the ocean. This fish grew to become the powerful shark god that is featured in many Hawaiian chants and hulas.

Keonelele Sand Dunes are just a few miles west of Moʻomomi. If you venture here, you'll feel as if you've entered a desolate wasteland. Hawaiians of yesteryear used this area as a burial site. There are no facilities and the area is completely deserted, except for an occasional geologist who visits to search for clues to the island's geological history.

Route 460 continues east until it forks and one direction veers south toward Kaunakakai, turning into Highway 450, while the other direction heads north to Kualapuʻu as Highway 470.

NORTH MOLOKAI, KUALAPUʻU TO KALAUPAPA

When Del Monte was harvesting pineapples on Molokai, **Kualapuʻu** was a booming town. Today, it's a small stop on the way north. At the Kualapuʻu Market, you can stock up on food and gas. It's open Monday through Saturday, 8:30 A.M. to 6:00 P.M.; 567–6243.

Kualapuʻu Cook House is located in upcountry Molokai, 4 miles or so from Hoʻolehua Airport on the way to Kalaupapa Overlook. The Cook House is a busy local standby, with good burgers of beef, chicken, or fish; plate lunches are offered, too. Pies are homemade by restaurant owner Nanette Olmstead and are outstanding; try the mac nut–chocolate chip pie for a taste thrill. Just a block off State Hwy. 470; 567–6185. $.

In town, you can't miss the huge water reservoir—it holds 1.4 billion gallons and is the largest of its kind in the world!

A few minutes' drive heading north will land you in the tiny town of Kalae. Don't miss the **Molokai Museum and Cultural Center,** built around the old **R. W. Meyer Sugar Mill,** listed on the National Register of Historic Places. The mill was constructed in 1878, and has since been restored. Visitors will be able to watch the various stages of processing sugar, from its natural cane form to the white powdery stuff you put on your cereal. The museum and cultural center focuses on Hawaiian crafts, such as lei-making, lauhala weaving, quilting, and woodcarving. The museum is open Monday through Saturday, 10:00 A.M. to 2:00 P.M. Admission is $2.50 for adults, $1.00 for children. For more information, call 567–6436.

The road ends at **Palaau State Park,** where the facilities and the views make it the best place to camp on the island. From the parking lot, a sign directs visitors to one of Molokai's most famous landmarks, the **Phallic Rock.** Hawaiian legend says that Nanahoa, the male god of fertility, once stopped here to admire a beautiful young girl who was gazing at her own reflection in a pool. Nanahoa's wife, Kawahuna, became so enraged with jealousy that she pulled out all the young girl's hair. In retaliation, Nanahoa struck his wife, sending her over a cliff, where she turned to stone. Nanahoa also turned to stone and today inhabits the Phallic Rock, which is shaped like what its name implies.

For centuries, allegedly barren women have come to pray for fertility at this rock—and local townsfolk are full of their success stories.

Also near the entrance to Palaau is the **Kalaupapa Overlook,** from where you can see the famous Kalaupapa Peninsula projecting out into the ocean, 1,600 feet below. The story of Kalaupapa involves one of the most tragic, yet inspiring, periods of Hawaiian history. In mid-1800s, many of the Hawaiian people were afflicted with leprosy, which later became known as Hansen's disease. It was a highly contagious infection that affected the skin and central nervous system, creating grotesque ulcers that over time grew into hideous deformities.

To halt the spread of infection, the sick were banished to remote Kalaupapa, where the steep cliffs on one side and the rough ocean on the other formed a complete barrier to the rest of society. Paranoia rampaged through the island chain, and anyone, regardless of age and gender, with a suspicious-looking skin color or sore was banished forever to Kalaupapa. No one was sent to care for these terminally ill people—food and supplies were packaged in tight containers and thrown overboard from passing ships. The Kalaupapa residents were forced to swim out to the rough channel to collect the packages.

Then, in 1873, Father Damien de Veuster, a Belgian priest, arrived at Kalaupapa, intending to stay a few weeks and provide some spiritual relief and compassion to the residents. He ended up remaining on this isolated peninsula for the rest of his life, unceasingly and selflessly caring for the forgotten people for sixteen years. He himself eventually became ill with the disease and died in Kalaupapa. During his years here, he built homes, a hospital, and St. Philomena Church, still standing today, and cared for the sick in what may be the greatest example ever of aloha and brotherly love.

Modern drugs have stopped the threat of Hansen's disease, allowing the longtime residents of Kalaupapa to leave if they wish. But most choose to remain here, acting as tour guides to the area, forever grateful to their savior, Father Damien.

Today, there are several methods of exploring **Kalaupapa National Historic Park**: by boat, by air, or by mule. All visitors must procure advance permission, however, and unfortunately children under age sixteen are not allowed. For more information, contact Damien Tours, 567–6171, or Destination Molokai, (800) 800–6367.

Standing at the overlook, you'll see the start of the mule trail to the right. The curvaceous trail leads 1,600 feet to Kalaupapa, and is one of the more popular ways to visit the peninsula, as the expansive vistas offer immense beauty.

Air Molokai and Aloha IslandAir offer round-trip flights, but you still must prearrange for a resident escort to meet you upon landing.

East of Kalaupapa, the **world's highest sea cliffs** surround isolated valleys that dot the northeastern coastline, culminating with the town of Halawa. You can't get to the area before Halawa via car, and only the most experienced hikers can navigate the dangerous mountain trails on foot. By helicopter, however, it's entirely possible, and a trip to **Kahiwa Falls** is certainly worth it. Here the water plummets 1,750 feet, making Kahiwa among the highest falls in all Hawaii. Most of the helicopter companies are headquartered on other islands. For information on helicopter companies, call Molokai Visitors Association.

KAUNAKAKAI

This is the major town of the island, the site of the post office, and the main place for shopping and banking, and it won't take you more than an hour to explore it completely. It's a quiet, quaint place. Businesses such as a health-food store, markets, a drug store, and a small selection of souvenir shops are situated along Ala Malama Street, the main drag.

Be sure to stop at **Kanemitsu Bakery,** home of the world-famous Molokai Sweet Bread. Many bakeries throughout the state try to imitate this delectable treat, but none have a product as close to perfect as Kanemitsu's. The front half of the building is bakery, the back half is restaurant, and it has all been run by the same family for seventy years. The bakery makes nineteen kinds of bread each day, and the restaurant is open for breakfast, lunch, and dinner. Fare is basic and inexpensive. At 79 Ala Malama; 553–5855. $.

Pau Hana Inn is just a half-mile from downtown Kaunakakai, right on the beach, and is a great place to celebrate the day's end with a tall cool drink and a nice dinner under the huge banyan tree. Food is simple but good, with generous portions. It's a local favorite. At the Pau Hana Resort, Kaunakakai; 553–5342. $.

Molokai Fish and Dive is a snorkel shop that not only rents equipment but will provide you with directions to the island's most colorful underwater spots. The staff can also arrange excursions. The store at 63 Ala Malama and is open daily 8:00 A.M. to 6:00 P.M., but hours are flexible, depending on the demand. For more information, call 553–5926.

Sailing trips are available through **Molokai Charters,** which offers half-day or full-day trips around the island and whale-watching tours in season. For more information, call 553–5852.

A quick walk west of Kaunakakai leads to the **Royal Kapuaiwa Coconut Grove.** These trees were planted during Kamehameha V's reign in the 1860s to furnish privacy and shade for the *ali'i* who bathed in the series of naturally formed pools here.

Statewide, Molokai is known for its abundance of **fishponds.** These were constructed in shallow waters with a wall, usually built of coral, that had a small opening. Young fish would swim inside the pond, fatten up, and then be unable to swim out, thus providing fishermen with large schools of easy-to-catch fish. The southeastern coast of the island is ideal for this form of aquaculture since it features miles of flat, shallow waters. In ancient times, the area housed an extensive network of ponds, many of which remain today. Driving east from Kaunakakai on Route 450, the Kamehameha Highway, **Kaloko'eli Pond** is just a few miles away from town, easily seen from the road. A few more minutes' drive east, look for the large **Ali'i Fishpond,** right before **Oneali'i Beach County Park.**

Oneali'i is a great place for families; the swimming is safe virtually year-round and picnic facilities are present.

SOUTHEAST COAST, KAWELA TO HALAWA

Continuing on Route 450, you'll be treated to a beautiful country drive. This was once the most populated section of Molokai, and around almost every bend in the road is an important site, whether a religious temple or an ancient battleground. You'll pass tropical deserted beaches, more fish-ponds, ancient *heiau,* picturesque churches, and wonderful parks. Many important historical sites are unmarked, however, so it's a good idea to ask for some hints from the local residents.

Soon after Oneali'i, look toward the mountain for the **Kawela Place of Refuge** and, just beyond, the **Pakuhiwa Battleground,** the site of a large battle between Molokai's chief Pakuhiwa and Kamehameha the Great. Then you'll pass **Kakahaia Beach Park,** a picturesque crescent of sandy beach that offers great swimming conditions.

You'll next arrive at **Kamalo Harbor,** where the wharf used to be the center of oceangoing activity before Kaunakakai's harbor assumed that role. Look around the next bend for the small **St. Joseph Church,** built by Father Damien in 1876. A metal sculpture of Father Damien sits outside the church.

A few miles beyond is the site of the **Smith and Bronte Landing.** In 1927 aviators Ernest Smith and Emory Bronte were forced to make a crash landing here after completing the first civilian flight in the Pacific region. They started at Kapiolani Park, Oahu, and it took them more than twenty-five hours to reach the soggy banks of south Molokai. Although they

crashed, they instituted air travel to these remote islands that now welcome more than six million airborne visitors annually.

At mile marker 13 sits the **Wavecrest Resort Condominium,** a
good stop to pick up food and drinks before continuing east. Next, look for
the fortresslike **Kalua'aha Church,** built in 1844 by Protestant missionaries Reverend and Mrs. Harvey Rexford Hitchcock. It was the first Christian
church constructed on Molokai and is well preserved.

Next, look toward the mountain for **Ili'ili'opae Heiau.** Legend says
this massive structure was built in one night by menehune who formed a
body-to-body chain and passed the stones from Wailau Valley, on the
northeast coast of the island. Ili'ili'opae was a *luakini,* a temple of human
sacrifice. It's one of the largest heiau in all Hawaii, and, although on private
land, it's designated a National Historic Landmark. The heiau is surrounded by vegetation, and the interior is as big as a football field.

Permission must be granted to visit the heiau. For more information,
call 558–8113, or ask any of the staff at the island's hotels how to make
the proper arrangements. To get there from Route 450, look for a bridge
right after the Mapulehu Mango Grove on the right. On the left, there's a
green gate. You have to park and walk around the gate; after a short trek
inland you'll see the trail heading into the woods where the heiau sits.

As long as you're in the neighborhood, stop at **Mapulehu Glass
House,** a colorful, fragrant nursery that will ship fruits and flowers home
for you. You can also take a free guided tour of the historical home and gardens on weekdays at 10:30 A.M. The Glass House is open Monday to Friday, 7:00 A.M. to noon; 558–8160.

Near the Mapulehu Mango Grove is the start of the **Molokai Wagon
Ride,** a wonderful cultural experience that offers a great glimpse into
Molokai's history. The wagon travels through the mango grove, planted by
the Hawaiian Sugar Company in the 1930s. It's one of the largest of its
kind in the world. After the mango grove, the trip goes to Ili'ili'opae Heiau,
then returns to the beach where guides demonstrate such local activities as
net fishing, coconut husking, and hula. Throughout the trip, the guides
entertain guests with local lore, legends, and songs. The trip costs $35.00
for adults, $17.50 for children three to twelve. For more information, call
558–8132.

Pukoo Beach Park fronts a small boat harbor and a sandy lagoon that offers wonderful swimming. A few minutes beyond Pukoo, you'll see a large stone that's been painted white, sitting at the side of the road. Locals refer to this as the **octopus stone,** and it's believed to hold magical powers having once marked the site of a cave that was home to a mythical octopus.

Wailua Beach is considered among the island's best for first-time surfers, snorkelers, and swimmers. It's tame and shallow. A short walk east will land you at another shallow beach where you can walk all the way to the reef.

Farther east, **Murphy's Beach Park** features another swimmable sandy beach with restroom facilities and expansive, breathtaking views. Another great beach is at mile marker 20, where there's a wide stretch of sand and a protected lagoon makes for great snorkeling.

Discover the adventures that abound at Hawaii's vast array of beaches. (Courtesy Aston Hotels and Resorts)

EAST MOLOKAI, HALAWA

Beyond Murphy's Beach, prepare yourselves for a thrilling car ride to Halawa Valley. The road follows each little nuance of the curving coastline, and the views are spectacular. You'll see cozy deserted beaches, picturesque bays, and craggy cliffs. Eventually the road bends inward and heads to the Puu O Hoku Ranch and **Kalanikaula,** a kukui grove that's considered Molokai's most sacred spot. It was planted when Molokai's most powerful kahuna, Lanikaula, died, and people are asked to maintain a quiet and respectful attitude when visiting here.

The road ends at the dramatic **Halawa Valley Lookout,** truly one of the most majestic sites in all Hawaii. Looking hundreds of feet below, you'll see a series of sparkling waterfalls cascading down cliffs carpeted in velvety-green vegetation. The turquoise ocean, full of foamy, frothy whitewater, drifts into and out of the bay.

Halawa Valley is Molokai's first permanent settlement; historians believe that Hawaiians lived here as early as the seventh century. People gravitated to this fertile valley for hundreds of years, farming taro and living off the land and sea. In 1946, a humongous tidal wave inundated the valley, leaving hefty ocean salt deposits in its wake, thus rendering much of the land unusable.

The paved road leads right into the valley and stops at a beautiful freshwater stream, suitable for swimming. You can also swim in the ocean here, which is safe year-round, but don't venture beyond the bay as the currents can be quite strong. Conditions for snorkeling, surfing, and fishing are optimum.

If your children are hardy hikers, and if the weather is cooperating, don't miss the chance to hike to **Moalua Falls.** From the parking lot at the end of the road, continue on foot along a small dirt road that turns into an even smaller footpath. A stone wall will be on your left. Ignore the signs and follow the waterpipe that's situated at the left of Halawa Stream. Keep bearing left as the trail branches out in other directions, and listen for the falls. If it's rained recently, the stream, and consequently the falls, will be a rushing torrent. Rain also makes for a mosquito-laden, muddy trail—use good judgment and caution. The trail can be difficult.

Hawaiian legend tells the story of *mo'o,* a female lizard who lives in a pool at the bottom of this picturesque 250-foot falls. Every so often, she gets lonely and will lure an unsuspecting swimmer to her underwater home. You can prejudge her disposition, which changes frequently, by throwing a *ti* leaf in the water. If it floats, the swimming is fine; feel free to jump in the cool pool. If it sinks, however, beware of the lonely *mo'o* and swim at your own risk.

Beyond Moalua, the trail is quite difficult and not recommended for children. Beyond Halawa, rounding the tip of the island, are the aforementioned tall seacliffs, forming the valleys of Waikolu, Pelekunu, and Wailau.

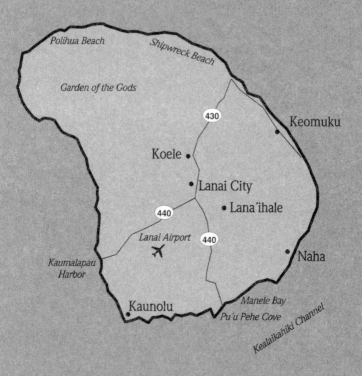

Polihua Beach   Shipwreck Beach

Garden of the Gods

430   Keomuku

Koele

Lanai City

440   Lana'ihale

Lanai Airport   440

Kaumalapau   Naha
Harbor

Kaunolu   Manele Bay
Pu'u Pehe Cove

Kealaikahiki Channel

Lanai

Lanai

U ntil the recent advent of tourism here, Lanai, nicknamed the Pineapple Island, always had been something of a silent, mysterious neighbor. Only 2,426 people, mostly pineapple plantation workers and their families, lived on its 41.2 square miles. There were—and still are—no traffic lights and just one school. The few visitors who ventured here came for hunting and stayed at the quaint, old-fashioned ten-room Hotel Lanai. A few Maui resorts offered day trips here as part of their recreational menu.

While other islands were competing for the almighty visitor industry to grace their shores, Lanai quietly kept to itself—harvesting batch after batch of what was once one of Hawaii's most famous agricultural products.

The majority of the island is owned by Castle & Cooke, one of five major Hawaii-based corporations. Dole Foods, once the world's primary pineapple harvesting company, is a subsidiary of Castle & Cooke. Residents lived the epitome of a small-town existence. Everyone knew one another and life moved slowly.

In the late 1980s, as pineapple operations were phased out, construction began on two five-star megaresorts. Residents went from living plantation lifestyles to servicing tourists in a prime resort destination. Today, the **Lodge at Koele** sits in the center of the island and resembles an English hunting lodge. The beachfront **Manele Bay Hotel** is on the southern coast and has a classic Mediterranean design. Both are pretty pricey and ultra deluxe, and beckon visitors with beautiful accommodations, recreational activities, and attractions. The notable activities are diving and sailing—said to be the best in all Hawaii.

The transition has been executed flawlessly, and Lanai is now a full-fledged attraction with plenty of family-oriented activities, from bountiful tidepools waiting to be explored to secluded bays beckoning to picnickers. The island is known for its bevy of artists. The Lodge at Koele and Manele Bay feature a visiting artist program that has attracted world-famous celebrities who host small, personal receptions. In Lanai City, the only "town" on the island, the Art Center (565–7503) is a combination school, gallery, cultural center, and studio. Programs throughout the year include seasonal exhibits, one-person shows, storytelling, visitor classes, and art services.

There's still much undiscovered terrain here, and several campsites are available throughout the island. Permits must be obtained from Castle and Cooke's Koele Company at P.O. Box L, Lanai City, HI 96763; 565–6661.

Kids at Manele Bay Hotel enjoy creating such tropical masterpieces as this Hawaiian fish mural. (Courtesy Sheila Donnelly & Associates)

Flights from Oahu are available on Aloha Island Air, Hawaiian, and Mahalo. There is only one airport. If you're going to rent a car, reserve one early—there's only one place that offers rentals: Lanai City Service, 1036 Lanai Avenue, Lanai City, HI 96763; 565–6780. It's a good idea to rent a four-wheel-drive vehicle because much of the good sightseeing requires one. Every visitor who rents a car is given a free map of the island. This map clearly identifies all the trails mentioned in this chapter.

NORTHERN LANAI

A definite don't-miss is the **Garden of the Gods** at the northwestern tip of the island. This is an unusual, eerie-looking geological formation of rock piles set in red dirt. The whole place changes colors throughout the day. Depending on the cloud cover and the sun's position, the spectrum of colors ranges from red to gold to brown to pink to orange—it's especially vibrant at sunrise and sunset.

To get there from Lanai City, take Fraser Avenue north. After the pavement ends (four-wheel-drives are recommended), stay on the road for a half-mile, then turn right. Keep going for 5.5 miles. The garden is a half-mile beyond the sign for Lapaiki Road.

If your kids are up for a hearty hike, you may want to travel the 3-mile **Awalua Trail** from the Garden of the Gods to **Shipwreck Beach.** The trail is overgrown and therefore a bit difficult; don't forget to bring plenty of water.

Shipwreck Beach is so named because of the grounded World War II ship that sits offshore. Of all the north-shore beaches, this is the easiest to get to, but you'll still find it very private. From here, there are great, expansive views of Molokai and West Maui. While the shallow reef makes the waters calm, it also makes swimming a little difficult because of sharp coral. It is safe, however, to swim in the shallow, sandy-bottom pools.

It's a beautiful drive to Shipwreck and one of the few destinations on Lanai that don't require a four-wheel-drive vehicle. Simply take the Keomuku Road from Lanai City to the end of the road. The dirt road forks left (north) to Shipwreck Beach or straight ahead (south) to the abandoned town of Naha. You'll see the beached freighter to the left. There are no facilities here, so bring some snacks and water.

JULIE'S TOP FAMILY ADVENTURES ON LANAI

1. Exploring the Garden of the Gods
2. Visiting Luahiwa Petroglyphs
3. Snorkeling in Hulopoʻe Bay
4. Riding on horseback around Koele
5. Beachcombing for treasures at Shipwreck Beach
6. Playing lawn bowling at the Lodge at Koele
7. Exploring the tide pools at Hulopoʻe Bay
8. Taking a snorkeling excursion on *Trilogy*
9. Learning how to putt at the putting course
10. Visiting scenic Sweetheart Cove

Along the drive, you'll see several small stones piled atop larger boulders. These are called *uhu* and are a traditional Hawaiian offering for good luck while traveling. Feel free to make your own, but never under any circumstances should you disturb the ones already there.

Once at the beach, don't miss the opportunity to look for treasures in the sand. This is relatively untouched land here, and you never know what you may find. The most sought-after treasures are glass floats that have drifted over thousands of miles of open ocean from Japanese fishnets.

Nature lovers shouldn't miss northern **Polihua Beach,** the longest, widest spot on the island. It's not great for swimming, even for adults, because the currents are strong and unpredictable. But if you don't mind the long, bumpy drive out there, the views are absolutely exquisite. Especially noteworthy here are the abundance of endangered green sea turtles. This is a popular breeding ground for them and you can usually spot them swimming around.

Finding Polihua is tricky, however. The route involves several unmarked roads. It's best to ask someone at the service station for directions.

CENTRAL LANAI

Horseback-riding tours are arranged through the activities desk at the Lodge at Koele. The Paniolo Ride costs $65 per person and lasts two hours. Children must be over 4 feet tall to participate in the adult rides; if they're too short, they can go on pony rides for $10 for fifteen minutes. Private trail rides cost $50 for one hour and $95 for two hours.

At 3,370 feet, **Lanaihale Ridge** is the highest point on the island. Be sure to take the road all the way to the top, where expansive views permit you to see all the other major islands in the Hawaiian chain. It's a good idea to bring along a guidebook detailing native plants, for you'll see a few interesting species here. Look for *ohia, pili* grass, and mountain *naupaka.*

You'll also see quite an abundance of Norfolk pines, and you'll probably think that they look out of place on a tropical island. You're right. They were planted by George Munro back in 1910. Munro was a New Zealand transplant who was hired to manage the Lanai Ranch. He believed, correctly, that the pines would help cool the area, and create moisture for other crops to flourish. Be sure to bring some warm clothes, because it gets quite chilly here.

The island's most famous hike is **Munro Trail,** which crosses Lanaihale Ridge. The trek is a little difficult and therefore not recommended for small children. There is quite a gain in elevation, but you needn't attempt to traverse the whole thing. The views are outstanding from every turn. Depending on cloud cover and how far you make it on the trail, you'll be able to see at least three, sometimes five, of the other islands. If your kids tire easily, you'll still be treated to expansive views from early points on the trail.

An easier alternative to the Munro Trail is the **Kaiholena Trail.** It's a four-hour loop that can be crossed with minimal difficulty. Be sure to pack some snacks and plenty of water. You'll see the trailhead on the way to the Munro Trail.

East of Lanaihale, on the coast in **Keomuku,** is the **Kalanakilo o Ka Malamalama Church.** This ancient roadside church currently is undergoing a restoration by the community. To get there, take the main road, Keomuku, which crosses Lanaihale heading northeast.

SOUTHERN LANAI

On the south side of the island, **Hulopoe Bay** is one of the most beautiful, calm, and picturesque sites in all Hawaii. It fronts the Manele Bay Resort and offers perfect swimming conditions for kids. Offshore, the waters are part of a marine-life conservation area, which means that fishing is illegal. This translates into great snorkeling.

Guests at either the Manele Bay Resort or the Lodge at Koele may enroll their children in Manele's children's program; the agenda includes lei-making, Hawaiian games and crafts, relay events, waterfall picnics, kite flying, and even movie production.

Lanai offers some of the state's best snorkeling, and **Spinning Dolphin Charters** provides half-day and full-day trips from Manele Harbor, on the southern tip of the island. Children are welcome aboard, and the guides always make sure the kids have a great time. Weather permitting, you can snorkel, fish, or customize your own sail and swim trip. For more information, contact Spinning Dolphin at P.O. Box 491, Lanai City, HI 96763; 565–6613.

Also, **Trilogy Ocean Sports** offers a variety of scuba and snorkel excursions. Best for kids is the morning snorkel, sail, and scuba trip. The crew possess expert knowledge about the local marine life, and they will patiently teach snorkeling skills to those who have never seen a mask and snorkel before. The catamaran whisks away the passengers to the clear, unspoiled, and protected waters where snorkeling is first-rate. The cruise lasts from 8:30 A.M. to 1:00 P.M. and includes a hearty gourmet lunch prepared by the chefs at Manele Bay Hotel. It costs $85 for adults, $42.50 for children under twelve. Trilogy also offers whale-watching trips in season. For more information, call (800) 874–2666.

Around the bend to the left of Hulopoe are some large tide pools. These are great discovery places for kids to see a variety of marine plants and animals. A little farther beyond the pools is picturesque **Sweetheart Rock,** also known as Pu'u Pehe Cove, where legend says a man hid his sweetheart (Pehe) and later she was drowned.

Pu'u Pehe Cove is much more secluded than Hulopoe so expect to do a little climbing on the way. Once there, however, the views are breathtaking. The beach is small, a tiny slice of sparkling sand bordered by 20-foot craggy cliffs. It's quite private here; you may have the beach all to yourselves.

Back on the road and farther south, don't miss the National Historic Landmark of **Kaunolu.** In precontact Hawaii, before Western civilization arrived, agrarian communities filled this area, purportedly growing yams in the nearby **Palawai Basin.** When pineapple harvesting was going full force, the area was filled to the hilt with the prickly fields. Today the fields remain fallow, but Kaunolu Village itself is full of archaeological treasures.

You'll see a series of ancient stone terraces and house sites where villagers lived and worked. There are remnants of a heiau (an ancient place of worship) and several **petroglyphs** that offer a glimpse into forms of written communication used by the Hawaiians of old. Kamehameha the Great, the first king to unite all the Hawaiian islands under one rule, is said to have erected a shrine in Kaunolu to his fishing god.

To get to the ruins, take Manele Road toward the boat harbor. When the road hooks left and uphill (about 3.5 miles from Kaumalapau Highway), go straight onto Kaupili Road. (It's a dirt road and may not be marked.) Follow this for 2.5 miles and turn left at the intersection. In half a mile, you'll come to another dirt road on the left. Turn here, and just up this road on the right is the trailhead. From the road to the ruins is 3.3 miles of flat terrain. Bring lots of water; it's very dry here and the temperature will get quite warm.

Luahiwa Petroglyphs are considered some of the best-preserved ancient rock carvings in all the islands. To get there, however, requires some perseverance. Heading south on Manele Road, look for the sign on the left for Hoike Road. This is the former main pineapple road, once paved, but now turned to gravel. On Hoike you'll pass two irrigation ditches; turn left at the second one, making sure the ditch remains on the right of your car. After a while, you'll see a NO TRESPASSING sign, where you should park. Follow the trail that leads off to the left up the hill until you see the large brown boulders. Most of the petroglyphs are found on the south faces of the rocks.

Some are drawings of symbolic circles; others are pictorial images, complete with canoes gliding under unfurled sails, dogs snarling with their jaws agape, and horses galloping. The petroglyphs were drawn on the rock faces more than 100 years ago.

Annual Events

H awaii travelers have a variety of year-round festivals, ethnic fairs, and cultural exhibits from which to choose. Some statewide; others happen on only one island. Most of the following events occur annually, but the exact dates fluctuate depending on community support and funding and on weather. For detailed information, it's recommended that you read the calendar sections of the local newspapers, the *Honolulu Advertiser* and the *Star-Bulletin.*

January

The **Hula Bowl** is the nationally televised college all-star football game. It's always played the first Saturday in January at Honolulu's Aloha Stadium. Call 947–4141.

The **NFL Pro Bowl** is the annual all-star professional game played by the top-rated NFL and AFC players. It's normally in late January or early February, also at Aloha Stadium. Information: 486–9300.

Honolulu's **Cherry Blossom Festival** starts in late January and lasts through March. It includes a Japanese tea ceremony, flower-arranging demonstrations, a queen and princess pageant and coronation ball, and a cultural show.

The **Narcissus Festival** commences with celebrations for the Chinese New Year, ranging from mid-January to early February. Honolulu's Chinatown comes alive with color, and there are fireworks, lion dances in the street, a beauty pageant, and a coronation ball.

The **Morey Boogie World Bodyboard Championships** are held on Oahu's North Shore. Competition days are determined by the best wave action. Information: 396–2326.

Molokai celebrates its **Makahiki Festival** with traditional Hawaiian games, food booths, and arts and crafts. Information: 553–3876.

February

Don't be misled into thinking the **Punahou School Carnival** is just an ordinary high school fundraiser. This is one of the longest-running events in Hawaii. In addition to the traditional rides and games, you'll find rows of food booths selling local delicacies, a white elephant sale, and arts and crafts booths. Usually held in early February. Information: 944–5753.

The **Carole Kai Bed Race** is a fundraising event of costumed volunteers pushing beds that are decorated in various themes and set on wheels. On Maui, the race travels down Front Street in Lahaina; on Kauai, it's at Kukui Grove Center in Lihue. In Honolulu, it usually heads down Kalakaua Avenue in early March.

On Oahu's North Shore, the **Haleiwa Sea Spree** is a four-day festival that includes outrigger canoe races, ancient Hawaiian sports, and surfing contests.

In Waimea, Kauai, the annual **Captain Cook Festival** commemorates the spot where Captain James Cook first landed. The festival features entertainment, a mini-marathon, and lots of food booths.

Buffalo's Annual Big Board Surfing Classic at Makaha Beach, Oahu, involves top-rated longboard surfers in an annual two-day competition. Weather and waves permitting, the event is held the last weekend in February and the first weekend in March.

The **Hilo Mardi Gras** in an annual New Orleans–style party on the Big Island, including a parade, ethnic food, and costumes. Information: 935–5111.

For snow bunnies, the annual **President's Cup Ski Tournament** is held atop on Mauna Kea during President's Day weekend, snow permitting. For more information, call Ski Guides Hawaii, P.O. Box 1954, Waimea, HI 96743; 885–4188.

March

The **Carole Kai Bed Race** travels down Waikiki's main drag, Kalakaua Avenue. There is usually a free concert at the Waikiki Shell the night before.

Music fans shouldn't miss the **Hawaiian Song Festival and Song Composing Contest,** held at the Kapiolani Park Bandstand in Waikiki. It's free, and it features top-notch entertainment.

The **Annual Hawaii Challenge International Sport Kite Festival** is at Kapiolani Park, Oahu. Kids will love watching the colorful kites float in the sky. Information: 922–5483.

The **Kamehameha Schools Annual Song Contest** includes competition between the high school classes at Kamehameha Schools, where only students of Hawaiian ancestry may attend. It's held at the Blaisdell Center in downtown Honolulu and is a wonderful chance to see young local musical talent. Information: 842–8338.

Prince Kuhio Day is a statewide holiday on March 26. It pays tribute to Prince Jonah Kuhio, a member of the royal family and Hawaii's first delegate to the U.S. Congress. Celebrations vary between the islands.

The **O'Neill International Windsurfing Championships** are held March and April in Paia, Maui.

At the week-long **Merrie Monarch Festival** in Hilo, you'll see the best hula dancers in the state. Competition is by invitation only and includes the modern and ancient styles. You have to write ahead of time for tickets, and make hotel, rental car, and airline reservations way ahead of time. This is the most popular hula competition of the year. Information: 935–9168.

April

An annual **Easter Sunday Sunrise Service** is held at the National Memorial Cemetery of the Pacific in Punchbowl Crater. This is a longstanding island tradition for locals and visitors.

The **Annual Hawaiian Festival of Music** is a competition that offers a huge compilation of musicians from throughout the state and the Mainland. It's held at the Waikiki Shell. You'll hear everything from Hawaiian to classical symphony as music is celebrated in all its forms.

The **Aloha Basketball Classic** at Honolulu's Blaisdell Center Arena features top-rated college seniors who compete in charity games.

If there's snow, the **Paniolo Ski Meet** is held atop the Big Island's Mauna Kea. Information: 885–4188.

May

May Day is "Lei Day" in Hawaii, and colorful, fragrant celebrations expand to all the islands. This is the best time of the year to see all the different designs of leis. Look for the most popular to be strung from plumeria, puakinikini, orchids, ginger, carnations, and maile, a fragrant green leaf found in local forests. There are lei-making contests, where prizes are given to the most unique and distinctive garlands, and a lei queen. Information (Oahu): 233–7300.

Arts and Crafts Festival at Seabury Hall, Maui, is a fundraiser for this private school and a great place to pick up handcrafted souvenirs. Information: 572–7235.

The **Captain Cook Festival** at Kailua-Kona, on the Big Island, features Hawaiian games and music.

Lanai is the site of the annual **Pineapple Festival,** which features arts and crafts, displays, demonstrations, an on-shore fishing tournament, a tennis tournament, local and ethnic music, and dancing. Information: 565–7600.

In Honolulu's Ala Moana Park,, the **Pacific Handcrafters Guild Fair** involves local craftspeople and a slew of colorful objects for sale. Information: 254–6788.

The annual **World Fire Knife Dancing Competition** is really something to see. It's held at the Polynesian Cultural Center, Oahu, and sometimes a junior division is added, for dancers ages seven to sixteen. Information: 293–3333.

The **Filipino Fiesta** is a month-long celebration of Hawaii's Filipino population.

Cowboy fun is at the **Annual Western Week at Honokaa,** on the Big Island. The festivities include a parade, dance, and rodeo.

The **outrigger canoe season** runs from May through August, and the races, or regattas, are an awesome spectacle, as teams race from one part of the island to the other. Check local papers for specific events. Information: 396–9164.

For **Memorial Day,** services are held at Honolulu's National Memorial Cemetery of the Pacific at Punchbowl.

The annual **Prince Albert Music Festival** occurs on Kauai. Festivities include classical concerts and a statewide hula competition for children. Information: 826–2286.

The **50th State Fair** begins in late May and lasts for four consecutive weekends. Events include entertainment, rides, games and agricultural exhibits, and plenty of local-style fare. At Aloha Stadium in Honolulu, 536–5492.

The third Saturday in May is the **Molokai Ka Hula Piko Festival,** a celebration of the birth of Hula. Molokai is believed to be the traditional birthplace of the hula, and this cultural celebration traces its roots from ancient times to today. Information: (800) 800–6367.

June

Kauai County Fair, at the Kauai War Memorial Convention Hall in Lihue, is a typical county fair offering wonderful samplings of produce and local delicacies.

On Oahu, the **Mission Houses Museum Fancy Fair** involves the island's talented craftspeople and artists. There's also entertainment and food booths. Information: 531–0481.

King Kamehameha Day falls in mid-June and celebrates the reign of Kamehameha I, the first king to unite all of the Hawaiian islands. Many of the islands feature a floral parade. Information: 586–0333.

The **Annual King Kamehameha Traditional Hula and Chant Competition** is held at Brigham Young University in Laie, Oahu. Information: 536–6540.

The **Annual Upcounty Fun Fair** is held in Makawao, Maui, and includes cowboy-style competitions and craft and food booths.

The **Annual Hawaiian Festival of Music at the Waikiki Shell,** Honolulu, is the same as the festivities that occur in April, when local and Mainland musicians compete in all types of music.

The **Annual Orchid Society Show** in Hilo offers a chance to see the vivid varieties of orchids that grow in the Orchid Capital of Hawaii. It's held at the Hilo Civic Auditorium and, depending on the recent crops, is sometimes postponed until midsummer.

The **Annual Big Island Bonsai Show** in Hilo's Wailoa Center features the finest statewide examples of these miniature plants. Information: 933–4360.

Bon-Odori is an annual Japanese festival that honors the souls of the departed. Activities include candlelighting ceremonies and dances at numerous Buddhist temples throughout the state. The highlight is a Floating Lantern Ceremony. Information: 261–6615 or 595–2556.

July

The **Makawao Statewide Rodeo** at the Oskie Rice Arena in Maui is an old-fashioned rodeo that offers lots of knee-slappin' good times. Information: 572–2076.

Hawaii celebrates the **Fourth of July** in different ways on all islands. For fireworks displays, festivities, and parades on Oahu, call 261–2727; on the Big Island, 885–7311; on Kauai, 245–7277.

The **Annual Fourth of July Parker Ranch Rodeo and Horse Races** are held in Waimea, on the Big Island. It's the biggest, most prestigious of all Hawaii's rodeos. Information: 885–7311.

The Fourth of July is always **Turtle Independence Day** at Mauna Lani Bay Hotel on the Big Island. Adult sea turtles raised in protected seawater ponds at the resort are released into the ocean in cooperation with Sea Life Park. It's quite a sight to see all the turtles waddling freely from sand to ocean. Information: 885–6677.

The **Hawaiian Islands Tall Ships Parade** sails off the coast of Oahu during the Fourth of July. Tall-masted ships from various Hawaiian harbors parade from Koko Head to Sand Island and back to Diamond Head.

The **Annual Pan Am Windsurfing Pacific Cup** occurs at select beaches around Oahu, determined by wind conditions. Check local newspapers for sites and times.

The **International Festival of the Pacific** in Hilo is also referred to as the Pageant of Nations. It includes folk dances with authentic costumes from all of Asia and the Pacific islands. Information: 934–5334.

Prince Lot Hula Festival offers an ideal chance to witness expert hula troupes, and it's a lot more accessible than the springtime Merrie Monarch Festival. It's held on Oahu, at Moanalua Gardens, 839–5334.

The **Annual Ukulele Festival** at Kapiolani Park Bandstand, Oahu, features hundreds of ukulele from throughout the state. Free. Information: 732–3739.

There's another **Pacific Handcrafters Fair** in July, at Thomas Square, a repeat of the May event. Information: 254–6788.

July brings an annual production of **Shakespeare in the Park** to Hilo, sponsored by East Hawaii Culture Center.

Koloa Plantation Days, on Kauai, commemorates the anniversary of Hawaii's first sugar cane production. The Koloa plantation began in 1837. The week-long festival includes a parade, Hawaiian-style Olympics, various races and sporting events, song and dance events, food booths, local entertainment, and crafts. Information: 322–9201.

August

Pu'ukohola Heaiu, in Kawaihae on the Big Island, hosts the **Annual Cultural Festival,** which celebrates the heritage of ancient Hawaii. Information: 882–7218.

The annual **Bankoh Ki'hoalu Hawaiian Slack Key Guitar Festival,** also referred to as the Gabby Pahinui/Atta Isaacs Hawaiian Slack Key Guitar Festival, is free and is held in Honolulu. Information: 239–4336.

The **Queen Liliuokalani Keiki Hula Competition** is held in Honolulu's Blaisdell Center and is a thoroughly charming event to watch; the children of Hawaii compete in ancient and modern hula dance styles. Information: 521–6905.

Honolulu Zoo Day in Waikiki offers families the chance to visit the animals, plus a day-long schedule of great entertainment.

Annual Keiki Hula Festival features children from Honolulu's Summer Fun program. It's held at Kapiolani Park Bandstand.

The **Kapalua Music Festival** on Maui includes chamber music performances by nationally acclaimed artists.

The first weekend in August is **Establishment Day.** It's celebrated at the Big Island's Pu'ukohola Heiau, with traditional lei and hula workshops. Information: 882–7218.

The **Hawaiian Professional Championship Rodeo** is held in Waimanalo, Oahu. Cowboys and bullriders from throughout Hawaii and the Mainland, bullfighting clowns, outdoor barbecue, live country music, and dancing make this rodeo one of the biggest outdoor events in Hawaii. Information: 235–3691.

The **Macadamia Nut Harvest Festival** is in Honokaa on the Big Island and features a harvest ball, sporting events, and horse racing.

August 17 is **Admissions Day,** a statewide holiday commemorating the day when Hawaii became the fiftieth state.

The **Annual Kauai County Fair** offers the Garden Island's gardeners and craftspeople the chance to showcase their finest products. It's held at the War Memorial Center in Lihue.

The **Kona Hawaiian Billfish Tournament** is a precursor to the **International Tournament.** In this round, American teams compete for entry to the latter event, usually held about one week later. It's fun for kids to watch the large fish hoisted from the boats. Information: 329–6155.

Kauai's **Annual Tahiti Fete** is held in mid-August. It's an exchange between Hawaiian and Tahitian cultures and includes entertainment and arts and crafts. It's at the Kukui Grove Park and Pavilion Center in Lihue. Information: 826–9343.

Toward the end of August, the **Annual Parker Ranch Round-up** is a Western-style event that includes a horse race relay, bull riding, wild cow milking, and calf roping. Information: 885–7447.

September

In the **Annual Waikiki Rough Water Swim,** swimmers glide through a 2-mile open ocean course, from Sans Souci Beach to the Hilton Hawaiian Village. The swim is open to all ages and ability levels.

The **Hawaii County Fair** in Hilo is on the grounds of Hilo Civic Auditorium. Sponsored by Hilo Jaycees, the fair includes food, exhibits, music, and rides. Information: 965–9522.

The annual **Molokai Music Festival** in Kaunakakai, at Meyer Sugar Mill, features entertainment, hula performances, craft demonstrations, and lots of *ono* (delicious) food. Information: 567–6436 or (800) 553–0404.

The **Annual Honomu Village Fair,** on the Big Island, commences with a 46-mile Volcano-to-Honomu team relay race, followed by volleyball and mountainball tournaments. There's also lots of local foods and arts and crafts.

The **Kauai Mokihana Festival** encompasses a variety of cultural events, the main one being the Kauai Composers Contest and Concert. Here, attendees have the chance to listen to performers from throughout the island. Other activities include an arts and entertainment day, lei-making competitions, and a folk arts workshop. Some events are free, others charge a small admission fee. Information: 822–2166.

Perhaps the most popular September events are the **Aloha Festivals.** The tradition began fifty years ago and started as a week-long party designed to honor and preserve the island's heritage. Today, the festivals have expanded into a two-month period and they circulate among the six major islands: Oahu, Maui, Hawaii, Kauai, Lanai, and Molokai.

The festival is partially funded through the sale of Aloha Festivals ribbons, which are available for less than $5.00 at retail stores throughout the state. The ribbons come with a program guide that details all of the events. Ribbon wearers are admitted for free or for a discounted admission at many of the functions. The activities range from a steel guitar contest to floral parades, to singing and dancing celebrations. Information: 944–8857.

Often scheduled as part of Aloha Week, the **Made With Aloha Festival** in Waikiki features Hawaii-made products, music and hula performances, and local food. Information: 591–6599.

On the Big Island, in Kona, the Keauhou Shopping Center hosts an annual **Lei Contest and Steel Guitar Festival.**

The **Molokai-to-Oahu Canoe Race** for women (men in October) is the finale of the competitive paddling season. Women teams navigate outrigger canoes from Molokai to Fort DeRussy Beach in Waikiki, where they're met with a whopping fun celebration.

October

Maui County Fair at the Maui War Memorial Complex in Wailuku involves a parade, arts and crafts, ethnic foods, amusements, and a grand orchid exhibition. Information: 244–9570.

The Kona Surf Resort and Country Club, Big Island, leads a **Historic Walk** to Kuamo'o Battleground, where the king's warriors fought traditionalists over abandonment of the ancient religion. Information: 322–3411.

The **Pacific Handcrafters Guild Fair** is held again at Ala Moana Beach Park. Information: 254–6788.

The **Makahiki Festival** at Waimea Falls Park, Oahu, includes traditional Hawaiian games, crafts, and dances. In olden days, the Makahiki was a traditional celebration to honor fruitful harvests. Information: 638–8511.

The men's version of the **Molokai-to-Oahu Canoe Race** is held on the same course as the women's race in September.

The **Annual Orchid Plant and Flower Show** is held at the Blaisdell Center Exhibition Hall. Information: 527–5400.

The **Bishop Museum Festival** entices visitors with special tours of the museum and neighboring planetarium. Information: 847–3511.

The **Ironman World Triathlon Championship** at Kailua-Kona, on the Big Island, is the granddaddy of all triathlons, sure to inspire anyone who's lucky enough to be a bystander as the athletes pass. The Ironman encompasses a 2.4-mile open ocean swim, followed by a 112-mile bike ride, and topped off by a full marathon. Information: 329–0063.

Hawaii **Winter League Baseball** plays from mid-October to early December at Wailuku Stadium. Top-rated American, Japanese, and Korean prospects compete on their way to the major leagues. Information: 242–2950.

Hilo's **Annual Macadamia Nut Festival** is always fun, with entertainment, food, booths, games, crafts, a parade, a recipe contest, and cooking demos. Information: 966–9301.

The place to be on Halloween is definitely Lahaina, Maui, where the wackiest, zaniest, creepiest costumes are seen in the **Annual Halloween Parade.** Information: 667–9175.

November

The **Kona Coffee Cultural Festival** is a week-long celebration honoring one of Hawaii's most famous crops. Activities include coffee-picking contests, crowning of Miss Kona Coffee, parades, and food and craft booths. Information: 326–7820.

The **World Invitational Hula Festival** at the Waikiki Shell, Honolulu, includes *halau* (dance troupes) from Canada, Europe, Japan, Mexico, and the Mainland. Information: 486–3185.

The **Annual King Kalakaua Keiki Hula Festival,** is held in Kailua-Kona, on the Big Island. Children come from throughout the state to perform.

Kamehameha Schools **Ho'olaule'a** is an old-fashioned Hawaiian festival featuring continuous hula, Hawaiian and contemporary entertainment, arts and crafts, Hawaiian children's games, and food. Information: 842–8444.

The **Hui Noeau Christmas Craft Fair** is in upcountry, Maui, and features unique crafts and gifts—an ideal place to jump-start your holiday shopping. Information: 572–6560.

The **O. P. Pro Surfing Championship** is the first contest in the annual triple crown of surfing. This is when the big waves really pound Oahu's North Shore beaches and the best surfers from around the world come to test their skills. Competition is held on the best four or five days during the waiting period. Alii Beach Park, Haleiwa, Oahu. Information: 377–5850.

Kauai's **Annual Taro Festival,** held either in November or December, pays tribute to Hanalei's famous agricultural product. Taro was the staple of ancient Hawaiian diets, used as much as Americans use potatoes. Events include arts and crafts, a produce market, and entertainment. Information: 826–6522.

The Big Island also hosts an **Annual Aloha Taro Festival** in Honokaa that highlights the growing and production of taro and related products with entertainment, a farmer's market, arts and crafts, and food booths. Information: 775–0233.

At the **Annual Molokai Ranch Professional Rodeo and Stew Cook-Off,** riders and ropers from across the state and the Mainland compete under the bright lights of Molokai Ranch's arena. Information: 552–2741.

Annual Christmas in the Country Gala in Volcano, on the Big Island, features artworks by local artisans in a special holiday atmosphere. Volcano Art Center. Information: 967–8222.

December

Maui's **Na Mele O Maui Festival,** in Kaanapali and Lahaina, features native art, music, and dance. Information: 661–3271.

Kauai Museum's **Holiday Festival** is an annual Christmas event known for offering the island's best in handcrafted items and home-baked goodies. Information: 245–6931.

Kamehameha Schools Christmas Concert is open to everyone and lifts the Christmas spirit at the Blaisdell Center Concert Hall, Honolulu. Information: 842–8211.

Pacific Handcrafters Guild Christmas Fair, Thomas Square, Honolulu, is a great stop for holiday shopping. Information: 732–4913.

Triple Crown of Surfing continues on Oahu's North Shore, at Ehukai Beach. Information: 377–5850.

Two NCAA football teams play in the annual **Jeep Eagle Aloha Bowl Football Classic** on Christmas Day. Information: 947–4141.

The **Rainbow Classic** is held in Honolulu, usually in the last week of December. The tournament features men's college basketball teams. Information: 956–6501.

The **First Night Honolulu** festivities are ideal for families on New Year's Eve. It's an alcohol-free community festival of arts and entertainment, encompassing more than 250 events at seventy-five downtown Honolulu locations—music, jugglers, dance, magic, and theater arts. Information: 523–3131.

GENERAL INDEX

ACTIVITIES INDEX

NATURAL ATTRACTIONS

THEATERS, SHOWS, ZOOS